The Law Commission
Consultation Paper No 140

DAMAGES FOR PERSONAL INJURY: NON-PECUNIARY LOSS

A CONSULTATION PAPER

HMSO

ISBN 0 11 730225 2

Printed in the United Kingdom for HMSO
Dd 301912 12/95 C20 59226

THE LAW COMMISSION

DAMAGES FOR PERSONAL INJURY: NON-PECUNIARY LOSS

CONTENTS

A NOTE ON CITATIONS

For the sake of convenience, and where appropriate, the following sources are hereinafter referred to in their abbreviated form:

ABBREVIATION	*FULL REFERENCE*
Access to Justice (1995)	*Access to Justice*, Lord Woolf's Interim Report to the Lord Chancellor on the civil justice system in England and Wales, June 1995
APIL	Association of Personal Injury Lawyers
CITCOM	Citizen Action Compensation Campaign
Harris *et al*, *Compensation and Support for Illness and Injury* (1984)	D Harris, M Maclean, H Genn, S Lloyd-Bostock, P Fenn, P Corfield and Y Brittain, *Compensation and Support for Illness and Injury* (1984)
JSB *Guidelines*	The Judicial Studies Board's *Guidelines for the Assessment of General Damages in Personal Injury Cases* (2nd ed 1994) and (1st ed 1992) (references are to the second edition unless otherwise stated)
Kemp and Kemp	Kemp and Kemp, *The Quantum of Damages*
(1971) Law Com Working Paper No 41	Personal Injury Litigation - Assessment of Damages (1971) Law Com Working Paper No 41
(1973) Law Com No 56	Report on Personal Injury Litigation - Assessment of Damages (1973) Law Com No 56
(1994) Law Com No 225	Personal Injury Compensation: How Much Is Enough? (1994) Law Com No 225
Pearson Report	The Pearson Commission, Report on Civil Liability and Compensation for Personal Injury (1978), Cmnd 7054-I
The trilogy	*Andrews v Grand & Toy Alberta Ltd* (1978) 83 DLR (3d) 452; *Arnold v Teno* (1978) 83 DLR (3d) 609; *Thornton v Board of School Trustees of School District No 57* (1978) 83 DLR (3d) 480 (a series of decisions determined simultaneously by the Supreme Court of Canada)

PART I
INTRODUCTION

1.1 This consultation paper is published as part of our review of the law of damages, particularly personal injury damages.[1] In this paper we examine the principles governing, and the method of assessing, damages for non-pecuniary loss in cases of actionable personal injury.[2] Where a plaintiff is injured as a result of the defendant's tort or breach of contract, he or she may incur consequential pecuniary losses, for example loss of earnings or medical expenses. But the injury will also have non-pecuniary consequences. For instance, the plaintiff may experience pain and distress and may be subject to some physical incapacity. In addition to receiving compensation for the pecuniary loss,[3] a plaintiff in a personal injury action will also be compensated for these non-pecuniary consequences of injury. In respect of these it is said that the plaintiff recovers damages for "pain and suffering and loss of amenity". It is with such damages that this paper is concerned. As we shall explain in due course, we have also found it necessary to consider the vexed question of the assessment of damages by juries in defamation cases.

1.2 We should emphasise at the outset that, in line with our terms of reference,[4] we are looking at the remedy of damages as applicable within the traditional common law system and we shall not be considering alternative forms of compensation outside that system. While we are, of course, aware of the many criticisms made of the existing tort system, our role in this project is not to advocate its replacement (whether wholesale or in particular areas) but rather, assuming its continued existence, to recommend improvements to it. It is therefore outside our terms of

---

[1] Fifth Programme of Law Reform (1991) Law Com No 200, Item 11; and Sixth Programme of Law Reform (1995) Law Com No 234, Item 2. The other papers and reports so far published are Structured Settlements and Interim and Provisional Damages (1992) Consultation Paper No 125 and (1994) Law Com No 224; Aggravated, Exemplary and Restitutionary Damages (1993) Consultation Paper No 132; Personal Injury Compensation: How Much Is Enough? (1994) Law Com No 225; and Liability for Psychiatric Illness (1995) Consultation Paper No 137. For the Law Commission's previous review of the assessment of damages in personal injury litigation, see Report on Personal Injury Litigation - Assessment of Damages (1973) Law Com No 56, which followed a working paper on the subject, (1971) Working Paper No 41. That Report led to reforms enacted in the Administration of Justice Act 1982.

[2] Personal injury includes illness. Damages awarded for the death of another person pursuant to the Fatal Accidents Act 1976, including bereavement damages, will be the subject of a separate consultation paper.

[3] The principles for determining *future* pecuniary loss were in part addressed by us in Structured Settlements and Interim and Provisional Damages (1992) Consultation Paper No 125; and (1994) Law Com No 224. The *main* pecuniary losses for which damages are awarded comprise loss of earnings and the 'cost of care'. The latter includes medical, nursing and hospital expenses; and the cost of buying, fitting out and moving to special accommodation. Other examples of pecuniary losses include the cost of employing a housekeeper.

[4] See the description of Item 11 of the Fifth Programme of Law Reform (1991) Law Com No 200.

reference to consider in this paper whether, for example, a threshold for non-pecuniary loss should be introduced as a trade-off for the introduction of some sort of new no-fault accident compensation scheme.[5]

1.3　The leading authorities on the principles applicable to damages for pain and suffering and loss of amenity remain two decisions of over thirty years' standing - *Wise v Kaye*[6] and *H West & Son Ltd v Shephard*.[7] These cases established that plaintiffs who are rendered permanently unconscious, or who are so severely brain-damaged that they have little appreciation of the condition to which they have been reduced, are nonetheless entitled to receive a substantial award as non-pecuniary loss: and it is irrelevant whether the damages will, or can in fact, be used to comfort or otherwise benefit the plaintiff. The cases also endorsed a comparative approach to assessment, whereby similar types of injury are compensated by similar sums (within a given range). Although subsequent cases have elaborated upon and illuminated the discussion which took place in *Wise* and *West*,[8] there has been no decision of equal significance on principle since then.[9] Nor has there been any statutory reform in this area since the Administration of Justice Act 1982, implementing some of the proposals put forward by us[10] and the Pearson Commission,[11] made limited changes to the principles involved.[12] The relevant principles therefore seem relatively settled; and the comparative approach to assessment has led to the development of a flexible judicial tariff of compensation, which affords some certainty and predictability in awards.

1.4　There are criticisms, however, that the task of assessment remains a particularly difficult one and that its complexity and obscurity make it both incomprehensible

---

[5]　See para 4.25, n 84 below.

[6]　[1962] 1 QB 638 (CA).

[7]　[1964] AC 326 (HL).

[8]　See, especially, *Andrews v Freeborough* [1967] 1 QB 1; *Fletcher v Autocar & Transporters Ltd* [1968] 2 QB 322; *Croke v Wiseman* [1982] 1 WLR 71; *Wright v British Railways Board* [1983] 2 AC 773; and *Housecroft v Burnett* [1986] 1 All ER 332.

[9]　In *Lim Poh Choo v Camden and Islington AHA* [1980] AC 174, the House of Lords declined to overrule the approach taken by the majorities in *Wise* and *West*, but indicated that (in relation to damages for personal injury generally) "a radical reappraisal of the law is needed." See also *Hansard* (HL) 22 February 1994, vol 552, cols 509-10 (the Lord Chancellor).

[10]　Report on Personal Injury Litigation - Assessment of Damages (1973) Law Com No 56.

[11]　Report of the Royal Commission on Civil Liability and Compensation for Personal Injury (1978) Cmnd 7054-I.

[12]　By abolishing damages for loss of expectation of life as a separate head of loss and by providing that any suffering caused by a plaintiff's awareness that his or her life has been shortened by the injuries should be taken into account only as part of the assessment of damages in respect of pain and suffering. See paras 2.6-2.9 and 2.11 below.

and inaccessible to the non-specialist.[13] In addition to these concerns, our review takes place against a background of a certain amount of disquiet in some quarters about the levels of awards for pain and suffering and loss of amenity, it being said by some that the sums awarded are far too low.[14] Indeed the Lord Chancellor has said that the existence of this feeling was one of the reasons for his referring issues relating to damages to this Commission.[15] Concern about the levels of awards also constituted the primary motivation behind a private member's Bill introduced into the House of Commons in 1988,[16] which contained proposals for the creation of a Compensation Advisory Board charged with the task of recommending new and, it was hoped, higher levels of awards for pain and suffering and loss of amenity. That Bill also provided for the sum of bereavement damages awarded under section 1A of the Fatal Accidents Act 1976[17] in cases of death to be increased to a minimum of £10,000, subject to a maximum of £50,000, and expanded the class of persons entitled to claim it. The Bill eventually ran out of parliamentary time. It did not therefore result in any change to the law, although the Lord Chancellor conducted a consultation on the level of bereavement damages soon afterwards[18] and then went on to increase the fixed statutory award for bereavement from £3,500 to £7,500 in 1990.[19]

1.5   An important development in this area was the publication in 1992 of the Judicial Studies Board's *Guidelines for the Assessment of General Damages in Personal Injury Cases*. The 1992 *Guidelines*, and a revised edition published in 1994,[20] were compiled by a working party of the Board's Civil and Family Committee with the aim of assisting judges and practitioners who deal with personal injury cases and in the hope that they would facilitate a more uniform approach to the assessment of

---

[13]   On the assessment of damages for personal injury, Lord Ackner has stated that the calculation of pecuniary loss is "simple, straightforward and ... wholly intelligible to the man in the street"; but that, in contrast, "I can well understand criticism being made as to how one evaluates the pain and suffering and the loss of amenities." See *Hansard* (HL) 16 June 1994, vol 555, col 1849. See also para 4.3, n 17 below.

[14]   See paras 4.28ff below.

[15]   *Hansard* (HL) 9 March 1992, vol 536, col 1168.

[16]   The Citizens' Compensation Bill, promoted by Mr Lawrence Cunliffe MP and sponsored by the Citizen Action Compensation Campaign (CITCOM). See paras 4.28, 4.30 and 4.68-4.70 below.

[17]   As inserted by s 3(1) of the Administration of Justice Act 1982.

[18]   Damages for Bereavement: A Review of the Level (March 1990), Lord Chancellor's Department.

[19]   The Damages for Bereavement (Variation of Sum) (England and Wales) Order 1990, SI 1990 No 2575.

[20]   This second edition, revised to take account of inflation and decisions reported since 1991, and including new sections dealing with post-traumatic stress disorder and work-related upper limb disorders, was published in October 1994.

damages for pain and suffering and loss of amenity.[21] They suggest, on the basis of previous cases and the working party's own collective experience, the appropriate bracket of non-pecuniary award for particular types of injury - for instance, that in 1994 the sum awarded for quadriplegia should be in the range of £105,000 to £125,000.[22] The *Guidelines* represent the first attempt to provide official guidance on the appropriate non-pecuniary sum to be awarded in a form which is simple, clear and easily accessible. We understand that all judges hearing personal injury cases are issued with the *Guidelines* and that they are now widely used by both judges and practitioners. We consider below the practical benefits of the *Guidelines* and the implications they have for the scope of our own law reform task.

1.6   In October 1994 we published a report that sets out the findings of research conducted on our behalf into the experiences of victims of personal injury who had received compensation by way of damages.[23] The survey sought to elicit the views of plaintiffs themselves concerning damages for non-pecuniary loss.[24] In addition, the report contains information about the long-term non-pecuniary effects of personal injury: the experience of pain, psychological problems and any physical impairment, as well as the wider effects that an injury may have had on daily life. Its findings serve, at the very least, to illustrate graphically the impact which non-pecuniary aspects of personal injury have upon an individual's quality of life and social relationships.[25] We have made use of these findings and the views contained in that report wherever they are relevant to the issues which we discuss in this paper.

1.7   In our Working Paper in 1971, we referred to the central importance in the legal system of claims for personal injuries.[26] This is equally true today. In 1988, the Lord Chancellor's Department estimated that the number of tort claims for personal injury (and death) made each year was in the region of 340,000[27] and, although the great majority of claims are settled without recourse to the courts,[28] in 1986 personal injury and death cases formed the majority of all types of civil cases tried

---

[21]   The JSB *Guidelines* (1st ed 1992) p 1.

[22]   *Ibid*, (2nd ed 1994) p 5.

[23]   (1994) Law Com No 225.

[24]   See paras 4.5-4.6 below.

[25]   See (1994) Law Com No 225, especially ch 3.

[26]   (1971) Law Com Working Paper No 41, paras 5, 8-9 and Appendix 2.

[27]   Civil Justice Review, Report of the Review Body on Civil Justice (June 1988) Cm 394, para 391.

[28]   Civil Justice Review, Report of the Review Body on Civil Justice (June 1988) Cm 394, para 391, reported that only 1% of tort claims for personal injury are disposed of by trial and that some 300,000 claims are settled without the issue of a writ. See also *Access to Justice* (1995) p 116 para 61.

in the county court or High Court.[29] This evidence is supported by more recent statistics collected by the Lord Chancellor's Department, which show that in each year between 1990 and 1994 personal injury (and death) cases comprised over 55 per cent of all hearings in the High Court (Queen's Bench Division) and over 23 per cent of cases in the county courts.[30]

1.8 It is also important to bear in mind recent important developments in procedure and professional practice relating to personal injury claims. Under the High Court and County Courts Jurisdiction Order 1991[31] personal injury claims up to £50,000 should now normally be tried in the county court rather than the High Court. The Court of Appeal has also endorsed the importance of the county court arbitration procedure for smaller personal injury claims, and has resisted the temptation of interpreting exceptions provided by the County Court Rules so as to make it easier for such claims to be taken out of the arbitration procedure.[32] In 1993, as part of the growing movement towards specialisation among solicitors and in the legal profession generally, the Law Society established a panel of solicitors specialising in personal injury litigation;[33] and since 5 July 1995 personal injury cases can be undertaken on a "no-win no-fee" basis.[34]

1.9 Even more radical changes will take place in the future if the recommendations made by Lord Woolf in his interim report on the civil justice system[35] are implemented. These would include the creation of a "multi-track" system, with

[29] Civil Justice Review, Report of the Review Body on Civil Justice (June 1988) Cm 394, para 390(i); and Civil Justice Review, Consultation Paper on Personal Injuries Litigation (February 1986) para 15.

[30] For the High Court, the figures are: 68% in 1990, 60.8% in 1991, 53% in 1992, 61.6% in 1993 and 58% in 1994. For the county courts, they are: 27.5% in 1990, 23.9% in 1991, 28.4% in 1992, 27.6% in 1993 and 30.4% in 1994. The information is drawn from two, one month samples of cases tried in the Queen's Bench General List and county courts, the data collected having been grossed up to represent annual figures. We are very grateful to the Court Service for these figures.

[31] SI 1991 No 724, art 5. The Order was made under the Courts and Legal Services Act 1990.

[32] *Afzal v Ford Motor Co Ltd* [1994] 4 All ER 720 (CA). For criticism of this decision as leading to the situation where solicitors will not take on small personal injury claims (as costs cannot be recovered under the small claims arbitration procedure and correspondingly defendants' insurers will not pay such costs in settling small claims) see the representations made to Lord Woolf detailed in *Access to Justice* (1995) ch 16 para 58.

[33] The panel now contains about 1,950 members. The increased consciousness of personal injury litigation as a specialised area of practice has also resulted in the formation of the Association of Personal Injury Lawyers (APIL) and the Personal Injuries Bar Association (PIBA).

[34] Conditional Fee Agreements Order 1995, SI 1995 No 1674; and Conditional Fee Agreements Regulations 1995, SI 1995 No 1675, both made under the Courts and Legal Services Act 1990.

[35] *Access to Justice* (1995).

significantly streamlined procedures, particularly for cases in the fast track, and much more active case management on the part of the courts. Lord Woolf envisages that claims under £10,000 which are relatively simple, including "running down" cases and other straightforward personal injury claims, would be dealt with on the fast track. The small claims procedure, which would cover claims of up to £3,000, would not apply to personal injury cases.[36] The changes he recommends in relation to expert witnesses, which would involve in some cases the use of experts appointed by the courts, and the elimination, in cases of less complexity or financial value, of oral evidence by the parties' expert witnesses, would have a particularly powerful effect on personal injury cases.

1.10   The arrangement of this paper is as follows. Part II is concerned with the present law. In Part III we look at the law in other jurisdictions. In Part IV we address the relevant policy issues and suggest options for reform. Part V contains a summary of the consultation issues and our provisional conclusions.

1.11   We gratefully acknowledge the assistance of the following people, who all helped us with various aspects of this paper: The Honourable Mr Justice Tuckey, His Honour Judge Roger Cox, Desmond Browne QC, David Eady QC, Charles Gray QC, Michael Harvey QC, Henry Witcomb, Gerhard Dannemann of Worcester College, Oxford, Laura Hoyano of the University of Bristol, Eoin O'Dell of Trinity College, Dublin and Sinéad Agnew of St Edmund Hall, Oxford, and Andrew Bell of the University of Manchester who, in addition to his invaluable help on the section on French law in Part III, presented a paper on damages for non-pecuniary loss at a conference which we organised with the Torts group of the Society of Public Teachers of Law and the Faculty of Law at the University of Manchester.[37]

---

[36] The Lord Chancellor has announced that the small claims limit in the county court will be raised (except, for example, for personal injury claims) from £1,000 to £3,000 from 8 January 1996.

[37] The title of the conference, which was held on 31 March - 1 April 1992, was *Compensation for Personal Injuries : Prospects for the Future*.

PART II
THE CURRENT LAW

1. INTRODUCTION

2.1 The aim of compensatory damages is to restore the plaintiff to the position he or she would have been in if the relevant tort (or breach of contract) had not been committed.[1] In other words, an injured plaintiff is entitled to compensation for the past, present and future losses that are consequent on his or her actionable personal injury. The application of this principle to pecuniary losses is relatively straightforward. This is not the case, however, in relation to non-pecuniary loss, since money cannot restore a broken limb or renew a shattered frame.[2] The award of damages is a monetary remedy, and non-pecuniary losses are losses which are "not susceptible of *measurement* in money."[3] They are such that, by definition, they cannot be measured by reference to the market.[4]

2.2 In a few jurisdictions, these problems have been avoided by the denial of damages for non-pecuniary losses,[5] but in England, as in most other countries, awards of damages on this account are well-established. Since at least the mid-nineteenth century[6] juries and courts have therefore been faced with the difficult task of assessing or valuing losses that are not readily measurable in money. After 1965,[7] the completion of the shift from jury to judge as the tribunal of assessment in personal injury actions has allowed the principles upon which damages for non-

---

[1]   See *Livingstone v Rawyards Coal Co* (1880) 5 App Cas 25, 39; *McGregor on Damages* (15th ed 1988) para 9. See also Aggravated, Exemplary and Restitutionary Damages (1993) Law Com Consultation Paper No 132 for circumstances in which tort damages are awarded on a different, non-compensatory, basis. Compensatory principles prevail in the context of personal injury damages (eg *British Transport Commission v Gourley* [1956] AC 185, 208).

[2]   *West v Shephard* [1964] AC 326, 346, *per* Lord Morris of Borth-y-Gest.

[3]   *Wright v British Railways Board* [1983] 2 AC 773, 777C, *per* Lord Diplock (emphasis in original). Similar observations are frequently made by the courts: eg *The Mediana* [1900] AC 113, 116-117; *West v Shephard* [1964] AC 326, 345-346.

[4]   *Warren v King* [1964] 1 WLR 1, 8, *per* Sellers LJ.

[5]   As was formerly the case in some socialist and Islamic jurisdictions: see H McGregor, Personal Injury and Death, Int Enc Comp L XI/2 Torts (1986) ch 9 ss 35-38, 46-47; and S H Amin, "Law of Personal Injuries in the Middle East" [1983] LMCLQ 446.

[6]   See *Blake v Midland Railway* (1852) 18 QB 93; *Fair v London & NW Ry Co* (1869) 21 LT 326, 327; *Phillips v London and South Western Railway Co* (1879) 4 QBD 406, (1879) 5 QBD 78, (1879) 5 CPD 280. For a history of damages for non-pecuniary loss, see J O'Connell & R J Simon, "Payment for Pain and Suffering: Who Wants What, When and Why?" (1972) 1 Univ Illinois Law Forum 1, Appendix V, especially at pp 87-93, 98-99.

[7]   In *Ward v James* [1966] 1 QB 273 a five-judge Court of Appeal held that a judge ought not to order trial by jury in a personal injury case, save in exceptional circumstances. For a very rare reported instance of an order for trial of a personal injury case with a jury, see *Hodges v Harland & Wolff Ltd* [1965] 1 WLR 523 (decided a month after *Ward v James*). Note that by s 69(1) of the Supreme Court Act 1981 and s 66(3) of the County Courts Act 1984 there continues to be a right to jury trial of a claim for false imprisonment, libel, slander and malicious prosecution or where there is a charge of fraud.

pecuniary loss are based and the process by which they are calculated to be articulated more fully. This change, in conjunction with a new need to itemise damages for the purpose of awarding interest,[8] has led to the emergence of sub-categories, or "heads", of non-pecuniary loss and to the development of a tariff by virtue of which a measure of consistency and predictability in awards for non-pecuniary loss is achieved.

2.3   Before examining the different heads of loss and the tariff system, it is important to explain that, at a theoretical level, English law adopts what may be labelled a "diminution in value" approach to the assessment of damages for non-pecuniary loss. Under this approach the purpose of an award of damages is to put a value on what the plaintiff has lost, irrespective of the use to which the damages may be put.[9] Moreover, in applying this approach, English law regards both subjective loss (loss which is dependent on the plaintiff's awareness of it) and objective loss (loss which is not dependent on the plaintiff's awareness of it) as compensatable.[10] A competing approach, which is explicitly favoured in some other jurisdictions,[11] is labelled "the functional approach" in a seminal article by Professor Ogus.[12] Under this approach damages for non-pecuniary loss are awarded as a solace or comfort for the plaintiff's misfortune by enabling him or her to purchase substitute sources of satisfaction. A key feature of this approach is that damages are subjectively assessed, since there is obviously no possibility of the damages being used to provide solace to a plaintiff who has no awareness of the injuries he or she has suffered.

---

[8]   See para 2.22, n 93 and paras 2.41-2.47 below.

[9]   See *The Mediana* [1900] AC 113, 116-117; *Wise v Kaye* [1962] 1 QB 638, 649-650; *West v Shephard* [1964] AC 326, 349; *Parry v Cleaver* [1970] AC 1, 22. J Munkman, *Damages for Personal Injuries and Death* (9th ed 1993), in particular pp 17-22, is a strong advocate of this approach. For rare indications of support by English judges for the alternative 'functional' approach, see the dicta in *Fletcher v Autocar and Transporters Ltd* [1968] 2 QB 322, 352, *per* Diplock LJ; and in *Lim Poh Choo v Camden and Islington AHA* [1979] 1 QB 196, 216 (CA), *per* Lord Denning MR.

[10]   The meaning of the words "subjective" and "objective" is a constant source of confusion in this area. Throughout this paper we treat these terms as relating to the question whether the plaintiff's own awareness of his or her position is a relevant consideration. A competing meaning, which we avoid, is derived from asking whether damages take account of the plaintiff's particular circumstances: ie it refers to the extent to which the assessment is particularised or standardised.

[11]   The most important example is Canada where, in 1978, the Supreme Court expressly adopted this approach in three contemporaneous decisions, widely referred to as "the trilogy": *Andrews v Grand & Toy Alberta Ltd* (1978) 83 DLR (3d) 452; *Arnold v Teno* (1978) 83 DLR (3d) 609; *Thornton v Board of School Trustees of School District No 57* (1978) 83 DLR (3d) 480. See also Windeyer J's judgments in the Australian cases *Teubner v Humble* (1963) 108 CLR 491, 507 and *Skelton v Collins* (1966) 115 CLR 94, 130-133. See paras 3.22 and 3.38-3.48 below.

[12]   A Ogus, "Damages for Lost Amenities: For a Foot, a Feeling or a Function?" (1972) 35 MLR 1. See also O Kahn-Freund, "Expectation of Happiness" (1941) 5 MLR 81, 86; H Luntz, *Assessment of Damages for Personal Injury and Death* (3rd ed 1990) pp 159-160; P Cane, *Atiyah's Accidents, Compensation and the Law* (5th ed 1993) pp 352-353.

2. THE RECOVERABLE LOSS: HEADS OF NON-PECUNIARY LOSS

2.4   The two principal heads of non-pecuniary loss in English law are pain and suffering, and loss of amenity.[13] The legal literature on damages for non-pecuniary loss in personal injury actions uniformly adopts this classification, and judges, lawyers and commentators will be familiar with it. However, it is important to stress that it remains the general practice of the courts when awarding damages in respect of non-pecuniary loss to make a global award.[14] In other words, damages for non-pecuniary loss are not usually sub-itemised in practice. One consequence of this is that, unless there is specific discussion of the matter by the judge in a particular case, it is difficult to analyse different awards in order to discover how much of them relate to 'pain and suffering' and how much to 'loss of amenity'. Moreover, in most cases it would be misleading to regard 'pain and suffering' as sharply distinct from 'loss of amenity'.[15] Indeed, judges sometimes make the point that it would be inappropriate to attempt to separate each item of non-pecuniary loss, as they are obliged to when assessing financial loss,[16] and that the most relevant factor is the *total* of the consequences of the injury (physical and mental) to the particular plaintiff.[17]

2.5   Nevertheless, there are situations or types of injury in which pain and suffering and loss of amenity can be sensibly distinguished, and it is therefore convenient to follow the customary classification and to consider each separately. Further, although "loss of expectation of life" no longer exists as an independent head of damage, its history and development remain important, since the issues raised by this concept, as addressed by the courts, find a parallel in the award of loss of amenity, in particular in relation to the unconscious plaintiff.[18] We shall therefore examine this defunct head of loss first, and then go on to set out the present law relating to pain and suffering and loss of amenity.

---

[13]   Damages may be recovered for both past (ie pre-trial) and prospective loss.

[14]   *West v Shephard* [1964] AC 326, 365; *Fletcher v Autocar and Transporters Ltd* [1968] 2 QB 322, 336C-E, 341-342, 364B-C; *Charlesworth & Percy on Negligence* (8th ed 1990) para 4-98.

[15]   *Povey v Governors of Rydal School* [1970] 1 All ER 841, 846d-e; (1971) Law Com Working Paper No 41, para 74; Pearson Report, vol 1, para 379; B S Markesinis & S F Deakin, *Tort Law* (3rd ed 1994) p 719. Note that there is only one tariff, organised by reference to the type of injury - as opposed to separate tariffs for pain and suffering on the one hand and loss of amenity on the other. See paras 2.21-2.37 below.

[16]   *Fletcher v Autocar & Transporters Ltd* [1968] 2 QB 322, 364B-C, *per* Salmon LJ. See also *West v Shephard* [1964] AC 326, 351. In Canada, the Supreme Court has also said that non-pecuniary loss *ought not* to be sub-itemised: *Andrews v Grand & Toy Alberta Ltd* (1978) 83 DLR (3d) 452, 478: see para 3.41 below.

[17]   *Fletcher v Autocar & Transporters Ltd* [1968] 2 QB 322, 364; *Frost v Palmer* [1993] PIQR Q14, Q20, *per* Ralph Gibson LJ. See also J Munkman, *Damages for Personal Injuries and Death* (9th ed 1993) p 119.

[18]   In some other jurisdictions loss of expectation of life is still treated as a separate head of non-pecuniary loss. See para 3.11 below (Ireland) and 3.20 below (Australia).

(1) A defunct head of loss: loss of expectation of life

2.6   It appears that before 1934, in cases where a plaintiff's mental suffering was exacerbated by the knowledge that his or her life had been shortened as a result of the injuries inflicted by the tortfeasor, this factor was taken into account to increase the damages awarded under the head of pain and suffering.[19] In 1934, the Court of Appeal in *Flint v Lovell* held that the shortening of life could form the basis of a claim for damages for "loss of expectation of life", as a separate and independent head of non-pecuniary loss, quite apart from any suffering caused to the plaintiff by this realisation.[20] Although the plaintiff in *Flint v Lovell* was in fact aware that his life expectancy had been reduced, the House of Lords subsequently confirmed in *Rose v Ford* that this new principle was correct.[21] It allowed this head of damages to be recovered by the estate of a woman who had died four days after being injured, although she had no knowledge that her life had been shortened because she was unconscious during that time.[22] It thus recognised this head of non-pecuniary loss as an independent and objective one, in the sense that it did not depend on the plaintiff's own awareness of the loss.[23]

2.7   The assessment of damages under this head presented difficulties. When claimed as a separate head of loss (usually by the estate in cases of instant or near-instant death), the assessment involved the courts in an unpalatable attempt to measure the value of life. In the years which followed *Rose v Ford*, their efforts produced widely divergent and rapidly increasing awards,[24] with some judges calculating the appropriate sum by reference to the victim's pre-accident life expectancy. Approaching assessment by reference to the injured person's or the deceased's pre-accident life expectancy clearly tended to inflate the award, especially in cases

---

[19]   See O Kahn-Freund, "Expectation of Happiness" (1941) 5 MLR 81, 82-83; (1971) Law Com Working Paper No 41, para 62; (1973) Law Com No 56, para 95.

[20]   [1935] 1 KB 354.

[21]   [1937] AC 826.

[22]   The claim formed part of a survival action under the Law Reform (Miscellaneous Provisions) Act 1934, as to which see paras 2.48-2.52 below. The principle in *Flint v Lovell* might have been confined to claims by plaintiffs who were alive at the trial of the action, but who experienced no suffering through the knowledge that their lives had been shortened because, eg, they were unconscious. However, the (perhaps unintended) effect of applying the newly enacted provisions of the Act of 1934 - which for the first time allowed a cause of action to survive the death of the plaintiff - was to extend the principle to claims made by the estates of deceased persons, even where death was instantaneous.

[23]   "I regard impaired health and vitality not merely as a cause of pain and suffering but as a loss of a good thing in itself. Loss of expectation of life is a form in which impaired health and vitality may express themselves as a result. In such a loss there is a loss of a temporal good, capable of evaluation in money though the evaluation is difficult.": *Rose v Ford* [1937] AC 826, 859, *per* Lord Roche.

[24]   See the comments in *Benham v Gambling* [1941] AC 157, 161-162; *Mills v Stanway Coaches Ltd* [1940] 2 KB 334, 346-347; *West v Shephard* [1964] AC 326, 342, 347, 367; A L Goodhart, "Viscount Simon, 1873-1954" (1954) 70 LQR 177, 180.

involving young children where the length of lost life was the greatest.[25] In *Benham v Gambling*[26] the House of Lords intervened and restricted the award for loss of expectation of life in the case of claims made on behalf of the estate of deceased persons to a moderate sum - £200 in December 1940. Rejecting the length of life that was lost as the basis of assessment and comparison, Viscount Simon LC indicated that "the thing to be valued is not the prospect of length of days, but the prospect of a predominantly happy life."[27] In other words, the task of the courts was to fix a figure which represented the loss of a measure of prospective happiness.[28] Bearing in mind that it was in fact the beneficiaries of the estate, not the injured person, who would benefit from the award; that the task of assessing lost happiness was an artificial one involving incommensurables; and that there was no necessary anomaly in awarding more to a living plaintiff than to a deceased one, the House of Lords concluded that only very moderate sums should be awarded for this head of damage.[29]

2.8 Following *Benham v Gambling*, damages for loss of expectation of life were awarded as a fixed, conventional sum, and although the new approach was formulated in the context of a claim made on behalf of the estate of a deceased person,[30] it was later also applied to claims by living plaintiffs.[31] It was still recognised, however, that in addition to this conventional award, damages under the head of pain and suffering might be increased, where there was any awareness by the plaintiff that his or her life expectancy had been reduced.[32] By 1985, the conventional sum, updated for inflation, had reached £1,750 in relation to an adult.[33]

---

[25] Eg *Turbeyfield v GWR Co* (1937) 158 LT 135 (girl of 8: £1,500); *Bailey v Howard* [1939] 1 KB 453 (girl of 3: £1,000); and *Gambling v Benham* [1940] 1 All ER 275 (CA) (boy of 2½: £1,200). Updated for inflation to May 1995 these sums are now worth £38,690, £26,714 and £32,057 respectively.

[26] [1941] AC 157.

[27] *Ibid*, 166.

[28] *Ibid*, 166.

[29] *Ibid*, 168. It has subsequently been observed that, although the House of Lords purported to justify the limitation imposed upon this head of damage by reference to the concept of 'lost happiness', the decision was in truth a pragmatic one based upon policy and the desire to control levels of awards: eg A L Goodhart, "Viscount Simon, 1873-1954" (1954) 70 LQR 177, 179-180; *West v Shephard* [1964] AC 326, 342, *per* Lord Reid.

[30] The award to the estates of deceased plaintiffs came to be perceived as operating in practice as a form of indirect bereavement award to their parents, at a time when bereavement damages could not be awarded to them directly.

[31] Eg *Wise v Kaye* [1962] 1 QB 638; *West v Shephard* [1964] AC 326.

[32] Eg *Davies v Smith* (1958) CA No 349, quoted in *Kemp and Kemp*, vol 1, paras 4-002 to 4-004, 4-014; *Forrest v Sharp* (1963) 107 SJ 536. See *Wise v Kaye* [1962] 1 QB 638, 649; *West v Shephard* [1964] AC 326, 349, 360, 370.

[33] *Kralj v McGrath* [1986] 1 All ER 54, 59g. The death in this case occurred before the commencement of the Administration of Justice Act 1982. See para 2.9, n 34 below.

2.9 Loss of expectation of life was abolished as a separate head of damages by section 1(1)(a) of the Administration of Justice Act 1982, but its relevance as an element of a claim for pain and suffering was left intact.[34] Hence any reduction in a plaintiff's life expectancy is now only to be taken into account in so far as the knowledge that his or her life has been shortened gives rise to any suffering.[35] In assessing damages the courts are not restricted to awarding the conventional *Benham v Gambling* sum. They should award an appropriate figure on the basis of the particular plaintiff's circumstances and attitude to the fact that life has been shortened.[36]

(2)   Pain and suffering

2.10 The expression "pain and suffering" is now almost a term of art.[37] In so far as they can be distinguished, "pain" means the physical hurt or discomfort attributable to the injury itself or consequent upon it. It thus includes the pain caused by any medical treatment which the plaintiff might have to undergo.[38] "Suffering" on the other hand denotes the mental or emotional distress which the plaintiff may feel as a consequence of the injury: anxiety, worry, fear, torment, embarrassment and the like. It is not, however, usual for judges to distinguish between the two elements.

---

[34] Section 1(1)(b). This followed the recommendations of the Law Commission (see (1973) Law Com No 56, paras 99 and 107) and the Pearson Commission (see Pearson Report, vol 1, paras 370-372).

[35] Section 73(3) of the Administration of Justice Act 1982 provides that s 1 has effect "where a person *has died* after the commencement of" the Act (emphasis added). This wording would appear to leave the fixed *Benham v Gambling* award for loss of expectation of life open in theory to a living (including an unconscious) plaintiff. However, there is no discussion of this point in the literature and we are not aware of it ever having been advanced by counsel on behalf of plaintiffs who are unconscious and who therefore experience no mental suffering from the knowledge that their life has been shortened.

[36] See *McGregor on Damages* (15th ed 1988) para 1531, whose author also believes that this consideration is likely to produce a sum exceeding the former conventional award. In practice, however, the sum representing the suffering attributable to the plaintiff's awareness that life expectancy has been reduced will simply be subsumed within the total award for non-pecuniary loss.

[37] *McGregor on Damages* (15th ed 1988) para 1517; *Kemp and Kemp*, vol 1, paras 1-007 and 2-001.

[38] *McGregor on Damages* (15th ed 1988) para 1517. Eg *Povey v Governors of Rydal School* [1970] 1 All ER 841, 846c-d (pain and discomfort from traction being applied to the plaintiff's skull).

2.11   Examples of matters which would be included under this head are: excruciating pain due to medical treatment without anaesthetic;[39] initial shock on impact;[40] fear that any future pregnancy may be problematic;[41] the mental stress of wondering whether one's eyesight will deteriorate further;[42] distress at being prevented from caring for loved ones;[43] and the misery resulting from awareness of one's disability.[44] Also included under this head is the embarrassment and humiliation felt as a consequence of disfigurement.[45] In addition, where a plaintiff's life expectancy has been reduced, any suffering attributable to awareness that it has been so reduced falls to be considered as part of the damages for pain and suffering.[46]

2.12   Pain and suffering is an inherently subjective head of non-pecuniary loss, in the sense that it is dependent on the plaintiff's awareness of it.[47] Hence an unconscious plaintiff who feels no pain and has no mental suffering receives nothing under this head.[48] Nor does a plaintiff whose lack of awareness of pain is due to anaesthesia or the effect of pain-relieving drugs.[49] It is cases like these, where the plaintiff can

---

[39]   *Kralj v McGrath* [1986] 1 All ER 54 (prolonged attempt to deliver baby in transverse position); *Phelan v East Cumbria Health Authority* [1991] 2 Med LR 419 (deep cutting and drilling of bone while conscious but unable to speak).

[40]   *Kaufman v Ocean Steamship Co* (1969) CA No 448 (shock on receiving blow from heavy block swinging against the face); *Skinner v Ministry of Defence* (1971) CA No 239 (shock of severe blows on face, with glass entering the face and jaw being fractured), both cases quoted in *Kemp and Kemp*, vol 1, para 2-017, n 31.

[41]   *Kralj v McGrath* [1986] 1 All ER 54, 63c (following terrifying and excruciatingly painful delivery due to medical negligence).

[42]   *Hamp v Sisters of St Joseph's Hospital Mount Carmel Convent School*, 26 July 1973 (CA), *Kemp and Kemp*, vol 2, para D2-100.

[43]   *Rourke v Barton*, The Times 23 June 1982. This case illustrates the proposition that the suffering need not be caused solely by concern for oneself. In *Re Jones (SA)*, 13 April 1994, *Kemp and Kemp*, vol 3, para J3-018, the applicant's unsightly burns caused such an acute psychiatric reaction in his young son that the son required treatment, which itself caused further anguish to the applicant.

[44]   *West v Shephard* [1964] AC 326, 340-341, 343, 351; *Housecroft v Burnett* [1986] 1 All ER 332.

[45]   Eg *Doughty v North Staffordshire Health Authority* [1992] 3 Med LR 81 (facial disfigurement giving rise to chronic post-traumatic stress disorder); *Comber v Greater Glasgow Health Board* 1992 SLT 22 (misshapen face causing mental distress falling short of clinical depression); *Laker v Townsend* [1986] CLY 996 (facial scarring causing self-consciousness, distress and embarrassment). For some physical injuries the element of disfigurement tends to become the predominant one in the assessment of damages - particularly in the case of facial or readily visible disfigurement. The JSB *Guidelines*, p 45, include a category for "Facial Disfigurement".

[46]   Section 1(1)(b) of the Administration of Justice Act 1982. See para 2.9 above.

[47]   *West v Shephard* [1964] AC 326, 349, *per* Lord Morris.

[48]   *Wise v Kaye* [1962] 1 QB 638, 649, 652, 654, 659, 660; *West v Shephard* [1964] AC 326, 340, 346, 349.

[49]   *West v Shephard* [1964] AC 326, 354.

establish no pain and suffering, which have contributed to the emergence of loss of amenity as a distinct, objective head of loss. It appears, however, that the subjectivity of the assessment for pain and suffering is not carried to the lengths of awarding lesser damages to a plaintiff who puts a brave face on his or her injury than to someone who appears miserable.[50]

2.13 We noted above that the courts do not usually divide damages for non-pecuniary loss into pain and suffering on the one hand and loss of amenity on the other.[51] Nevertheless, in addition to those cases where a plaintiff is unaware of pain or is unconscious (where no award of damages under this head can be made), in practice pain and suffering comes close to being a distinct head of damages where a plaintiff suffers only minor injuries or makes a complete recovery. Here most, if not all, of the award will consist of damages in respect of pain and suffering. Another example relates to claims for personal injury where an anaesthetist has failed to render the plaintiff unconscious during a serious operation.[52]

(3) Loss of amenity

2.14 Injuries may be such as to deprive plaintiffs of the capacity to do the things which before the accident they were able to enjoy, and to prevent full participation in the normal activities of life. A plaintiff who is blinded is no longer able to enjoy the amenities that are associated with sight, such as reading or painting; one who loses the use of both legs is no longer able to walk or play football; and a plaintiff who loses the use of both hands can no longer play the piano or lift things easily. This is what is meant by the term "loss of amenity", which is sometimes also referred to as "loss of enjoyment of life" or "loss of faculty". Loss of amenity includes the physical and social limitations inherent in the injury itself, but it extends also to the loss of special amenities which are peculiar to the particular plaintiff, such as no longer being able to engage in pre-accident hobbies or interests.[53] Loss of the capacity to use one's limbs[54] and the impairment of any one or more of the five

---

[50] *Wise v Kaye* [1962] 1 QB 638, 651; *West v Shephard* [1964] AC 326, 369; *Povey v Governors of Rydal School* [1970] 1 All ER 841, 846-847. Contrast Ireland (where damages otherwise recoverable under this head will be lessened if the plaintiff has adjusted well to his or her injured condition): see para 3.12 below.

[51] See para 2.4 above.

[52] See *Kemp and Kemp*, vol 1, paras 2-009 to 2-012 and vol 3, section L7. Cf also cases involving disfigurement (especially facial disfigurement), where most of the loss comprises mental suffering; and cases in which plaintiffs have died of mesothelioma after a prolonged period of pain: eg *Simpkins v BREL*, 5 December 1990, *Kemp and Kemp*, vol 2, para F2-018/4.

[53] See *West v Shephard* [1964] AC 326, 365, *per* Lord Pearce; and para 2.30 below.

[54] Eg through paralysis or amputation, recent examples of which are *Hunt v Severs* [1994] 2 AC 350 (paraplegia) and *Frost v Palmer* [1993] PIQR Q14 (below knee amputation).

senses[55] are matters which clearly fall to be considered under this head of loss. Loss of amenity also extends, for instance, to loss of marriage prospects;[56] loss of sexual function;[57] inability to play with one's children;[58] loss of a craftsperson's pleasure and pride in work;[59] and even to loss of enjoyment of a holiday.[60]

2.15   The courts have always taken into account the deprivations occasioned by the bodily (and more recently the psychiatric) injury sustained by a plaintiff as an element of his or her non-pecuniary loss.[61] But because the injured person was usually aware of his or her diminished capacity and inability to enjoy life as before, it was unnecessary to make a clear distinction, when awarding and assessing damages for non-pecuniary loss, between on the one hand the subjective mental suffering to which such deprivations and loss of amenity give rise, and on the other the objective fact of having been deprived of them. Loss of amenity only emerged clearly as a conceptually distinct head when the courts were confronted with one particular situation: where the injuries had rendered the plaintiff permanently unconscious.[62] The development of medical science, enabling plaintiffs who have suffered catastrophic injury to be kept alive, and kept alive for longer periods, has made this once unusual case a more common problem.[63] In this type of situation no damages are recoverable for pain and suffering since these depend on awareness. The difficult question is whether the plaintiff should nevertheless be entitled to an award for "loss of amenity"; and, if so, whether the award should be a substantial one at the top end of the conventional scale of values.

2.16   The question is a controversial one upon which the courts have been sharply divided, but it is now clear that in English law loss of amenity is a distinct and

---

[55] Eg *Cook v J L Kier & Co Ltd* [1970] 1 WLR 774 (loss of taste and smell); *Thompson v Smiths Shiprepairers (North Shields) Ltd* [1984] QB 405 (loss of hearing).

[56] *Moriarty v McCarthy* [1978] 1 WLR 155; *Hughes v McKeown* [1985] 1 WLR 963; *Housecroft v Burnett* [1986] 1 All ER 332, 345e.

[57] Eg *Cook v J L Kier & Co Ltd* [1970] 1 WLR 774; *Hale v London Underground Ltd* [1993] PIQR Q30.

[58] Eg *Hoffman v Sofaer* [1982] 1 WLR 1350; *Re Burleigh*, 11 September 1992 (CICB), *Kemp and Kemp*, vol 2, para C2-004.

[59] Eg *Morris v Johnson Matthey & Co Ltd* (1968) 112 SJ 32.

[60] Eg *Ichard v Frangoulis* [1977] 1 WLR 556; *Hoffman v Sofaer* [1982] 1 WLR 1350.

[61] Eg *Fair v London NW Railway* (1869) 21 LT 326; *Phillips v London & South Western Railway Co* (1879) 4 QBD 406, 407, *per* Cockburn CJ ("the bodily injury sustained").

[62] See H McGregor, "Compensation Versus Punishment in Damages Awards" (1965) 28 MLR 629, 650; and *West v Shephard* [1964] AC 326, 359.

[63] *Lim Poh Choo v Camden and Islington AHA* [1979] 1 QB 196, 216, 217 (CA), [1980] AC 174, 183H-184A (HL); *Croke v Wiseman* [1982] 1 WLR 71, 75B-C; and see also Mental Incapacity (1995) Law Com No 231, para 2.37. But cf *Winfield & Jolowicz on Tort* (14th ed 1994) p 648, n 53, which suggests that, notwithstanding medical advances, such cases may be less frequent after *Airedale NHS Trust v Bland* [1993] AC 789 (HL).

objective head of loss in the sense that the loss exists without the injured person being aware of it.[64] This issue was first addressed directly by the courts in *Wise v Kaye*,[65] a case where the brain-injured plaintiff had been unconscious since the date of the accident and had no prospect of recovery. A majority of the Court of Appeal held that, although her lack of awareness meant that she could recover nothing as damages for pain and suffering, the plaintiff was still entitled to a substantial sum for "loss of amenity", the latter being a "separate and distinct"[66] head of loss.[67] To award an unconscious plaintiff only the *Benham v Gambling* sum in respect of loss of expectation of life would be to treat her loss as comparable to that suffered by a deceased person, and the Court of Appeal refused to do so.[68]

2.17 This recognition of an objective element in a plaintiff's non-pecuniary loss was subsequently confirmed by the House of Lords in *West v Shephard*.[69] Lord Morris of Borth-y-Gest said:

> An unconscious person will be spared pain and suffering and will not experience the mental anguish which may result from knowledge of what has in life been lost or from knowledge that life has been shortened. The fact of unconsciousness is therefore relevant in respect of and will eliminate those heads or elements of damage which can only exist by being felt or thought or experienced. The fact of unconsciousness does not, however, eliminate the

[64] *Wise v Kaye* [1962] 1 QB 638 (Sellers and Upjohn LJJ; Diplock LJ dissenting); *West v Shephard* [1964] AC 326 (Lords Tucker, Morris and Pearce; Lords Reid and Devlin dissenting); and *Lim Poh Choo v Camden and Islington AHA* [1980] AC 174 (HL).

[65] [1962] 1 QB 638. The matter had deliberately been left open by the Court of Appeal in *Oliver v Ashman* [1962] 2 QB 210, 224 (decided 5 months before *Wise*), in the knowledge that the *Wise* case was pending.

[66] [1962] 1 QB 638, 652, *per* Sellers LJ.

[67] [1962] 1 QB 638 (Sellers and Upjohn LJJ; Diplock LJ dissenting). The Court of Appeal refused to interfere with Finnemore J's assessment of £15,000 for loss of amenities. Although Diplock LJ dissented on the principles to be applied, he would still have awarded the plaintiff *something* for her non-pecuniary loss, in addition to the *Benham v Gambling* sum for loss of expectation of life; but he would have set this at the much lower figure of £1,500.

[68] *Wise v Kaye* [1962] 1 QB 638, 654, 659. But Diplock LJ (dissenting) thought that an unconscious plaintiff's loss corresponded closely, except for the survival of "mere existence", with a deceased plaintiff's loss: *ibid*, 673.

[69] [1964] AC 326. Lords Reid and Devlin dissented on the sum which should be awarded as pain and suffering and loss of amenities, but they both recognised the objective element of the loss. Lord Devlin only did so, however, because he believed that authority required him to, the House of Lords having decided in *Rose v Ford* [1937] AC 826 and *Benham v Gambling* [1941] AC 157 that there was an objective element to damages for loss of expectation of life: *West v Shephard* [1964] AC 326, 360, 362. He would otherwise have preferred to award the unconscious plaintiff nothing as damages for non-pecuniary loss.

actuality of the deprivations of the ordinary experiences and amenities of life which may be the inevitable result of some physical injury.[70]

And in Lord Pearce's words:

> The practice of the courts hitherto has been to treat bodily injury as a deprivation which in itself entitles a plaintiff to substantial damages according to its gravity.[71]

The House differed, however, on the relative weight which should be attached to the objective element (that is, the fact of deprivation) in comparison with the subjective element (the plaintiff's own feeling about what had been lost). Regarding deprived capacity as a grave loss in itself, the majority awarded the plaintiff, a severely brain-damaged paraplegic who may have had some limited insight into her condition,[72] £17,500 as damages for pain and suffering and loss of amenity.[73] Lords Reid and Devlin, on the other hand, would have awarded a much smaller sum.[74] It was their belief that a plaintiff's subjective suffering was the more important loss, and they drew support for this from the decision in *Benham v Gambling*,[75] which in their view illustrated the point that when damages for non-pecuniary loss are assessed on an objective basis, they should only give rise to moderate sums.

2.18 The majority decisions in *Wise* and *West* have been the subject of criticism both here[76] and in other jurisdictions.[77] In 1979, however, the House of Lords, whilst

---

[70] *Ibid*, 349. Like Sellers and Upjohn LJJ in *Wise*, the majority of the House of Lords in *West* were also concerned that a living plaintiff should not be treated as if she were already dead: [1964] AC 326, 368-369.

[71] *Ibid*, 365.

[72] But Lord Devlin indicated that the case had been pleaded as one of unconsciousness: *ibid*, 353.

[73] For similar cases see *Deeley v McCarthy and Leeds AHA*, 29 July 1977, *Kemp and Kemp*, vol 3, para L5-025 (maximum brain damage consistent with continuance of life: £15,000 for loss of amenities, there being no pain and suffering); *Duhelon v Carson*, 18 July 1986, *Kemp and Kemp*, vol 2, para A4-006 (severe brain damage: £65,000 for loss of amenity, the plaintiff being "unaware" of her predicament and not in pain). Cf also *Murray v Shuter* [1976] 1 QB 972, 981A (£11,000 non-pecuniary damages awarded to the estate of a plaintiff who died four years after suffering severe brain injury, the element of pain and suffering being almost entirely excluded).

[74] Lord Reid would have awarded the plaintiff £5,000 for her actual physical injuries and £4,000 for her pain and suffering: [1964] AC 326, 343. Lord Devlin did not find it necessary to decide upon an alternative figure, although he did think that the sum awarded for mental suffering should be generously assessed because any uncertainty as to the exact extent of the plaintiff's awareness - she being unable to express herself - was attributable precisely to the defendant's negligence: *ibid*, 363.

[75] [1941] AC 157. See paras 2.6-2.9 above.

[76] Eg *Andrews v Freeborough* [1967] 1 QB 1, 12, 18; *Croke v Wiseman* [1982] 1 WLR 71; Pearson Report, vol 1, paras 393-398, which recommended that non-pecuniary damages should no longer be available for permanent unconsciousness; *McGregor on Damages* (15th

---

lamenting the "complexities" of the law on personal injury damages and recognising the need for "a radical reappraisal" of it,[78] refused to overrule *West v Shephard*, in the belief that any change in this area of the law should only take place "legislatively within the context of a comprehensive enactment dealing with all aspects of damages for personal injury."[79]

2.19 The cases of the permanently unconscious or severely brain-damaged plaintiff are the best examples of those cases where loss of amenity acquires independent status as a separate head of non-pecuniary loss. Another situation where loss of amenity tends to attain prominence is where the plaintiff is seriously injured in terms of physical capacity but the administration of drugs relieves the sensation of bodily pain.[80]

2.20 It is sometimes suggested that one must separate loss of amenity from "the injury itself" and that a plaintiff is entitled to damages for both.[81] But even if this is correct it will be a very rare case where one can say that the plaintiff is being compensated for the injury as distinct from its consequences (be they pain, suffering or loss of amenity). As the editor of *Winfield and Jolowicz on Tort* says: "It is .... sometimes said that the injury itself is a proper subject of compensation, quite apart from pain and suffering and loss of amenity. While this may be correct as a matter of principle and while there may be injuries which will lead to no disability, it is not very likely that they will be unaccompanied by pain and suffering so as to require the court to give express recognition to the injury as a head of damage."[82] For example, in *Church v Ministry of Defence*[83] the plaintiff had developed asbestos

---

ed 1988) para 1525; K M Stanton, *The Modern Law of Tort* (1994) p 255.

[77] For example in Australia: see paras 3.21-3.22 below.

[78] *Lim Poh Choo v Camden and Islington AHA* [1980] AC 174, 182F-G.

[79] *Lim Poh Choo v Camden and Islington AHA* [1980] AC 174, 189C. However, the sum of £20,000 awarded to the plaintiff for her non-pecuniary loss was a good deal lower in real terms than the sums which were awarded to the plaintiffs in *Wise* and *West*. See para 4.48 below. It has therefore been suggested that the *result* in *Lim* may have represented a modest move in the direction of the minority in *West*, despite following the majority in principle: see *Winfield & Jolowicz on Tort* (14th ed 1994) pp 649-650; and *Knutson v Farr* (1984) 30 CCLT 8, 27 (BCCA).

[80] But in this last instance there may be a large element in respect of mental suffering.

[81] See, eg, J Munkman, *Damages for Personal Injury and Death* (9th ed 1993) pp 120-121; B S Markesinis & S F Deakin, *Tort Law* (3rd ed 1994) p 722; *Charlesworth & Percy on Negligence* (8th ed 1990) paras 4.99-4.100.

[82] *Winfield & Jolowicz on Tort* (edited by Professor Rogers) (14th ed 1994) pp 650-651.

[83] *The Times* 7 March 1994 (Sir Peter Pain): cf *Sykes v Ministry of Defence, The Times* 23 March 1994 in which, in a similar pleural plaques case, Otton J awarded £1,500 damages for three elements; the physiological damage itself; the risk of further complications; and anxiety. J Munkman, *Damages for Personal Injury and Death* (9th ed 1993) p 121, n 4 argues that in *Forster v Pugh* [1955] CLY 741, in which the plaintiff's spleen was removed, "[a]llowing for pain and suffering and for the scar left by the operation, a substantial part

pleural disease (a symptomless thickening of the lung pleura by "plaques"). While the plaintiff was held to have suffered an actionable personal injury by reason of the "injury itself" the damages of £1,500 were based entirely on the increased risk that the plaintiff would develop asbestosis and the anxiety associated with the realisation that this might occur.

3. QUANTIFICATION: VALUING THE LOSS
(1) The judicial tariff system

2.21 As non-pecuniary loss cannot be compensated in a precise or literal sense, the courts have often talked in this context of awarding "fair and reasonable compensation":[84] and what is fair and reasonable is to be assessed in the context of the social, economic and industrial conditions which prevail in England and Wales.[85] This suggests a wide discretion in the assessment of damages for non-pecuniary loss. It also presents a real danger of widely divergent awards. In an effort to control the levels of awards and to ensure a measure of consistency and predictability (this in turn encouraging out-of-court settlements), the requirement of fairness is understood to import the proposition that like cases should be treated alike and unlike cases should be treated differently from one another.[86] The result is a comparative approach to assessment. Thus, although the fixing of the general level of awards may not be susceptible of 'rational' or 'logical' analysis,[87] once the general level has been decided on, the assessment process can be governed by the twin principles of comparability and proportionality.[88] Comparative values are attributed

of the award is clearly for the loss of the organ itself". But the report is too brief to substantiate that comment. In *Hamilton v Burdon* [1962] CLY 859 it would appear that no damages were awarded for loss of a spleen as such because there was no evidence that the spleen was useful or desirable.

[84] *Phillips v London & South Western Railway Co* (1879) 4 QBD 406, 407, 408. See, similarly, *British Transport Commission v Gourley* [1956] AC 185; *West v Shephard* [1964] AC 326, 356-357, 358-359; *Wise v Kaye* [1962] 1 QB 638, 650; *Warren v King* [1964] 1 WLR 1, 7, 9, 11, 14; *Fletcher v Autocar and Transporters Ltd* [1968] 2 QB 322, 335, 362.

[85] *Jag Singh v Toong Fong Omnibus Co* [1964] 1 WLR 1382 (where the Privy Council said that the appropriate level of award for non-pecuniary loss may vary in differing social and economic conditions in different parts of the world); *Selvanayagam v University of West Indies* [1983] 1 WLR 585 (PC); and *Li Ping Sum v Chan Wai Tong* [1985] 1 Lloyd's Rep 87 (PC). See also *Simpson v Harland and Wolff Plc* [1988] NILR 432, 440H-441A, *per* Lord Lowry LCJ: "I would reject the suggestion that our calculations of general damages are 'wrong' if they do not conform to standards observed in other jurisdictions since Northern Ireland, like Scotland and the Republic of Ireland, constitutes a separate legal jurisdiction with its own judicial and social outlook".

[86] *Hennell v Ranaboldo* [1963] 1 WLR 1391, 1392, 1393; *Ward v James* [1966] 1 QB 273, 293-294, 296, 300; *West v Shephard* [1964] AC 326, 346; *Wright v British Railways Board* [1983] 2 AC 773, 777C-D.

[87] *Wise v Kaye* [1962] 1 QB 638, 669; *Every v Miles* (1964) CA No 261, quoted in *Kemp and Kemp*, vol 1, para 1-003.

[88] Eg *Bird v Cocking & Sons Ltd* [1951] 2 TLR 1260; *Rushton v National Coal Board* [1953] 1 QB 495, 501; *Waldon v War Office* [1956] 1 WLR 51; *Wise v Kaye* [1962] 1 QB 638, 650, 664-665, 669, 671; *West v Shephard* [1964] AC 326, 346, 366.

to different types of injury (for example, loss of an eye or amputation of a leg) according to the seriousness of the injuries (in terms of the duration and gravity of the loss of amenity and pain and suffering associated with them),[89] thereby allowing a scale or tariff to emerge.

2.22   The pursuit of consistency and predictability has been facilitated by the disappearance, for all practical purposes, of the jury (which could not be referred to previous awards) in personal injury actions.[90] Indeed, that these aims could not otherwise be properly achieved was the rationale behind the decision to remove virtually all personal injury actions from the jury.[91] It is this change which, in conjunction with the publication of collections of awards,[92] has enabled a tariff to develop more fully.[93]

2.23   Damages for pain and suffering and loss of amenity are therefore assessed by reference to awards made in previous cases. Whilst it is true that no two cases will ever be identical, certain *types* of injury (for example, those involving paralysis or those affecting the senses) can be isolated and may recur with sufficient frequency for a body of awards to develop and a pattern eventually to emerge.[94] In addition, "some injuries are more susceptible to some uniformity in compensation than others" - tetraplegia, for instance, where the variables are fairly limited.[95] In this way, the range of appropriate awards for a particular form of injury is established. The range can be found by consulting the reports of previous awards made in respect of similar injuries.[96]   This can be a quite time-consuming and complex

---

[89]   *Wise v Kaye* [1962] 1 QB 638, 650, 651, *per* Sellers LJ; *West v Shephard* [1964] AC 326, 349, 365; *Rose v Ford* [1937] AC 826, 859.

[90]   However, it has been suggested to us by the Association of Personal Injury Lawyers that changes to the jurisdiction of the county court, resulting in most personal injury cases being tried at that level, increase the prospect for inconsistency between awards for similar injuries: APIL Preliminary Submission to the Law Commission (1992).

[91]   *Ward v James* [1966] 1 QB 273, a decision of the full Court of Appeal. See para 2.2, n 7 above.

[92]   See S Chapman, Review of *Kemp and Kemp on Damages* (1962) 78 LQR 275, 278-279; (1971) Law Com Working Paper No 41, para 210.

[93]   The separation of pecuniary and non-pecuniary losses, required after the Court of Appeal's interpretation in *Jefford v Gee* [1970] 2 QB 130 of interest provisions introduced by s 22 of the Administration of Justice Act 1969, has also contributed to the development of a scale for non-pecuniary loss. See, further, paras 2.41-2.47 below. There can be no scale for pecuniary losses, where the principle of full compensation or exact assessment is more meaningful; *Lim Poh Choo v Camden and Islington AHA* [1980] AC 174, 189, 190 (HL).

[94]   H Luntz, *Assessment of Damages for Personal Injury and Death* (3rd ed 1990) para 3.1.4.

[95]   *Housecroft v Burnett* [1986] 1 All ER 332, 337c-d.

[96]   Details of awards, which assist practitioners and the judiciary, are collected systematically in, eg, *Kemp and Kemp*; *Current Law*; *Quantum* (Casewatch); *New Law Journal*; *Halsbury's Laws Service Monthly Review*; and (in computerised form) LEXIS and LAWTEL.

process and, because the facts of each case inevitably differ, must be approached on a very broad, flexible basis. However, the task has been facilitated by the Judicial Studies Board's publication in 1992 of *Guidelines for the Assessment of General Damages in Personal Injury Cases*, indicating the appropriate bracket of award for particular injuries and listing features which might affect the level of the award within the bracket.[97] They are proving to be a very useful aid to litigants and practitioners as well as to those judges for whom they were intended. Nevertheless, they remain guidelines only, lacking any authoritative status, and need not be adhered to.[98] It has been stressed by the Court of Appeal that the *Guidelines* "are not in themselves law", which is to be found in greater bulk elsewhere, and that they can provide no substitute for looking to the primary sources.[99]

2.24 The Court of Appeal has taken upon itself the function of laying down authoritative guidelines as to the quantum of damages appropriate for a commonly occurring injury.[100] This assistance may be particularly necessary where there is a wide divergence among awards by different judges for a relatively new injury, or where it is likely that cases concerned with a particular form of injury will in the future come before the courts with more frequency.[101] Alternatively, a new guideline may be desirable and the conventional bracket adjusted where the general pattern of awards comes to be perceived as being at the wrong level[102] or in order to take into account advances in medical knowledge which make a certain injury less disabling than it used to be or which disclose hitherto unknown effects.[103] In addition, awards must always be adjusted for inflation,[104] in order to take into account any fall in the value of money. For this purpose, the court should have recourse to a table of retail

---

[97] See para 1.5 above. A second edition, revised and updated to take account of inflation and decisions reported since 1991, was published in October 1994.

[98] See the comments of the Judicial Studies Board itself in the Introduction to the JSB *Guidelines*, pp 1-2; and cases in which judges have departed from the *Guidelines*, eg *McLaughlin v QDF Component* [1995] 2 CL 165, p 41; *Wilson v Clarke* [1995] 3 CL 177, p 44; *Re Matthews* [1995] 4 CL 137, p 35; and *Johnson v Edwards* [1995] 4 CL 137, p 36.

[99] *Arafa v Potter* [1994] PIQR Q73, Q79, *per* Staughton LJ ("In this Court we ought to look to the sources rather than the summary produced by the Judicial Studies Board").

[100] *Wright v British Railways Board* [1983] 2 AC 773, 784-785.

[101] Eg *Smith v British Rail Engineering Ltd, The Times* 27 June 1980: loss of hearing due to noise exposure. The Court of Appeal observed that there were 2,000 writs outstanding against the defendant rail company and it therefore recognised that "to some extent [its] decision would provide some general guidance to judges who had to deal with similar cases." It would also facilitate settlements.

[102] Eg because awards have failed sufficiently to take into account the fall in the value of money: *Walker v John McLean & Sons Ltd* [1979] 1 WLR 760, 764H-766C.

[103] *Wright v British Railways Board* [1983] 2 AC 773, 785F. But the guideline must not be altered too frequently, as this would deprive it of its usefulness in providing a degree of uniformity and predictability: *ibid*, 785C-D.

[104] This is necessary, not discretionary: *Wright v British Railways Board* [1983] 2 AC 773, 782C-D.

price indices in order to ascertain the value in real terms at the date of trial of earlier comparable awards.[105] The guidelines do not represent binding precedents.[106] Instead, the plaintiff's individual circumstances are relevant and they will lead to the basic award being adjusted up or down. The process of assessment is thus a flexible one.[107]

(2) Examples of variables affecting the level of the award in a particular case

2.25 Whilst the informal tariff or scale establishes a bracket for injuries of the same type, considerations which make the non-pecuniary loss in a particular case more or less *severe*, together with the *duration* of the loss, will affect the precise level of the award within the bracket. The factors which may in any particular case affect the level of the award are infinitely variable, but those which will feature most frequently are set out below.[108]

(a) Gravity or Severity

(i) The intensity of the pain

2.26 In the case of pain, the concept of 'gravity' requires an evaluation of the intensity of the physical pain suffered by the plaintiff.[109]

(ii) Level of insight

2.27 The extent to which the plaintiff appreciates his or her altered circumstances is an important variable which may affect the element of the award attributable to suffering.[110] This factor is particularly relevant in cases of brain injury or coma. A

---

[105] *Wright v British Railways Board* [1983] 2 AC 773, 782D-F; and *Kemp and Kemp*, vol 1, para 7-001.

[106] *Wright v British Railways Board* [1983] 2 AC 773, 785C. Cf also Cumming-Bruce LJ's words of warning in *Walker v John McLean & Sons Ltd* [1979] 1 WLR 760, 765B; and *Bird v Cocking & Sons Ltd* [1951] 2 TLR 1260, 1263 (there can be no fixed and unalterable standard, but comparable cases do represent a guide to the appropriate figure).

[107] *Pickett v British Rail Engineering Ltd* [1980] AC 136, 168A, *per* Lord Scarman (there is "a flexible judicial tariff, which judges will use as a starting-point in each individual case, but never in itself as decisive of any case."). Cf *McCamley v Cammell Laird Shipbuilders Ltd* [1990] 1 WLR 963, 965-966.

[108] Some of these factors are mentioned in the JSB *Guidelines*. But in general the *Guidelines* confine themselves to laying down quantum brackets arranged according to a broad (eg quadriplegia) or more specific (eg arm amputated at the shoulder) description of the injury.

[109] Cf *Wise v Kaye* [1962] 1 QB 638, 650, where Sellers LJ stated that the intensity of pain which is a bodily hurt, such as toothache, can perhaps be assessed and compared; but that suffering which involves mental anguish and distress is more difficult to assess.

[110] Eg *Housecroft v Burnett* [1986] 1 All ER 332, 338d; *Fletcher v Autocar & Transporters Ltd* [1968] 2 QB 322, 351E; *Rialas v Mitchell*, 10 November 1982, *Kemp and Kemp*, vol 2, para A2-010. In *Fallon v Beaumont*, 16 December 1993, *Kemp and Kemp*, vol 3, para L7-023, a man who suffered 65% burns died 30 days after the accident. During that time he experienced no pain from 50% of the burns and had only partial periods of consciousness, but when conscious he would have had significant insight into his condition. He was also

22

plaintiff who has no insight whatsoever into his or her condition will still receive a substantial sum under the head of loss of amenities,[111] but a plaintiff with similar physical injuries who also has some awareness of his or her condition will be awarded more.[112]

(iii)   Age or stage of life

2.28   It is sometimes suggested that the stage of the plaintiff's life at which the accident occurred is relevant to the assessment of damages for non-pecuniary loss.[113]   For instance, it has been said that a child who is catastrophically injured necessarily suffers less mental suffering and less loss of amenity than a similarly injured adult;[114] and that a young person on the brink of life is deprived of more than one in old age.[115] But this view must be doubted and it has been contradicted by other judicial statements which are to the effect that it is impossible to know whether the amenities of life are more valuable at, for example, the age of seventeen, than they are at the age of eight:[116] in another case, it was assumed that a baby of 21 months with severe brain injury had been deprived of more, not less, than an adult in early

conscious during the time that he was trapped in his burning car and appeared to be aware of the attendance of a priest on his admission to hospital, when he was not expected to survive the night. His estate was awarded £10,000 damages for pain, suffering and loss of amenity in the 30 days between injury and death. Compare this with the £1,500 (£2,785 updated to 1994 for inflation) awarded in *Doleman v Deakin*, 24 January 1990 (CA), *Kemp and Kemp*, vol 3, para L5-027, to the estate of a man who died 6 weeks after the accident, but who was unconscious for the entire period.

[111] *Wise v Kaye* [1962] 1 QB 638; *West v Shephard* [1964] AC 326.

[112] *West v Shephard* [1964] AC 326, 365. In *West* a severely brain-damaged plaintiff who had some insight into her condition was awarded £2,500 more than the plaintiff in *Wise v Kaye* [1962] 1 QB 638, who was severely brain-damaged but in a permanent coma. This was despite the fact that the plaintiff's life expectancy in *West* was much shorter. The JSB *Guidelines*, pp 5 and 6, suggest the same bracket of award (£105,000 - £125,000) for quadriplegia as for plaintiffs with severe brain injury, including those in a vegetative state; but in relation to brain injury indicate that "insight" is one of the factors which will affect the precise level of the award within the bracket.

[113] Eg *Housecroft v Burnett* [1986] 1 All ER 332, 339d-h, *per* Kilner Brown J; *Wise v Kaye* [1962] 1 QB 638, 675, *per* Diplock LJ; *Kemp and Kemp*, vol 1, para 3.003. Compare, in the context of the former claim for loss of expectation of life, *Benham v Gambling* [1941] AC 157, 167, where it was suggested that damages should be reduced in the case of a very young child.

[114] *Andrews v Freeborough* [1967] 1 QB 1, 14C, *per* Willmer LJ: child of 8 cannot feel as much mental anguish, through insight, as is probable in the case of an adult; and 21B-E, *per* Winn LJ (dissenting): at 8, a child's deprivation is more limited in scope, kind and quality compared with the deprivation of bodily capacity suffered by an adult.

[115] *Housecroft v Burnett* [1986] 1 All ER 332, 339e, g-j, *per* Kilner Brown J. It seems that the younger a person is, the higher the sum they will be awarded in cases of facial disfigurement (see the JSB *Guidelines*, pp 45-46).

[116] *Andrews v Freeborough* [1967] 1 QB 1, 19B-C, *per* Davies LJ; *Housecroft v Burnett* [1986] 1 All ER 332, 339g-340b (CA) (wrong to award a higher non-pecuniary sum to a 16 year old girl on the ground that she is in a worse state than a man of 22 and in a far worse state than a woman of 35 who had borne a child).

middle age.[117] The better view is therefore that age is not significant in itself and that its significance relates rather to the question of life expectancy (in terms of the period for which the pain and suffering and loss of amenity will last) or to the fact that the injury may be of a type which affects an elderly person more severely than it would do a younger one or vice versa.[118]

(iv) Reduced life expectancy

2.29 The fact that an injury has shortened the plaintiff's life expectancy has a twofold significance. On the one hand, the more reduced the plaintiff's life expectancy the shorter the duration of the loss and thus the smaller the damages.[119] On the other, if the plaintiff is aware that life has been substantially cut short, a sum may be awarded in respect of the mental suffering caused thereby.[120]

(v) Pre-injury hobbies or amenities

2.30 If the plaintiff enjoyed a particular activity before his or her injury that he or she is no longer able to pursue, the damages for non-pecuniary loss will be correspondingly increased.[121] For instance, the amateur footballer who loses a leg will be awarded more than the physically inactive scholar, in order to reflect his or her greater loss.[122]

(vi) Pre-existing disability

2.31 Applying normal principles of liability (going to causation and remoteness), a plaintiff's pre-existing disability is relevant in identifying the personal injury or injuries for which damages (whether for pecuniary or non-pecuniary loss) are to be awarded.[123] The standard principle is that a defendant "takes his victim as he finds

---

[117] *Croke v Wiseman* [1982] 1 WLR 71, 85C-E, *per* Shaw LJ.

[118] Eg *Frank v Cox* (1967) 111 SJ 670 (hip injury for which operation was desirable but impractical in the plaintiff's case because of his advanced age); see the JSB *Guidelines*, p 14, which indicate that a different sum may be appropriate for deafness according to whether the injury was sustained at an early age, with the result that it has had an effect on speech, or in later life. See also *Nutbrown v Sheffield HA* [1993] 4 Med LR 187 (indicating the correct approach to the assessment of non-pecuniary damages for a 76-year-old man).

[119] See para 2.35 below.

[120] See s 1(1)(b) of the Administration of Justice Act 1982, giving statutory recognition to what was already the case at common law; and paras 2.9 and 2.11 above.

[121] *West v Shephard* [1964] AC 326, 365.

[122] *Wise v Kaye* [1962] 1 QB 638, 664-665; (1971) Law Com Working Paper No 41, para 77. Examples are *Moeliker v Reyrolle & Co Ltd* [1977] 1 All ER 9 (fishing); *Miller v Tremberth*, 25 November 1982, *Kemp and Kemp*, vol 2, para D2-014 (blind plaintiff unable to continue pre-accident hobbies of sketching and painting, stamp collecting, reading and DIY).

[123] Similarly, where there is a risk that the plaintiff would have developed the injury or illness in any event, the damages will be discounted to reflect that risk (as they will be for the ordinary contingencies of life).

him".[124] This can operate to a defendant's disadvantage or advantage. For example, where a foreseeable injury is made much worse because of the plaintiff's "thin skull" the defendant is liable for the full extent of the injury whether foreseeable or not. In contrast, where a plaintiff already has a badly injured leg, but is then involved in an accident requiring the leg to be amputated, he or she can recover damages only for the difference between an amputated leg and an already injured leg (and not for the difference between an amputated leg and a good leg).[125]

2.32 Of more direct concern to this paper is the fact that a plaintiff's pre-existing disability may mean that a particular injury has especially serious consequences for that plaintiff (albeit that the existence of the pre-existing disability does not mean that one injury triggers off further injuries). The most obvious examples are the cases where a plaintiff who has already lost an eye or arm loses the other eye or arm. A one-eyed man who loses the sight in his other eye has in effect suffered a worse injury (blinding) than one who was fully sighted before suffering the same injury.[126] Clearly the damages awarded for non-pecuniary loss should reflect this. On the other hand, leaving aside the causation issue discussed in the previous paragraph, it is far from clear that damages should be reduced on the ground that a plaintiff's pre-existing disability means that a particular injury has less serious consequences for the plaintiff than for others. For instance, in *Mustard v Morris*,[127] the defendant argued that because the plaintiff (a diabetic suffering from pre-existing arterial insufficiency which caused pain in his right leg and which would have become increasingly burdensome) was seriously unfit at the time of the injury (which necessitated an above knee amputation of his left leg), the award of damages for non-pecuniary loss should be less than that to a man who had been fit before being injured. The Court of Appeal held that the argument was "misconceived", Watkins LJ adding that "[i]ndeed, an argument to the contrary might well be made. To impose upon a man who, through natural causes has been made ill to a certain extent, very grave injuries such as were sustained in this plaintiff and which reduces his capacity to bear natural ill health, is in my judgment more likely to increase than

---

[124] *Smith v Leech Brain & Co Ltd* [1962] 2 QB 405, 414, *per* Lord Parker CJ, restating what "has always been the law".

[125] The House of Lords assumed this to be the case in *Baker v Willoughby* [1970] AC 467 (where there were successive torts), when discussing the robbers' liability to pay damages for the second injury they caused. Although the decision in *Baker v Willoughby* was subsequently doubted by the House of Lords in *Jobling v Associated Dairies Ltd* [1982] AC 794, their Lordships again assumed that the damages for the second injury ought to recognise that the plaintiff was already to some extent incapacitated. See also *Cutler v Vauxhall Motors Ltd* [1971] 1 QB 418.

[126] The facts are those of *Paris v Stepney BC* [1951] AC 367, although the issue there was liability rather than damages. See *Bickerton v Snare* [1963] CLY 968a where, in awarding damages to a blind woman who sustained a broken leg, Paull J said that had she been in full possession of her faculties the general damages would have been £750; but, because of her blindness, they were £1,500.

[127] 21 July 1981 (CA), *Kemp and Kemp*, vol 3, paras I2-106 and I2-604.

reduce damages". Similarly, a terminally ill woman with only a few years left to live who sustains a permanently disabling injury, such as the loss of an arm, will suffer the loss for a shorter period of time than would a person with a normal life expectancy; but, on the other hand, her quality of life is impaired at a time during which the amenities of life would have been "sweetest", and in circumstances which are likely to lead to greater distress.[128]

(vii) Gender

2.33 The gender of the plaintiff will sometimes be relevant to the level of the award. Women, for instance, tend to receive higher awards than do men in cases of disfigurement.[129] Similarly, loss of marriage prospects seems to be treated as more relevant to or more damaging to women.[130]

(viii) Circumstances in which the injury was sustained

2.34 The circumstances in which the injury was sustained may be relevant. So, for instance, if the injury to the plaintiff was inflicted in horrific or terrifying circumstances, the damages for pain and suffering may take into account any additional suffering which was caused in this way.[131] Thus, a traumatic amputation may give rise to a higher award than a surgical amputation carried out under

---

[128] Cf *Rides Pty Ltd v Gauci* (1984) Aust Torts Reports 80-637, where the Supreme Court of South Australia dismissed the defendant's appeal against the sum awarded for non-pecuniary loss, the appeal being based on the argument that because of the plaintiff's pre-accident disabilities (brain damage at birth), his capacity to enjoy life was already impaired.

[129] R Colbey, "Quantifying Awards of General Damages for Scarring" (1989) 9 Lit 57, 58; *Kemp and Kemp*, vol 2, paras C1-022 and C5-001; the JSB *Guidelines* indicate a bracket of up to £30,000 for a woman, but up to only £20,000 for a man, pp 43, 45-46. But see *Wynn v Cooper* [1992] PIQR Q140, Q142 where the Court of Appeal, noting that "it has always been accepted" that young girls suffer embarrassment on scarring, held that this effect is not confined to girls and may affect boys as well.

[130] See *Kemp and Kemp*, vol 1, paras 1-008 and 3-001(referring to loss of marriage prospects "*of a young woman*" (emphasis added). Examples are *Hughes v McKeown* [1985] 1 WLR 963, 966D; *Aloni v National Westminster Bank*, 20 May 1982, *Kemp and Kemp*, vol 2, para A3-007.

[131] Eg *Allot v British Steel Corpn*, 25 May 1989 (CA), *Kemp and Kemp*, vol 3, para J3-111 (where the Court of Appeal thought that the trial judge's assessment, for a man who had suffered severe burns in an explosion of fire, under-estimated the terrifying circumstances in which the accident occurred); *Allsopp v White* [1992] CLY 1614. See also *Phelan v East Cumbria HA*, 18 October 1991, *Kemp and Kemp*, vol 3, para L8-204 (£15,000 for awareness under anaesthetic during leg surgery, including £5,000 for the experience on the operating table). Horror and fear alone will not give rise to a cause of action, nor therefore damages, unless they result in a recognisable psychiatric injury or are accompanied by some physical injury: *Hicks v Chief Constable of S Yorkshire* [1992] 2 All ER 65. See Liability for Psychiatric Illness (1995) Law Com Consultation Paper No 137. Cf H Luntz, *Assessment of Damages for Personal Injury and Death* (3rd ed 1990) paras 3.1.4 and 3.2.5; and *Freudhofer v Poledano* (1972) VR 287. It should be noted that the suffering here recognised is not necessarily *consequent on* the injury.

anaesthetic.[132] The circumstances in which the injury is sustained may also be relevant to the seriousness of the injury for other reasons: for example, it is likely to be more difficult to adjust to sudden hearing loss than to hearing loss which occurs over a period of time.[133]

(b) Duration

2.35 The length of time for which the pain or suffering has lasted or will last, or for which the plaintiff is deprived of some capacity, is always relevant. The longer the period of the loss, the higher the award. However, in contrast to some jurisdictions, the English courts do not make mathematical comparisons or computations based on units of time: that is, English law does not favour a *per diem* method of assessment.[134] Where the plaintiff's life has been shortened by the injury there is in the case of permanent incapacity a question whether the deprivation is to be measured over the period for which the plaintiff will in fact be disabled (that is, the remainder of the plaintiff's life); or over the period of life which the plaintiff would have enjoyed but for the defendant's wrong. It is well settled that in English law the former applies.[135]

(3) Irrelevant factors

2.36 In *Phillips v London & South Western Railway Co*, Cotton LJ suggested that the plaintiff's wealth might be relevant to the assessment of damages for non-pecuniary loss and that a poor plaintiff ought perhaps to receive more than a rich one because he or she has less financial means out of which to alleviate his or her suffering.[136] On the other hand, it is sometimes suggested that the same sum represents greater

---

[132] Eg the JSB *Guidelines*, p 35, which indicate that a "traumatic amputation in a horrendous accident, where the injured person remained fully conscious" will place a below knee amputation at the top of the range for that injury; and, at p 42, that the level of award for amputation of all toes will be determined (*inter alia*) by the consideration whether or not the amputation was traumatic or surgical.

[133] See the JSB *Guidelines*, p 14.

[134] See, eg *Andrews v Freeborough* [1967] 1 QB 1, 13, 19 (rejecting counsel's argument at p 5); *McCann v Sheppard* [1973] 1 WLR 540, 551E. But cf *Doleman v Deakin*, 24 January 1990, *Kemp and Kemp*, vol 3, para L5-027, where the Court of Appeal accepted (in a case of permanent unconsciousness) that the need for an arithmetical calculation of this type might arise. According to this method of assessment a sum would be attached to a day's (or a week's, etc) pain or deprivation. This would then be multiplied by the number of days (or weeks, etc) for which the plaintiff is expected to experience the pain or deprivation in order to reach the appropriate figure in the particular case. In the USA, where damages are assessed by juries, the majority of jurisdictions accept that an argument based on the *per diem* method of assessing damages is within the bounds of legitimate advocacy. See para 3.60 below.

[135] Eg in *Rose v Ford* [1937] AC 826, damages for the loss of a leg were limited to the four days during which the plaintiff survived after the accident; *West v Shephard* [1964] AC 326, 349, 370. In contrast to the rule for non-pecuniary loss, a living plaintiff *can* recover damages for loss of earnings during the 'lost years': *Pickett v British Rail Engineering Ltd* [1980] AC 136.

[136] (1879) 5 CPD 280, 294. See also (1879) 5 QBD 78, 87.

compensation for a poor plaintiff than for a rich one.[137] However, it has long been clear that the plaintiff's wealth is *not* to be taken into account when assessing damages for pain and suffering and loss of amenities.[138] It is also irrelevant in English law that the plaintiff is unable to use or benefit from the award - because he or she is permanently unconscious, for instance. In *Wise v Kaye*[139] and *West v Shephard*[140] the Court of Appeal and House of Lords respectively were unanimous in holding that this circumstance ought not to exclude damages for non-pecuniary loss altogether. In *West v Shephard*[141] the House was divided, however, as to whether it should be regarded as relevant to the extent that it might justify a more moderate award. The majority view was that it should not be relevant even in this limited sense.[142]

(4) Multiple injuries

2.37 Multiple injuries are especially difficult to assess because, in the nature of things, the combination of injuries tends to vary from case to case and comparisons are therefore difficult to make.[143] In deciding what sum constitutes fair and reasonable compensation, the judge will take an overall view of the plaintiff's injuries, looking at the total effect they have produced upon the plaintiff's life and at his or her psychological state.[144] An attempt is made to fit the assessment into the tariff: that is, it is recognised that, as far as possible, the total sum awarded should not be out of step with awards currently being made in respect of injuries of comparatively more or less severity.[145] In some cases, particularly where the injuries involved are

---

[137] Pearson Report, vol 1, para 379.

[138] *Wise v Kaye* [1962] 1 QB 638, 658, 671; *West v Shephard* [1964] AC 326, 350, 364; *Fletcher v Autocar and Transporters Ltd* [1968] 2 QB 322, 340-341; *McGregor on Damages* (15th ed 1988) para 1521. In Germany, the economic circumstances of the plaintiff may be relevant to assessment, so as either to reduce or increase the award. See para 3.75 below.

[139] [1962] 1 QB 638, 653-654, 656-659, 671.

[140] [1964] AC 326, 341-342, 349-350, 363, 364.

[141] [1964] AC 326.

[142] *Ibid*, 349-350, 364 (Lords Tucker, Morris of Borth-y-Gest and Pearce; Lords Reid, at p 342, and Devlin, at p 363, dissenting). See paras 2.16-2.18 above.

[143] Eg *Channer v Lucas*, 7 February 1990 (CA), *Kemp and Kemp*, vol 2, para B2-104, *per* Farquharson LJ; *Rollason v Graham*, 7 July 1980 (CA), *Kemp and Kemp*, vol 2, para B2-100. The working party of the Civil and Family Committee of the Judicial Studies Board found, when compiling the JSB *Guidelines*, that multiple injuries presented particular difficulties and commented (2nd ed 1994, p 3) that "It is perhaps in this area more than in any other that the subjective views of the assessor as to the degree of priority to be accorded to the several injuries has its part to play."

[144] Examples of awards for multiple injuries, illustrating the process of assessment involved, are collected at paras B1-001 to B2-104 of *Kemp and Kemp*, vol 2.

[145] Eg *Jenkinson v Eagle International Freight Ltd & Keydril Ltd*, 26 January 1983 (CA), *Kemp and Kemp*, vol 2, para B2-103. In *Sharpe v Woods*, 16 July 1993, *Kemp and Kemp*, vol 2, para B2-002, a woman suffering devastating orthopaedic and cerebral injuries was regarded as being "in a worse position than a paraplegic but a better position than a

less serious and can be regarded as separate from each other, judges appear to have assessed the damages for non-pecuniary loss on an aggregate basis; that is, separate sums are assigned to the different injuries and then added up to produce a total figure for non-pecuniary loss.[146] However, in the Introduction to the Judicial Studies Board's *Guidelines to the Assessment of General Damages in Personal Injury Cases*, it is stated that it is "axiomatic that it is not appropriate separately to value the individual elements of a multiple-injury case and to aggregate the figures thus achieved. An overall view must be taken in which the largest single element will usually be the most serious of those injuries."[147]

(5) Overlap between damages for loss of earnings and damages for loss of amenity

2.38   A further question of some interest is whether there is an overlap, requiring a deduction, between damages for loss of earnings and damages for loss of amenity where the plaintiff's injury means that he or she saves the expense of paying for activities that he or she can no longer pursue.[148] In *Fletcher v Autocar and Transporters Ltd*[149] Lord Denning MR thought that this matter should lead to a reduction in damages for loss of earnings, since otherwise the plaintiff would be being compensated for his pleasures and recreations as if they were free. Similarly Diplock LJ suggested that the sums awarded for loss of amenity should reflect the fact that the plaintiff is being awarded full loss of earnings and yet is being saved the expense of paying for the pleasures of life. Salmon LJ, in his dissenting judgment, took a slightly different view, saying that where the court is to add a sum to that normally awarded for loss of amenity to reflect the loss of a special hobby (for example, because the plaintiff can no longer fish or shoot) account should be taken of the expense of that hobby since it will now be saved: but otherwise no such deduction should be made. All three approaches were, however, rejected by this Commission in our 1973 Report. We said: "If the loss of a special amenity has the

tetraplegic." See also *Hills, Mullarkey, Page, Ruane and Finn v Edmund Nuttall Ltd*, 9 December 1982, vol 2, para B2-004, where two of the plaintiffs were said to have injuries which, in total, were broadly comparable with those of a paraplegic.

[146] Eg *Skipp v Fisher*, 27 November 1990, *Kemp and Kemp*, vol 2, para B2-035; *Mitchel v Lewis*, 14 August 1992, *Kemp and Kemp*, vol 2, para B2-039.

[147] (2nd ed 1994) p 3.

[148] A different question of overlap between damages for pecuniary and non-pecuniary loss was raised by Lord Denning MR in *Smith v Central Asbestos Co* [1972] 1 QB 244, 262, who thought that damages for pain, suffering and loss of amenity might be reduced because it is a comfort for a plaintiff to know that he is receiving his full loss of earnings. This idea was rejected by us in (1973) Law Com No 56, paras 195-200; see also dicta of Lord Scarman in *Lim Poh Choo v Camden and Islington AHA* [1980] AC 174, 192C-E ("Upon the point of principle whether damages for non-pecuniary loss can properly be reduced to avoid an overlap with damages for pecuniary loss I express no final opinion. I confess, however, that I doubt the possibility of overlap..."); Pearson Report, vol 1, para 759; *Kemp and Kemp*, vol 1, para 1-022.

[149] [1968] 2 QB 322, 337, 341-342, 351-353, 364.

effect of increasing an award of damages for non-pecuniary loss above the conventional sum (as we think it can and should) we do not think it ought to be relevant to enquire what that amenity cost. The fell-walker and the fisherman should be equally compensated for their lost recreation although the fisherman may have spent large sums for fishing rights."[150] Certainly it is strongly arguable that the case for a deduction falsely treats the assessment of damages for non-pecuniary loss as if it were arrived at with the degree of precision possible for assessing pecuniary loss. And we are aware of no subsequent case in which the deduction suggested in *Fletcher* has been made. In the circumstances we do not regard this as being a major issue for consultation and we shall not be discussing it further in Part IV. **Nevertheless we would welcome the views of consultees, and particularly those with experience of personal injury litigation, as to whether the question of overlap (between damages for loss of earnings and damages for loss of amenity) raised in *Fletcher v Autocar and Transporters Ltd* gives rise to difficulty and, if so, what the solution to that difficulty should be.**

(6) Levels of compensation for non-pecuniary loss

2.39 In some jurisdictions, statutory ceilings are placed upon the amount that may be recovered as damages for non-pecuniary loss.[151] In Canada, as a result of a series of decisions of the Supreme Court,[152] the courts are subject to a self-imposed "rough upper limit" on compensation for non-pecuniary loss, which in 1978 stood at $100,000; and in Ireland, the Irish Supreme Court held in 1984 that damages for non-pecuniary loss should not exceed a sum in the region of £150,000 having regard to money values then current.[153] In contrast, although guidelines as to the appropriate levels of awards are from time to time set by the Court of Appeal, in English law there is neither a fixed upper limit[154] on, nor a lower threshold for,

---

[150] (1973) Law Com No 56, para 194. This approach derives some support from the Pearson Report, vol 1, para 759; the dicta of Lord Scarman referred to in n 148 above; and dicta of Lord Griffiths in *Dews v National Coal Board* [1988] AC 1, 14F. The editors of *Kemp and Kemp*, vol 1, at para 1-021, prefer Salmon LJ's approach to that of the majority in *Fletcher's* case.

[151] Eg Australia, where a number of states have introduced statutory ceilings and thresholds on the recovery of damages for non-pecuniary loss in relation to particular types of accidents, notably transport and industrial accidents. See paras 3.29-3.32 below.

[152] *Andrews v Grand & Toy Alberta Ltd* (1978) 83 DLR (3d) 452; *Arnold v Teno* (1978) 83 DLR (3d) 609; and *Thornton v Board of School Trustees of School District No 57* (1978) 83 DLR (3d) 480, widely known and referred to as "the trilogy". See paras 3.38-3.48 below.

[153] *Sinnott v Quinnsworth Ltd* [1984] IRLM 523. Note, however, that this judicial ceiling was imposed at a time when juries still assessed damages in personal injury actions in the High Court in Ireland and that the jury in *Sinnott* (a case of quadriplegia) had assessed damages for non-pecuniary loss alone at £800,000. Trial by jury was abolished for nearly all personal injury actions in the High Court by the Courts Act 1988, which came into force on 1 August 1988. See paras 3.14-3.17 below.

[154] *Croke v Wiseman* [1982] 1 WLR 71; *Young v Redmond*, 29 March 1982 (CA), *Kemp and Kemp*, vol 2, para C2-100; *Mustart v Post Office*, *The Times* 11 February 1982. But some legislation based on international transport treaties do place a cap on awards: see, eg, the Carriage by Air Act 1961 and the Carriage of Passengers by Road Act 1974. See also s 17

awards.[155] However, although the scale of awards is in theory a very flexible one, the decision of the Court of Appeal in *Housecroft v Burnett*,[156] in which it indicated that in April 1985 an award of £75,000 for pain and suffering and loss of amenity is appropriate for a typical case of tetraplegia, appears in practice to have imposed an unofficial cap on the level of awards in the most serious cases. It has also been argued that it has brought down the general level of awards in other cases, since these ought to bear a proportionate relationship to the guideline figure for tetraplegia.[157]

2.40 At the top end of the English scale stand catastrophic injuries such as quadriplegia, very severe brain injury and total blindness combined with total deafness, for which a plaintiff can expect to receive a maximum sum in the region of £125,000.[158] In contrast, at the bottom of the scale very minor injuries which give rise to little pain or incapacity and which result in a complete recovery, can attract sums of under £500.[159]

4. INTEREST ON DAMAGES FOR NON-PECUNIARY LOSS

2.41 In many cases the injured person may have to wait a number of years before receiving compensation from the defendant,[160] during which time the sum to which he or she is entitled could have been earning interest if prudently invested. The principle of full compensation suggests that he or she ought to be compensated for

of the Merchant Shipping Act 1979.

[155] The Pearson Commission was equally divided on the question of an upper limit on damages for non-pecuniary loss. Those who favoured one considered that it should be set at five times average annual industrial earnings (about £20,000 in 1977): vol 1, paras 390-392. As regards a threshold for non-pecuniary damages, the Pearson Commission recommended by a majority that no damages should be recoverable for non-pecuniary loss suffered during the first three months after the date of the injury: vol 1, paras 382-389.

[156] [1986] 1 All ER 332.

[157] *Kemp and Kemp*, vol 1, para 1-004/3; and APIL Preliminary Submission to the Law Commission. But see para 4.36 below.

[158] The JSB *Guidelines* suggest a rough maximum of £125,000 for these injuries in June 1994: see pp 2, 5, 6 and 12. The highest reported award for non-pecuniary loss of which we are aware is the award of £130,000 by Hidden J in February 1994 to a young woman suffering multiple injuries, including a severe closed head injury resulting in confinement to a wheelchair, loss of the ability to cry, laugh or speak and complete dependency on others but who was fully conscious and aware of her situation: *Whiteside v Howes, Kemp and Kemp*, vol 2, para B2-001.

[159] See the table at para K1-100 of vol 3 of *Kemp and Kemp*. Note that minor physical injuries can sometimes give rise to serious psychiatric illness, particularly where the injury was sustained in very frightening or unpleasant circumstances. Here, the psychological injury will be regarded as the primary injury, the most severe forms of which can give rise to awards of up to £45,000 (JSB *Guidelines*, p 10). See also *Kemp and Kemp*, vol 2, paras C4-013, C4-015.

[160] See, eg, (1994) Law Com No 225, para 4.2, pp 70-72, which found that a substantial proportion of the cases surveyed remained unresolved four years after the date of the accident; and *Access to Justice* (1995) pp 12-15, 184.

this loss. However, prior to 1970, it was not the courts' practice to make awards of interest on damages for personal injury, although they had the power to do so under section 3(1) of the Law Reform (Miscellaneous Provisions) Act 1934. In 1969, section 22 of the Administration of Justice Act[161] made the award of interest on damages exceeding £200 compulsory in personal injury claims, in the absence of special reasons to the contrary. The relevant statutory provisions are now found in section 35A of the Supreme Court Act 1981[162] and section 69 of the County Courts Act 1984.[163] Under these provisions, as under those which preceded them, the court must make an award of interest[164] on damages for personal injury exceeding £200 but it is given a discretion as to what part(s) of the total award should carry interest, in respect of what period, and at what rate.

2.42   The Court of Appeal and the House of Lords have from time to time given guidance on the exercise of this discretion, the non-pecuniary element of a plaintiff's damages having in particular given rise to some difference of opinion. In *Jefford v Gee*,[165] decided shortly after the award of interest was first made compulsory, the Court of Appeal explained that the reason pre-judgment interest on damages in personal injury cases is awarded to a plaintiff is *"for being kept out of money* which ought to have been paid to him."[166] The Court then went on to articulate the principles which should be applied when awarding interest in respect of the different elements of a plaintiff's damages for personal injury. As regards the non-pecuniary loss it was held that interest should be paid on the whole amount at the full short term investment account rate,[167] taking the average rate over the period for which

---

[161] Amending s 3(1) of the 1934 Act. This followed the recommendations of the Winn Committee (1968) Cmnd 3691: Report of the Committee on Personal Injuries Litigation.

[162] Inserted by s 15 of the Administration of Justice Act 1982. This applies to proceedings before the High Court.

[163] For proceedings in the county courts. This replaces s 97A of the County Courts Act 1959 (inserted by s 15 of the Administration of Justice Act 1982) and its terms are nearly identical to those which apply in the High Court.

[164] Which under the terms of the legislation is simple, not compound interest (although see R Bowles, "Interest on Damages for Non-Economic Loss" (1984) 100 LQR 192, 196-197, arguing that indexing awards to allow for inflation is tantamount to offering compound interest). We did not favour compounding interest in our Report on Interest (1978) Law Com No 88, Cmnd 7229, para 85. As the question of compounding goes to interest generally, and not merely to interest on damages for non-pecuniary loss, we shall not be reexamining it in this paper.

[165] [1970] 2 QB 130.

[166] [1970] 2 QB 130, 146A, *per* Lord Denning MR (emphasis in original). It is assumed that the plaintiff has lost the interest from investing the damages which the defendant ought to have paid, ie has been deprived of their use value: see *Wright v British Railways Board* [1983] 2 AC 773, 781D.

[167] This is now known as the special account. The rate reached a height of 15% in 1980 and in the period 1980-1987 never dropped below 11½%. Since 1991, the rate has been adjusted three times by the Lord Chancellor. The current rate, with effect from 1 February 1993, is 8%. See the Supreme Court Practice (1995) vol 2, Pt 5, para 1262.

interest is awarded where the rate has varied, but only from the date of service of the writ to the date of trial.[168] Although in principle it was thought that interest should not be awarded in respect of future (that is, post-trial) losses, since these have not yet occurred,[169] it was not considered possible to split a plaintiff's non-pecuniary loss into that occurring before trial and that after it,[170] and therefore interest should be awarded on the whole. However, because these losses are continuing losses and do not all occur at the time of the accident but are spread indefinitely into the future,[171] and because the defendant can only be said to have kept the plaintiff out of the sum representing them from the time when it ought to have been paid,[172] the Court held that interest should only run from the date of the service of the writ[173] (rather than from the date when the accident occurred[174] or the loss was actually sustained) to the date of trial. It was thought that this practice would incidentally encourage plaintiffs to serve the writ without delay and thus expedite the process of litigation.[175] Where there is gross delay by either party the Court suggested that courts might depart from the rule expounded above by altering the period for which interest is allowed.[176]

2.43   Less than a decade later, but after a period of rising inflation in the 1970s, the Court of Appeal in *Cookson v Knowles*[177] questioned, *obiter*, the guideline it had laid down for non-pecuniary loss in *Jefford v Gee*. Adopting the reasoning and conclusion we had put forward in our 1973 Report,[178] it took the view that interest ought not to be awarded at all on that part of the plaintiff's damages representing non-

---

[168] *Jefford v Gee* [1970] 2 QB 130, 147E-H, 148G- 149B, 151B-D.

[169] This reasoning is at the basis of the rule that as regards pecuniary loss interest should only be awarded on that actually sustained up to the date of trial (ie special damages) and not at all on future pecuniary loss (eg loss of future earnings and future medical expenses): *Jefford v Gee* [1970] 2 QB 130, 146B-147D, 151B. Indeed, sums representing future pecuniary loss are discounted to reflect the fact that the plaintiff has received a lump sum in advance.

[170] *Ibid*, 147F.

[171] *Ibid*, 147E-F.

[172] *Ibid*, 147F-G.

[173] The time might in some cases be taken to be the date of letter before action (*ibid*, 147G); but this would be only in the simplest type of case where liability was not seriously in doubt and the medical condition of the plaintiff had by then become stabilised: *Wright v British Railways Board* [1983] 2 AC 773, 779F-G, *per* Lord Diplock.

[174] As is the rule for pre-trial pecuniary loss, although the appropriate rate is halved to reflect the fact that the losses may not all have been sustained at this moment: *Jefford v Gee* [1970] 2 QB 130, 146B-147B, 151B.

[175] *Jefford v Gee* [1970] 2 QB 130, 147H.

[176] *Ibid*, 151F. This point was reiterated by the Court of Appeal as regards unjustifiable delay by the plaintiff in *Birkett v Hayes* [1982] 1 WLR 816, 825E-H.

[177] [1977] QB 913.

[178] (1973) Law Com No 56, paras 273-277, 286.

pecuniary loss.[179] Since damages are assessed at the date of trial and take inflation into account, it was reasoned that the plaintiff gets the benefit of a sum which is higher than that current at the date of the injury or at the date of the writ. The lapse of time between injury and trial might be, and often is, substantial and the Court thought that the plaintiff ought not to gain still more by having interest as well.[180] Although the plaintiff in *Cookson* appealed to the House of Lords, it was not necessary to decide the question of interest on damages for non-pecuniary loss and the House declined to do so.[181] The courts proceeded to follow the new guideline set by the Court of Appeal, and for the next five months plaintiffs in personal injury actions received no interest at all on their damages for pain and suffering and loss of amenities.[182]

2.44 In *Pickett v British Rail Engineering Ltd*[183] the House of Lords did address the question and chose to restore the *Jefford v Gee* guideline. The Court of Appeal's reason in *Cookson v Knowles* for prohibiting altogether the award of interest on damages in respect of pain, suffering and loss of amenities was, their Lordships pointed out, based on a fallacy regarding the relationship between interest and inflation:[184]

> Increase for inflation is designed to preserve the 'real' value of money: interest to compensate for being kept out of that 'real' value. The one has no relation to the other. If the damages claimed remained, nominally, the same, because there was no inflation, interest would normally be given. The same should follow if the damages remain in real terms the same.[185]

2.45 In *Birkett v Hayes*,[186] the Court of Appeal accepted that arguments based on inflation could not, after *Pickett*, exclude the award of interest altogether.[187] However, the Court considered itself free to determine what should be the *rate* of

---

[179] *Cookson v Knowles* [1977] QB 913, 921C-G.

[180] *Ibid*, 921D-E.

[181] [1979] AC 556, 573G.

[182] *Wright v British Railways Board* [1983] 2 AC 773, 780E, *per* Lord Diplock.

[183] [1980] AC 136, decided less than a year after *Cookson v Knowles* and in the same year that the Pearson Commission published its Report.

[184] The Pearson Commission had drawn attention to this fallacy at vol 1, para 746 of its Report.

[185] *Pickett v British Rail Engineering Ltd* [1980] AC 136, 151D-E, *per* Lord Wilberforce. In addition, Lord Scarman thought that the reasoning of the Court of Appeal was inconsistent with the statutory provisions on interest. Under those provisions the court is required to award interest in the absence of special reasons for giving none, and inflation, being of general application, cannot be regarded as a special reason: *ibid*, 173F-H.

[186] [1982] 1 WLR 816.

[187] *Ibid*, 820C, 821D, 822C.

interest and concluded that the relationship between interest and inflation justified a rate which was lower than the full market rate.[188] In times of high inflation, interest rates have a large inflationary element built in to them. Since the plaintiff's damages are already assessed on the basis of the value of the pound at the time of trial the Court thought that it would be unjust to award interest on those damages at a rate which carries an inflationary element, because this would amount to double recovery. Instead the plaintiff should be awarded interest at a rate which excludes the counter-inflationary element. Assuming a "real" rate of interest of 4 per cent, the Court settled on an appropriate rate of 2 per cent by first deducting 30 per cent to allow for the tax which the plaintiff would have paid had he or she been able to invest the damages, but would now not have to pay (reaching a net rate of 2.8 per cent);[189] and then by searching for an appropriate net figure below this, taking the view that the starting rate of 4 per cent gross was too high because it was unfair to assume that the defendant ought to have paid the damages at the moment of service of the writ.[190] A low rate of 2 per cent, the Court noted, was the approximate rate of return (net of tax) that an investor in index-linked (that is, inflation-proof) government stock could expect to receive.[191]

2.46   This low rate, and the reasoning upon which it was based, was subsequently approved by the House of Lords in *Wright v British Railways Board*.[192] Giving the sole speech, Lord Diplock observed that the rate of interest accepted by investors in index-linked government securities ought to provide a broad indication of the appropriate rate of interest, since these securities provide an investment protected against inflation at minimal risk;[193] and that the net return on medium and long-term index-linked issues available to private individuals liable to income tax was 2 to 2½ per cent.[194] However, he also suggested that the 2 per cent guideline might

---

[188] *Ibid*, 821D-E, 822H, 823D-G.

[189] Interest on damages is exempt from income tax under what is now s 329 of the Income and Corporation Taxes Act 1988. At the time that *Jefford v Gee* was decided and the full short term investment account rate favoured, the award of interest was taxable in the hands of the plaintiff. The tax exemption was introduced by s 19 of the Finance Act 1971.

[190] This, according to Eveleigh LJ, is because damages for non-pecuniary loss are difficult to quantify and indeed uncertain until the court assesses them, yet the plaintiff is in the best position to put a value on the claim; and because in many cases the plaintiff's condition will not have stabilised at the date of writ - by the time of trial it may have deteriorated (or improved), thus resulting in a larger (or smaller) award than he or she would have received if the damages had been assessed at the date of writ. Thus to award interest upon the damages sum "as though it were a debt is to call upon a defendant to pay interest upon a figure that was never demanded and which at the date of the writ is usually sheer guesswork": [1982] 1 WLR 816, 823G-825B.

[191] *Birkett v Hayes* [1982] 1 WLR 816, 824G-825B.

[192] [1983] 2 AC 773.

[193] Ie a plaintiff awarded damages for non-pecuniary loss can be regarded as holding the equivalent of index-linked stock.

[194] *Wright v British Railways Board* [1983] 2 AC 773, 782F-784C.

have to be re-examined and the rate raised, in the light of expert economic evidence, if and when currency became more stable again so that interest rates included only a very small counter-inflationary, or risk, element (and hence the assumptions made at the time of *Birkett v Hayes* would no longer hold good).[195] There was no material before the House to indicate that the time was ripe for this re-examination and it has not been embarked on in any subsequent case.

2.47   In summary, therefore, under the present law interest at a rate of 2 per cent is payable on damages for non-pecuniary loss in their entirety from the date of service of the writ to the date of trial. Unjustifiable delay by the plaintiff may, however, lead the court to reduce the period for which interest is awarded.

5. SURVIVAL OF DAMAGES FOR NON-PECUNIARY LOSS

2.48   A person with a cause of action for personal injury may die some time after being injured (either as a result of the injury or from some independent cause) but before he or she is able to obtain compensation from the defendant in a settlement or by judgment at trial. The effect of an individual's death upon his or her own subsisting cause of action (and corresponding claim to damages) depends upon the rules which govern the survival of actions for the benefit of the deceased's estate. Where death is due to the injuries caused by the defendant's wrong, it may also give rise to a claim by dependants under the Fatal Accidents Act 1976.[196]

2.49   Subject to a few exceptions, the old common law rule governing survival, expressed in the maxim *actio personalis moritur cum persona*, was that tort actions died with the person. Section 1 of the Law Reform (Miscellaneous Provisions) Act 1934 reversed this common law rule and it provides in general terms that all causes of action which are vested in a person shall survive on death for the benefit of his or her estate.[197] Except for creating a right to recover funeral expenses,[198] the Act creates no new cause of action, but merely ensures that rights which were vested in the deceased immediately before death are transferred to his or her estate. In contrast

---

[195]   *Ibid*, 784B-C, 785F-786B.

[196]   We will be considering the Fatal Accidents Act 1976 in a future consultation paper.

[197]   Defamation and claims for bereavement damages arising under s 1A of the Fatal Accidents Act 1976 are excluded: s 1(1) and (1A) of the 1934 Act. The 1934 Act was in fact principally directed at cases involving the death of the wrongdoer, rather than the death of the claimant, where the rule against survival operated to prevent an injured, living plaintiff from obtaining compensation from the defendant's insurer. In the case of the death of the claimant the more immediate concern of the proponents of the Act appears to have been to ensure the recoverability (whether by the estate or by third party dependants) of medical and funeral expenses actually incurred. See the Law Revision Committee's Interim Report (March 1934) Cmd 4540, paras 5-6; *Hansard* (HL) 2 May 1934, vol 91, col 990; and *Hansard* (HC) 15 June 1934, vol 290, cols 2112-2113.

[198]   Funeral expenses, for which the deceased could not of course have claimed had he or she lived, may be recovered by reason of s 1(2)(c) of the 1934 Act provided the death was caused by the defendant's wrong.

to the position in some other jurisdictions,[199] the right to damages which survives in a personal injury action is not restricted to the pecuniary loss suffered, but extends also to non-pecuniary loss. So for example, in *Fallon v Beaumont*,[200] the deceased was severely burned in a road accident and died from his injuries thirty days later. His estate was awarded £10,000 for his pain, suffering and loss of amenity during that period.

2.50   The principles upon which damages for non-pecuniary loss in Law Reform Act claims are assessed are the same as those which apply in the case of plaintiffs who are living at the time of trial.[201] In particular, the rule that damages for non-pecuniary loss cannot be recovered for the years after death[202] applies so that, even where death is due to the defendant's wrongful act, damages must be assessed over the period that the pain, suffering and loss of amenity was actually endured, that is (at most) the period between injury and death.[203] Although the principles are the same, death affects the measure of damages in that it fixes the term of the loss: the shorter the period between injury and death, the smaller the damages. In the case

---

[199] See paras 3.19, 3.25, 3.50 and 3.57 below. The original draft of the Law Reform (Miscellaneous Provisions) Bill excluded the recovery of damages "in respect of the mental or bodily suffering of [the deceased] before his death", but this restriction was removed at the Committee stage of the Bill: see *Hansard* (HL) 14 May 1934, vol 92, cols 332-334. See also the Law Revision Committee's Interim Report (March 1934) Cmd 4540, p 8, para 15(c).

[200] 16 December 1993, *Kemp and Kemp*, vol 3, para L7-023 (for the facts, see para 2.27, n 110 above). Other examples are *Rose v Ford* [1937] AC 826 (£22 for amputated leg with intermittent consciousness plus £1,000 for loss of expectation of life, death after 4 days); *Andrews v Freeborough* [1967] 1 QB 1 (£2,000 for unconsciousness plus £500 for loss of expectation of life, death after almost a year); *Murray v Shuter* [1976] QB 972 (death after 4 years: £11,000); *Doleman v Deakin*, 24 January 1990, *Kemp and Kemp*, vol 3, para L5-027 (death after 6 weeks: £1,500); *Kralj v McGrath* [1986] 1 All ER 54 (£2,500 for baby born with severe disabilities but no insight plus £1,650 for loss of expectation of life, death after 8 weeks); *Kerby v Redbridge HA* [1994] PIQR Q1 (£750 for baby born with severe disabilities but no insight, death after 3 days); *Mills v British Rail Engineering* [1992] PIQR Q130 (£15,000 for asbestos-induced lung cancer, death after 1 year). Cases involving industrial disease probably form a significant proportion of claims made under the 1934 Act (see paras 4.127 and 4.130 below).

[201] Cf *Andrews v Freeborough* [1967] 1 QB 1, 24-27, where Winn LJ (dissenting) expressed the view that damages for non-pecuniary loss should be assessed more moderately in the case of claims made by the estate because the deceased clearly cannot receive and enjoy the benefit of the award himself or herself. See also *Wise v Kaye* [1962] 1 QB 638, 659, *per* Upjohn LJ.

[202] See para 2.35 above. In the context of future *pecuniary* loss these are commonly termed the 'lost years'.

[203] This may seem so obvious as to be hardly worth saying, but the Scottish Law Commission felt the need to make specific provision to this effect and s 2(3) of the Damages (Scotland) Act 1976 (as substituted by s 3 of the Damages (Scotland) Act 1993) therefore directs the court, in assessing damages for non-pecuniary loss, to have regard only to the period ending immediately before the deceased's death. See Report on The Effect of Death on Damages (1992) Scot Law Com No 134, para 4.11. Note also that *McGregor on Damages* (15th ed 1988) para 1606 seems to regard this point as still being open to question in English law; but if living plaintiffs cannot recover non-pecuniary damages for the years after death, the estate can hardly be in a better position.

of living plaintiffs on the other hand, future non-pecuniary loss will often represent the larger element of the total non-pecuniary award. These considerations mean that the sums involved in claims made by the estate are often relatively small in comparison with those made by living plaintiffs. However, such awards will be by no means insignificant where the period between injury and death is long,[204] or where the pain and mental suffering is particularly severe.[205]

2.51 The fact that damages are assessed over the period between injury and death also excludes claims (other than claims for funeral expenses) on behalf of the deceased's estate where death is instantaneous.[206] It is not easy to identify any precise dividing line between instantaneous death (for which no damages may be recovered by the estate) and non-instantaneous death (for which they may). In *Hicks v Chief Constable of South Yorkshire Police*,[207] the deceased died from asphyxia due to crushing in the Hillsborough disaster. Unconsciousness would have occurred within seconds of the crushing injury, followed by death within minutes. The House of Lords held that the medical evidence in that case did not establish any pre-death injury for which damages might be awarded to the estates of the deceased under the 1934 Act.[208] It is unlikely in practice that claims will be pursued on behalf of the estate in cases of near-instant death, since in the majority of cases the sums involved will be insignificant and the persons who will in practice receive the benefit of the award can usually recover damages in their own right for loss of support or bereavement under the Fatal Accidents Act 1976.[209]

[204] Eg *Simpkins v BREL*, 5 December 1990, *Kemp and Kemp*, vol 2, para F2-018/4 (£32,000 for asbestosis, death after 2 years).

[205] Eg *Fallon v Beaumont*, 16 December 1993, *Kemp and Kemp*, vol 3, para L7-023: see para 2.49 n 200 above.

[206] Until s 1(1)(a) of the Administration of Justice Act 1982 abolished loss of expectation of life as a separate head of non-pecuniary loss, damages on this account could be recovered by the estate in a survival action even in cases of instant death. See, eg, *Gammell v Wilson* [1982] AC 27; and paras 2.6-2.9 above. Until 1983 the estate could also recover damages for pecuniary loss (loss of earnings) during the "lost years" but this too was prohibited by the Administration of Justice Act 1982, s 4, substituting a new s 1(2)(a) in the 1934 Act which provides that recovery by the estate of damages for loss of income is limited to the period prior to death. The combined effect of these changes is to confine the operation of survival claims by the estate (leaving aside funeral expenses) to cases of non-instantaneous death.

[207] [1992] 2 All ER 65. See also *Bishop v Cunard White Star Co Ltd* [1950] P 240, 247.

[208] In the *Hicks* case [1992] 1 All ER 690, 694a-b (CA), Parker LJ indicated that, if damages could be awarded for the pain and knowledge of impending death which he was prepared to infer the deceased had experienced in the few seconds before the onset of unconsciousness, such damages could only amount to a nominal conventional sum. But it was his view that "when unconsciousness and death occur in such a short period after the injury which causes death no damages are recoverable. The last few moments of mental agony and pain are in reality part of the death itself, for which no action lies under the 1934 Act."

[209] In *Hicks v Chief Constable of South Yorkshire Police* [1992] 2 All ER 65, the claim on behalf of Sarah Hicks' estate was the only claim which could be brought in respect of her wrongful death (*per* Lord Bridge at 67j). No action could be brought by the parents under

2.52 Until 1983, the damages (including those for non-pecuniary loss)[210] received by the estate under the Law Reform Act would be deducted from those awarded to the dependants under the Fatal Accidents Acts, if the dependants were also the beneficiaries of the estate.[211] Section 4 of the Fatal Accidents Act 1976 (as substituted by section 3(1) of the Administration of Justice Act 1982) now directs the court in assessing damages for dependency to disregard all benefits accruing to the dependants from the estate.[212]

the Fatal Accidents Act 1976 because there was no dependency and Sarah was not (at 19 years old) a minor in respect of whom a claim for bereavement damages could be made.

[210] But excluding accrued pecuniary loss.

[211] *Davies v Powell Duffryn Associated Collieries* [1942] AC 601. See eg *Murray v Shuter* [1976] 1 QB 972.

[212] After 1983 the value of the surviving claim is considerably less, since damages for loss of expectation of life may no longer be awarded in cases of instant death and loss of earnings can no longer be recovered for the "lost years": s 1(1)(a) of the Administration of Justice Act 1982; and s 1(2)(a)(ii) of the Law Reform (Miscellaneous Provisions) Act 1934, as substituted by s 4(2) of the Administration of Justice Act 1982. Section 4 of the 1976 Act will be considered in our consultation paper on the Fatal Accidents Act 1976.

PART III
OTHER JURISDICTIONS

3.1 In Part IV of this paper we shall be examining the options for reform of the law in England and Wales. Before we do so, we consider that it may be helpful to consultees to be aware of the approaches that are taken to similar problems[1] in other jurisdictions. We have made a brief sketch of the relevant law in Scotland, Ireland, the United States and a number of Commonwealth common law jurisdictions. We have also included similar summaries of the law in France and Germany as examples of European civil law jurisdictions.[2]

---

[1] Eg the heads under which damages for non-pecuniary loss are awarded; the problem of the unconscious plaintiff; the extent to which damages for personal injury are awarded by juries as opposed to judges; whether damages for non-pecuniary loss may survive on the plaintiff's death for the benefit of the plaintiff's estate; the award of interest on damages for non-pecuniary loss; and the quantum of awards.

In relation to quantum, we have expressed each figure in the currency in which the judgment was given. We have not attempted the very complex task of updating the figures to today's sterling rate. The following list of current exchange rates may be useful as a very general guide only:

Country	Currency	Rate
Ireland	Punt (£)	0.9765
Australia	Dollar ($)	2.0803
New Zealand	Dollar ($)	2.3882
Canada	Dollar ($)	2.1044
United States	Dollar ($)	1.5754
Germany	Deutschmark (DM)	2.2358
France	Franc (FFr)	7.8031

(*The Independent*, 17 October 1995).

[2] The law in some other European countries is also of interest. For example, in Belgium, in the absence of any scales of damages, official or unofficial, there are wide variations in the amounts of damages awarded for non-pecuniary loss, and the courts have rejected the claims of unconscious plaintiffs. In the Netherlands, the new Civil Code which came into force in 1992 makes provision for reasonable damages for "other loss than material damages": courts are to make allowance for all the circumstances of the case, but there are indications, at least from the parliamentary debates, that courts should take into account the likely use by the plaintiff of the amount awarded. Awards in respect of non-pecuniary loss in the Netherlands tend to be modest in comparison with other European countries. Damages for non-pecuniary loss in Italy fall under two heads: "moral damage", which is assessed on an equitable basis according to the circumstances of the accident, type of injury and extent of permanent disability, and "biological damage" reflecting the degree of violation of the plaintiff's psychological and physical integrity. In Switzerland, damages for non-pecuniary loss constitute a separately assessed sum (*Genugtuung*) comprising pain and suffering, loss of amenities, distress and disfigurement, but this sum is only recoverable if the injury causes lasting impairment or involves a long painful recovery process. Tort claims are less important in Sweden, in relation to the compensation system as a whole, because of the wide scope of compensation schemes involving insurance and strict liability. An interesting feature of these schemes is the use of tables produced by advisory boards which give opinions on the amount of compensation that should be paid. These advisory boards consist of judges, insurance officials and lay persons and are only consultative in nature, although they have considerable influence in practice. See generally W Pfennigstorf (ed), *Personal Injury Compensation* (1993).

40

SCOTLAND[3]

3.2 A person who has sustained actionable personal injury is entitled under Scottish law to *solatium* from the wrongdoer, in addition to patrimonial (that is, pecuniary) loss.[4] The solatium element of damages is awarded as compensation for pain and suffering and loss of amenities,[5] although in practice a single global award tends to be made.[6]

3.3 Solatium was previously capable of including an element for loss of expectation of life,[7] in the form of a modest conventional sum, following the same principles as those formerly applied in England.[8] However, in 1993 the law was reformed on the recommendation of the Scottish Law Commission,[9] and a similar approach was adopted to the one now applied in England. No damages are now recoverable, by way of solatium, for loss of expectation of life, except where the pursuer is, was, or is likely to become, aware of the reduction in life expectancy. In those circumstances the court will assess the damages, having regard to the extent to which the pursuer has suffered, or is likely to suffer, in consequence of his or her knowledge of the reduction.[10] Loss of expectation of life is therefore only compensated as part of the damages for the pursuer's subjective pain and suffering, and will not be compensated if, for example, he or she is permanently unconscious.

3.4 Between 1976 and 1992 the Damages (Scotland) Act 1976, which governed the survival of actions on the pursuer's death, rendered claims for solatium incapable of passing to the pursuer's estate.[11] The law has now been reformed on the advice

---

[3] We are grateful to the Scottish Law Commission for assisting us in the compilation of this section.

[4] The concept of solatium probably derives from the now obsolete claim for assythment, and before that from the even more ancient concept of *wergeld* (blood money): see D M Walker, *The Law of Civil Remedies in Scotland* (1974) p 941 and *M'Kendrick v Sinclair* 1972 SC 25 (HL).

[5] Sometimes referred to as loss of faculties and amenities: see, eg, *Dalgleish v Glasgow Corpn* 1976 SC 32, 53, *per* Lord Wheatley, Lord Justice-Clerk (2nd Division).

[6] See, eg, *Stark v Lothian and Borders Fire Board* 1993 SLT 652, 654C-D (OH). But cf *Dalgleish v Glasgow Corpn* 1976 SC 32, 53 (2nd Division) in which the Lord Justice-Clerk considered a solatium claim within the context of three separate heads of damage, namely (a) pain and suffering; (b) loss of faculties and amenities; and (c) expectation of life. See para 3.5 below.

[7] See *Dalgleish v Glasgow Corpn* 1976 SC 32, 53; cf *Balfour v William Beardmore & Co Ltd* 1956 SLT 205, 215 in which the Outer House appeared to regard the claim for loss of expectation of life as being separate from the claim for solatium.

[8] See paras 2.6-2.8 above.

[9] Report on The Effect of Death on Damages (1992) Scot Law Com No 134, paras 4.19 and 4.20.

[10] Damages (Scotland) Act 1976, s 9A, inserted by Damages (Scotland) Act 1993, s 5.

[11] Damages (Scotland) Act 1976, s 2(3) (unamended).

of the Scottish Law Commission.[12] As in England all rights to damages in respect of personal injuries vested in the pursuer now pass to his or her executor on the pursuer's death. As in England, too, the damages are restricted to the period up to the pursuer's death.[13]

3.5 In cases where the pursuer is unconscious the Scottish courts have adopted a similar approach, in the assessment of solatium, to the one adopted by the English courts. In *Dalgleish v Glasgow Corporation*,[14] for example, the victim had been rendered permanently unconscious. The court found for the defenders on the ground that the accident was not foreseeable but went on to consider the level of damages that would have been appropriate had the pursuer succeeded in the claim. The court adopted an objective approach to the assessment of damages for loss of amenity, and decided that a substantial award would have been appropriate in the context of the unconscious victim's injuries. In doing so, it referred to the English decisions in *Wise v Kaye*[15] and *West v Shephard*.[16] However, the fact that the victim was permanently unaware of her loss was relevant when assessing damages for pain and suffering, and no award was made under this head.[17]

3.6 Scottish law requires that the element of solatium that provides compensation for loss of amenity should be measured, as in England, with a degree of flexibility so as to reflect the pursuer's particular circumstances, such as the nature and consequences of the injuries, the age of the victim, and the period of life during which the pursuer is deprived of life's activities and amenities. In *Dalgleish* the court acknowledged that there was no mathematical formula for the purposes of assessing quantum: the sum was to be arrived at, with regard to the factors mentioned, "using a broad axe with a blunt edge".[18] However, the courts do refer to awards in clearly similar cases for guidance,[19] and they may also take into account awards made in

---

[12] Report on The Effect of Death on Damages (1992) Scot Law Com No 134, para 4.10. The recommendations followed public concern at perceived undercompensation occurring in the context of industrial diseases, and at the failure of the enhanced loss of society award provided for by the 1976 Act to lead to higher awards for non-pecuniary loss: for detailed consideration see para 4.127 below.

[13] Damages (Scotland) Act 1976, s 2, substituted for the old section by the Damages (Scotland) Act 1993, s 3, on the recommendation of the Scottish Law Commission in the Report on The Effect of Death on Damages (1992) Scot Law Com No 134, para 4.11.

[14] 1976 SC 32 (2nd Division).

[15] [1962] 1 QB 638. See para 2.16 above.

[16] [1964] AC 326. See para 2.17 above.

[17] *Dalgleish v Glasgow Corpn* 1976 SC 32, 54, *per* Lord Wheatley, Lord Justice-Clerk.

[18] *Ibid*, 54.

[19] See, eg, *McMillan v McDowell* 1993 SLT 311, 312, *per* T G Coutts QC. In 1969, however, any suggestion of a formal tariff was vehemently rejected in *McCallum v Paterson* 1969 SC 85, 90, *per* Lord Guthrie.

similar English cases.[20] In *Girvan v Inverness Farmers Dairy*[21] the Court of Session reviewed the level of awards for very serious injuries. After considering arguments from both counsel based on awards in other cases and after the pursuer's counsel had drawn the Court's attention to the guidelines issued by the Judicial Studies Board in England,[22] the Court took the view that previous awards, whether by judge or jury, could only be taken as a rough guide.[23] However, given that the highest Scottish award of solatium for paraplegia was £70,000[24] and that an award for quadriplegia could be expected to be something in excess of £100,000, the jury's award of £120,000 to the pursuer in *Girvan* for injuries less serious than paraplegia or quadriplegia[25] was held to be plainly excessive and a new trial was ordered.[26]

3.7   The court has power to award interest on damages.[27] Where the damages consist of, or include, solatium for personal injuries, the court is directed to exercise that power so as to include interest on the damages, including the solatium, or on such part as the court considers appropriate, unless the court considers that there are special reasons why interest should not be awarded.[28] Interest may be calculated for the period between the date when the cause of action arose and the date of the judgment, or for any part of that period. The principle governing the exercise of the court's discretion is that interest should be allowed on those damages which have been withheld from the pursuer due to the normal delay of litigation.[29] This means that interest may be awarded on different parts of the total damages award for

---

[20] *Allan v Scott* 1972 SC 59; *Dalgleish v Glasgow Corpn* 1976 SC 32; *MacShannon v Rockware Glass Ltd* [1978] AC 795.

[21] 1995 SLT 735 (2nd Division).

[22] See para 1.5 above.

[23] 1995 SLT 735, 738.

[24] *McMillan v McDowall* 1993 SLT 311.

[25] A fracture of the right elbow and lacerations to the head and knee: the injury to the elbow had a disabling effect and prevented the pursuer from following his special interest in competitive clay pigeon shooting.

[26] For other recent examples of the approach involving the use of comparable cases see *Stevenson v Sweeney* 1995 SLT 29 (OH); *McKenzie v Cape Building Products Ltd* 1995 SLT 695 (OH). However, in *Cole v Weir Pumps Ltd* Lord Johnston said: "...I am never convinced that other cases bear much on a decision in a particular case when an individual assessment [of solatium] has to be made.": 1995 SLT 12, 14. Awards for non-pecuniary loss have been said to be lower than those in England: see W Stewart, *An Introduction to the Scots Law of Delict* (1989) p 163.

[27] Interest on Damages (Scotland) Act 1958, s 1(1), substituted by Interest on Damages (Scotland) Act 1971, s 1.

[28] Interest on Damages (Scotland) Act 1958, s 1(1A), inserted by Interest on Damages (Scotland) Act 1971, s 1.

[29] *Macrae v Reed & Mallik Ltd* 1961 SC 68, 74. This case was decided under the wording of the Interest on Damages (Scotland) Act 1958 in force before it was amended by the Interest on Damages (Scotland) Act 1971, but the principle was affirmed in relation to the amended Act in *Smith v Middleton* 1972 SC 30, 38, *per* Lord Emslie.

different periods of time. In particular, interest will not be awarded on damages relating to future loss, for example, the part of solatium representing future pain and suffering. Courts will therefore award interest on the proportion of solatium intended to represent past loss, although this apportionment is made only for the purpose of calculating interest and does not represent a division of solatium into two separate awards.[30] The rate of interest tends to be about one half of the usual judicial rate in order to reflect the fact that the loss will have been incurred over a period of time which, in most cases, will be the whole of the period from the date of the accident to the date of judgment, and that it would therefore be inappropriate to award interest on the whole of the relevant amount at the full rate for the full period.[31]

3.8 It is still possible for actions for the recovery of damages for personal injuries in the Court of Session to be tried by jury,[32] and in the event of a jury trial the jury will also determine the amount of damages, including the amount of past and future solatium. The allowance of jury trial is not uncommon and demand for it on the part of pursuers has revived in recent years.[33] It is for the court to decide whether or not special cause exists for refusing to allow trial by jury. It has been said that one case is of little guidance in deciding whether jury trial will be ordered in another case.[34] Nevertheless, examples of circumstances which may constitute special cause include cases where questions of fact are difficult and complex, or where it is essential to ascertain precisely what the facts prove; or where a difficult question of law, or questions of mixed fact and law, arise so that a judge may not be able to give an effective direction to the jury.[35] On the other hand, the fact that the trial is one of quantum only, or that the amount of damages is, or is expected to be, small, is not generally regarded as constituting special cause for refusing to allow jury trial.[36]

IRELAND

3.9 In Ireland damages for pecuniary loss are recoverable on a similar basis to recovery in England, and damages for non-pecuniary loss resulting from personal injury are recoverable "for the pain, suffering, inconvenience and loss of the pleasures of life

[30] *McManus v British Railways Board* 1994 SLT 496 (2nd Division).

[31] See *McEwan and Paton on Damages in Scotland* (2nd ed 1989) para 3-09.

[32] Court of Session Act 1988, ss 9 and 11.

[33] *The Laws of Scotland: Stair Memorial Encyclopedia* (1989) vol 17 para 1412.

[34] D Maxwell, *The Practice of the Court of Session* (1980) p 296. See *Morris v Drysdale* 1992 SLT 186 (OH).

[35] D Maxwell, *The Practice of the Court of Session* (1980) p 297.

[36] *Ibid*, p 298.

which the injury has caused and will cause to the plaintiff."[37] In *Dunne v National Maternity Hospital*[38] the Irish Supreme Court isolated five factors which, on the facts of that case, were of particular relevance to the assessment of such damages. These were: (1) the extent to which the plaintiff had any appreciation or awareness of his damaged condition and of the amenities of living he had lost; (2) the extent to which the award of damages under separate headings made full and ample provision for the plaintiff's care and bodily needs; (3) the totality of the plaintiff's loss of amenity and happiness; (4) the plaintiff's life expectancy; and (5) the amount of the gross award for damages under all headings of which the amount of general damages formed a component part.[39]

3.10 The presence of the second of these factors appears to suggest that at least part of the rationale behind the award of damages for non-pecuniary loss is to provide for the plaintiff's care and bodily needs, in so far as this has not been completely achieved by the award for pecuniary loss. Similarly, in the earlier case of *Sinnott v Quinnsworth Ltd* the Supreme Court had expressed the view that regard should be had to "the things upon which the plaintiff might reasonably be expected to spend money".[40] In that case the plaintiff was a young man who had become quadriplegic as a result of a motor accident. The Supreme Court reduced a jury award of £800,000 for non-pecuniary loss to £150,000.

3.11 It seems that Ireland, unlike England, retains the principle that damages may be recovered under the head of loss of expectation of life. In arriving at a figure the trier of fact must be just and reasonable.[41] Awards must, however, be moderate. In *O'Sullivan v Dwyer*[42] the Supreme Court held that an award of about £10,000 in 1969 for the loss of expectation of between approximately 16 and 20 years of life was excessive, bearing in mind the fact that an allowance had already been made under the head of pain and suffering for the mental distress attributable to the knowledge of the loss of expectation of life. In the view of Walsh J "the loss of 16 to 20 years of life is considerably less in value than having to endure 21 years as a

---

[37] *Sinnott v Quinnsworth Ltd* [1984] ILRM 523, 531, *per* O'Higgins CJ.

[38] [1989] IR 91. The plaintiff in this case had been born with irreversible brain damage due to alleged medical negligence at the birth and at the time of the trial was quadriplegic with major mental handicap. The defendant's appeal was allowed in relation to both liability and quantum and a retrial ordered.

[39] *Ibid*, 118-119. Although the reference is to general damages, it is clear from the context that only general damages for non-pecuniary loss are being referred to, and not damages for future pecuniary loss.

[40] [1984] ILRM 523, 532, *per* O'Higgins CJ. See also *Reddy v Bates* [1983] IR 141, 148, *per* Griffin J.

[41] *McMorrow v Knott*, unreported, 21 December 1959 (Sup Ct: ref 29-1959) pp 3-4, *per* Maguire CJ.

[42] [1971] IR 275 (Sup Ct).

paraplegic."[43] Little will therefore be awarded for the loss of expectation of life *in itself* as opposed to the subjective *awareness* of that loss.

3.12   The case of the plaintiff who has no, or little, awareness of his or her injuries was considered by the Supreme Court in *Cooke v Walsh*.[44] The plaintiff in that case was not unconscious but in addition to his very severe physical injuries he had sustained brain injuries of such a degree that his mental age would not progress much beyond the age of two. The majority of the Supreme Court held that damages should be "moderate" on account of the plaintiff's limited appreciation of his condition.[45] It would appear therefore that although the plaintiff should still receive some compensation in these circumstances in recognition of the loss, there is a strong preference for the subjective approach whereby damages are gauged according to the degree of unhappiness and mental turmoil which the plaintiff has in fact sustained.[46]

3.13   The plaintiff in the *Dunne* case was brain damaged as a result of his injuries. He was not unconscious and, although he had little appreciation of the position he was in, he did display minimal signs of unhappiness or contentment on certain occasions.[47] Referring to previous cases including *Cooke v Walsh*[48] and *Sinnott v Quinnsworth Ltd*[49] the Supreme Court was satisfied that the sum of £467,000 awarded by the jury as general damages was excessive to a degree which rendered it unreasonable. Finlay CJ, giving the leading judgment, indicated that the range of general damages which he would expect to be awarded on the retrial of the case would be between £50,000 and £100,000.[50] However, he declined to express any view as to whether as a matter of principle a person who had no awareness of an impaired condition should be entitled to either no or nominal general damages.

3.14   The difficulties of proof and computation which arise when assessing damages for non-pecuniary loss led to the introduction of a rough upper limit by the Supreme

---

[43]   *Ibid*, 290.

[44]   [1984] ILRM 208. See J White, *Irish Law of Damages for Personal Injury and Death* (1989) para 6.3.08.

[45]   McCarthy J reserved his opinion as to the approach to be adopted in a case of this nature.

[46]   Another consequence of the subjective approach preferred by the Irish courts is that damages may be reduced where the victim responds with fortitude and good spirits to his or her injury: see, for example, *Prendergast v Joe Malone Self Drive Ltd*, unreported, 21 June 1967 (Sup Ct: ref 137-1966). See J White, *Irish Law of Damages for Personal Injury and Death* (1989) para 6.3.04.

[47]   [1989] IR 91, 118.

[48]   [1984] ILRM 208: see para 3.12 above.

[49]   [1984] ILRM 523: see paras 3.10 above and 3.14 below.

[50]   [1989] IR 91, 120.

Court in *Sinnott v Quinnsworth Ltd.*[51] In arriving at a figure of £150,000, the court expressed the view that the jury's award of £800,000 lacked "all sense of reality".[52] Awards of excessively large damages would lay courts open to the criticism that they were awarding damages on a punitive, rather than a compensatory basis, and they might also endanger the operation of public policy. It appears that this limit is still being applied by the Irish courts in practice.[53]

3.15 Although the plaintiff in *Sinnott* was conscious of what he had lost, it is possible to imagine cases in which the plaintiff's pain and suffering might be even more severe. Some commentators have therefore suggested that the £150,000 upper limit should not be regarded as the absolute maximum for general damages in tort actions.[54] It is also uncertain whether the £150,000 guideline simply represents a cap, or whether it has implications, in the form of a "scaling down" effect, for setting the quantum of general damages in *all* cases. There are indications that Irish courts are indeed scaling down other claims.[55]

3.16 Some of the concerns which gave rise to the establishment of this rough upper limit in 1984 were removed four years later by the abolition of the right to a trial by jury in nearly all actions for personal injury and death in High Court proceedings. The Courts Act 1988 provided that actions in respect of personal injuries caused by negligence, nuisance or breach of duty, including breach of a contractual or statutory duty, and wrongful death actions, would not be tried with a jury.[56] Jury trial is, however, still available where the action includes a claim for false imprisonment or intentional trespass to the person.[57] Before this time, awards were assessed by a jury with no reference to previous cases, no guidelines to amounts to be awarded, and no expert advice as to the level of the compensatory award it should make.[58]

---

[51] [1984] ILRM 523. See para 3.10 above. See also J White, *Irish Law of Damages for Personal Injury and Death* (1989) paras 6.5.05-6.5.06.

[52] [1984] ILRM 523, 532, *per* O'Higgins CJ.

[53] Letter from the President of the Law Reform Commission of Ireland, 30 June 1994.

[54] See B McMahon and W Binchy, *Irish Law of Torts* (2nd ed 1990) p 799.

[55] See, eg, *Griffiths v Van Raaj* [1985] ILRM 582 (Sup Ct).

[56] Courts Act 1988, s 1. The right to a jury in lower courts had previously been abolished by section 6 of the Courts Act 1971: see B McMahon and W Binchy, *Irish Law of Torts* (2nd ed 1990) pp 35-36.

[57] Courts Act 1988, s 1(3). This exception is, in turn, subject to an exception where damages are claimed both for false imprisonment or intentional trespass to the person and another cause of action, and it appears to the court that it is not reasonable to claim damages for false imprisonment or intentional trespass to the person: *ibid*, s 1(3)(b).

[58] P Szöllösy, "Recent Trends in the Standard of Compensation for Personal Injury in a European Context" (1991) 3 Nordisk Forsikringstidsskrift 191, 195.

3.17   The rising cost to the insurance industry, and, through increased premiums, to businesses, of personal injury claims in Ireland has continued to be a concern. The previous Irish government indicated a desire to introduce a statutory cap on awards for pain and suffering.[59] This gave rise to considerable debate, but the reform had not been implemented, and indeed no formal policy document had been published, at the time when a new government took office in 1994. The present Irish government has established an investigation into the possibility of capping and has, in accordance with a finding of a lack of empirical information, commissioned a study by independent management consultants.

3.18   Irish courts have the power to award interest on those elements of an award of damages for personal injuries which relate to loss which is pecuniary and to the period before the date of judgment: but there is no power to award interest on damages for non-pecuniary loss.[60]

3.19   The common law rule that a cause of action dies along with the person in whom it is vested[61] applied in Ireland until 1961. It was then abolished by the Civil Liability Act 1961 and, as a result, a cause of action will vest in the estate of the deceased and may be pursued by his or her personal representatives. However, section 7(2) of the Act precludes recovery of damages for "any pain or suffering or personal injury or for loss or diminution of expectation of life or happiness." It follows that a claim for damages for non-pecuniary loss will not survive the plaintiff's death.

AUSTRALIA

3.20   As in England, damages are recoverable for pain and suffering and loss of amenity. Damages can also be recovered for loss of expectation of life as a separate head of loss.[62] Pain and suffering are regarded as being purely subjective, so that damages are awarded only in so far as the plaintiff is aware of that loss.[63] Despite this subjective approach, the courts do not reduce the damages for pain and suffering where the plaintiff has borne injuries courageously.[64] Damages for suffering can include compensation for the plaintiff's awareness of the shortening of his or her life. Damages for loss of amenity are intended to reflect the loss of enjoyment which the plaintiff has suffered in life, and may take into account the activities in which he or

---

[59]   S Brennan TD, Minister of State for Commerce and Technology, in a speech to the Irish Insurance Federation on 18 May 1993: *Irish Times*, 19 May 1993.

[60]   Courts Act 1981, s 22(2). See J White, *Irish Law of Damages for Personal Injury and Death* (1989) vol 1 para 1.8.01.

[61]   The *actio personalis moritur cum persona* rule: see para 2.49 above.

[62]   Abolished in England and Wales by the Administration of Justice Act 1982, s 1: see paras 2.6-2.9 above.

[63]   *Skelton v Collins* (1966) 115 CLR 94.

[64]   *Cawrse v Cocks* (1974) 10 SASR 10; *Burke v Batchelor* (1980) 24 SASR 33, 40 *per* Wells J.

she engaged before the injuries were suffered, and which can no longer be pursued. Damages for loss of expectation of life as a separate head of loss are conventional and relatively small, following the English decision in *Benham v Gambling*.[65]

3.21 The Australian approach towards the assessment of damages for loss of amenity tends to place greater importance on the plaintiff's subjective awareness of his or her condition than in England. In other words, using Professor Ogus' labels, the Australian courts tend to prefer a subjective "personal approach" rather than an objective "conceptual approach".[66] In the leading case of *Skelton v Collins*,[67] in which the plaintiff, aged 19, had suffered brain damage in a road accident which rendered him permanently unconscious and reduced his life expectancy to a period of approximately six months after the trial, the judge at first instance had assessed his general damages (for loss of amenity and loss of expectation of life) as £1,500.[68] In doing so he had adopted the reasoning of the dissenting judgments of Diplock LJ in *Wise v Kaye*[69] and of Lord Devlin in *West v Shephard*[70] and applied a subjective test to the plaintiff's loss of amenities. The plaintiff appealed against this award,[71] but it was upheld by the High Court of Australia (Menzies J dissenting) which approved the judge's emphasis on the plaintiff's subjective experience.[72] Kitto J took the view that the correct approach was objective only in the limited sense that the plaintiff's loss should be measured in terms of the life which a person in the plaintiff's position might have been expected to lead if the injuries had not occurred, rather than the life which the individual plaintiff might have led. He did not, however, favour an approach which was objective in the sense of valuing the amenities lost by the plaintiff as if it were "a physical thing".[73] Taylor J, for his part, said:

> I find it impossible to ignore, or to regard merely as a minimal factor, what has been referred to as the subjective element. The expression 'loss of the amenities

---

[65] [1941] AC 157 (HL): see *Skelton v Collins* (1966) 115 CLR 94.

[66] A Ogus, "Damages for Lost Amenities: For a Foot, a Feeling or a Function?" (1972) 35 MLR 1: see para 2.3 above.

[67] (1966) 115 CLR 94.

[68] This was then reduced by 25% because of the plaintiff's contributory negligence. The Australian pound was superseded by the Australian dollar in 1966.

[69] [1962] 1 QB 638: see para 2.16 above.

[70] [1964] AC 326: see para 2.17 above.

[71] He also appealed against the award of damages for loss of earnings.

[72] For more recent examples of low sums for loss of amenity being awarded to permanently unconscious plaintiffs see, eg, *Densley v Nominal Defendant* [1993] ACL Reporter 500 (15 June 1993; Queensland Sup Ct) ($5,000 for loss of amenity); *Tille v Parkinson* [1992] ACL Reporter 467 (February 1992; Queensland Sup Ct) ($3,000 for loss of amenity).

[73] (1966) 115 CLR 94, 101.

of life' is a loose expression but as a head of damages in personal injury cases it is intended to denote a loss of the capacity of the injured person *consciously* to enjoy life to the full as, apart from his injury, he might have done.[74]

3.22 The judgment of Windeyer J placed special emphasis on the solace for the plaintiff afforded by the damages for non-pecuniary loss and the use to which they would be put: in Professor Ogus' terminology, he was adopting the "functional approach".[75] He said:

> Money may be a compensation for [the plaintiff] if having it can give him pleasure or satisfaction. ... But the money is not then a recompense for a loss of something having a money value. It is given as some consolation or solace for the distress that is the consequence of a loss on which no monetary value can be put ... [The judge at first instance], after carefully considering the problem created for him by conflicting decisions and inconsistent reasoning, thought that he should allow £1,500 in addition to economic loss. He said, however: 'I would merely add that if it is ultimately held that the correct principle is that there should be no award beyond economic loss unless there is at least a chance that the additional sum can be used for the advantage of the plaintiff then on the evidence and admissions in this case there should be no such additional award.' In my view, his Honour, having thus held that on the evidence there was not even a chance that the additional sum could be used for the advantage of the plaintiff, ought not to have awarded it. It could not bring any advantage or consolation to the plaintiff. Consolation presupposes consciousness and some capacity of intellectual appreciation. If money were given to the plaintiff he could never know that he had it. He could not use it or dispose of it.[76]

3.23 Nearly 30 years ago the High Court of Australia attempted to resist the employment of a tariff scheme or even reference to a norm or standard derived from a consideration of awards in comparable cases.[77] Instead, the paramount principle to be followed in assessing damages for non-pecuniary loss was that the amount of damages must be fair and reasonable compensation for the injuries that have been caused. The standards of reasonableness to be applied must be those prevailing in the community.[78] The Court in the *Planet Fisheries* case insisted that any award was to be "proportionate to the situation of the claimant party and not to the situation

---

[74] (1966) 115 CLR 94, 113 (emphasis in original).

[75] A Ogus, "Damages for Lost Amenities: For a Foot, a Feeling or a Function?" (1972) 35 MLR 1: see para 2.3 above.

[76] (1966) 115 CLR 94, 131-133.

[77] *Planet Fisheries Pty Ltd v La Rosa* (1968) 119 CLR 118. See also *Arthur Robinson (Grafton) Pty Ltd v Carter* (1968) 122 CLR 649, 656, *per* Barwick CJ.

[78] *O'Brien v Dunsdon* (1965) 39 ALJR 78.

of other parties in other actions, even if some similarity between their situations may be supposed to be seen."[79] The Court acknowledged that when making an assessment a judge would be aware of and give weight to "current general ideas of fairness and moderation", but this must be "a product of general experience and not formed ad hoc by a process of considering particular cases and endeavouring...to allow for differences between the circumstances of those cases and the circumstances of the case in hand."[80] Such an approach has, however, been criticised as a vague and unreliable means of ensuring that awards are proportionate to the circumstances of the case.[81] It would appear that, despite the High Court's opposition in the late 1960s, a tariff approach has indeed developed in the different states of Australia.[82] One attempt at reconciliation was made in *Hirsch v Bennett*,[83] soon after the decision in the *Planet Fisheries* case, in which the Supreme Court of South Australia acknowledged that a judge "must recognise that no two cases are wholly alike and that apparent similarities are often superficial..." but that it was not wrong for a judge to search for comparable cases and "use any current pattern as a guide in making his assessment in the case under consideration...".[84]

3.24 It is difficult to draw any general rules as to levels of damages for non-pecuniary loss from reported cases in the Australian jurisdictions, given the official lack of tariffs at common law and the fact that any *de facto* tariffs tend to apply within individual states or territories. Comparisons are made even more difficult by the existence of statutory rules that place limitations on the damages recoverable for certain types of accident.[85] It is possible, however, to give a very general impression. For example, in South Australia in 1992 there was an award of $320,000 for pain and suffering and loss of amenities to a plaintiff aged 13 at the time of the trial who had been rendered quadriplegic in a motor accident.[86] $90,000 was for past loss and $230,000 for future loss. In New South Wales there have been a number of awards of damages for quadriplegia exceeding $200,000 in relation to motor accidents,[87] where special statutory rules apply. In other states, for example Tasmania, awards for

---

[79] (1968) 119 CLR 118, 125 *per* Barwick CJ and Menzies and Kitto JJ in a joint judgment.

[80] *Ibid.*

[81] See, eg, H Luntz, *Assessment of Damages for Personal Injury and Death* (3rd ed 1990) para 3.1.5. See also *Sharman v Evans* (1977) 138 CLR 563, 572 *per* Gibbs and Stephen JJ.

[82] N Mullany, "A New Approach to Compensation for Non-Pecuniary Loss in Australia" (1990) 17 MULR 714, 714-715; H Luntz, *Assessment of Damages for Personal Injury and Death* (3rd ed 1990) para 3.1.9.

[83] [1969] SASR 493.

[84] *Ibid*, 499, *per* Travers and Walters JJ.

[85] See paras 3.29-3.32 below.

[86] *Burford v Allen* (1992) Aust Torts Reports para 81-184.

[87] Eg *Dillon v Salameh* (18 February 1994; NSW Sup Ct); *Farrell v Mackie* (11 February 1994; NSW Sup Ct).

comparable injuries appear to have been lower.[88] This tendency was recently criticised by the Tasmanian Full Court in *Motor Accidents Insurance Board v Pulford*[89] when it dismissed an appeal against an award of $90,000 to a plaintiff who had become paraplegic as a result of a motor accident. The court compared levels of damages for non-pecuniary loss in Tasmania with other Australian jurisdictions and called for a general increase.

3.25   In all the Australian states and territories legislation exists to provide for the survival of causes of action. In Queensland, South Australia, Western Australia and Tasmania, damages for non-pecuniary loss do not pass to the plaintiff's estate in any circumstances.[90] In the other states and territories the right to damages for non-pecuniary loss will survive where the death is independent of the tort.[91] In none of the Australian jurisdictions does the right to recover damages for non-pecuniary loss pass to a plaintiff's estate where the plaintiff's death has been caused by the tort to which those damages relate. This must be contrasted with the position in English law where damages for non-pecuniary loss survive irrespective of the cause of the plaintiff's death.[92]

3.26   Some civil actions in Australia are still tried by jury, but the importance of jury trial is said to be declining.[93] In Queensland, Tasmania, Victoria and (in cases other than those relating to motor accidents) New South Wales either party has a right to demand trial by jury.[94] In the Northern Territory, the Australian Capital Territory and Western Australia the mode of trial is in the court's discretion.[95] In motor accident cases in New South Wales, the court may in its discretion order trial by

---

[88]   We were informed that no awards in the region of $200,000 had been made to the knowledge of the Tasmanian Law Reform Commissioner: letter dated 12 May 1994.

[89]   (1993) Aust Torts Reports para 81-235, *per* Wright J.

[90]   **Queensland** Succession Act 1981, s 66; **South Australia** Survival of Causes of Action Act 1940, s 3; **Western Australia** Law Reform (Miscellaneous Provisions) Act 1941, s 4; **Tasmania** Administration and Probate Act 1935, s 27.

[91]   **NSW** Law Reform (Miscellaneous Provisions) Act 1944, s 2; **Victoria** Administration and Probate Act 1958, s 29; **Northern Territory** Law Reform (Miscellaneous Provisions) Ordinance 1956, ss 5-9; **Australian Capital Territory** Law Reform (Miscellaneous Provisions) Ordinance 1955, ss 4-8.

[92]   See paras 2.48-2.52 above. Queensland had originally enacted legislation that was modelled on the English provisions: Common Law Practice Act 1867, s 15D, repealed by the Succession Act 1981.

[93]   B C Cairns, *Australian Civil Procedure* (3rd ed 1992) p 461.

[94]   **Queensland** Rules of the Supreme Court 1965, O 39 r 4; **Tasmania** Rules of the Supreme Court 1965, O 39 r 6(1); **Victoria** General Rules of Procedure in Civil Proceedings 1986, r 47.02; **New South Wales** Supreme Court Act 1970, s 85.

[95]   **Commonwealth Australian Capital Territory** Supreme Court Act 1933, s 14(2); **Northern Territory** Juries Ordinance Act 1962, s 7; **Western Australia** Supreme Court Act 1935, s 42.

jury if either party requests it, and must do so if both parties request it.[96] The only Australian jurisdiction in which jury trial is generally unavailable is South Australia, where jury trial may only take place if a question may arise as to whether an indictable offence has been committed.[97]

3.27   The approach to the award of interest on damages differs between jurisdictions in Australia. In Western Australia interest may not be awarded on damages for non-pecuniary loss in respect of a claim for personal injuries.[98] In other jurisdictions, such awards may be made, although in some jurisdictions interest may not be awarded on future non-pecuniary loss.[99] The general rule for the award of interest follows two basic models: either the court must award interest unless good cause is shown to the contrary,[100] or the court's discretion is an open one.[101] The possible starting point for the period over which interest is calculated also differs: in Victoria and South Australia interest may only run from the date on which proceedings were commenced, but in the other jurisdictions interest may run from the date on which the plaintiff's cause of action arose.[102] Even in jurisdictions where interest can be awarded, courts nevertheless tend to refrain from awarding interest on damages for future loss. In the case of non-pecuniary loss, for example, courts tend to apportion damages between past and future loss and allow interest on the portion for past non-pecuniary loss only,[103] although where this is the practice there is still no strict rule that courts must exercise their discretion in this way in all cases.[104]

3.28   There are special rules governing interest on damages in relation to motor accidents in New South Wales, South Australia and Victoria. In New South Wales, interest is excluded unless one of certain specified conditions applies.[105] In Victoria interest

---

[96] **New South Wales** Supreme Court Act 1970, s 87.

[97] **South Australia** Juries Act 1927-1974, s 5.

[98] **Western Australia** Supreme Court Act 1935, s 32(2)(a), as amended by Acts Amendment (Actions for Damages) Act 1986.

[99] Such a prohibition is contained in the **Victoria** Supreme Court Act 1986, s 60(3); and the **Commonwealth Australian Capital Territory** Supreme Court Act 1933, s 53A(3).

[100] **Victoria** Supreme Court Act 1986, s 60; **South Australia** Supreme Court Act 1935, s 30c; **Commonwealth Australian Capital Territory** Supreme Court Act 1933, s 53A.

[101] See, eg, **NSW** Supreme Court Act 1970, s 94; **Queensland** Common Law Practice Act 1867, s 72.

[102] H Luntz, *Damages for Personal Injury and Death* (3rd ed 1990) para 11.3.6. For rates of interest, see para 4.122, n 389 below.

[103] See H Luntz, *Damages for Personal Injury and Death* (3rd ed 1990) para 11.3.7; *Vincent v Faehrmann* (1979) 21 SASR 503; *Paull v Gloede* (1979) 21 SASR 526. See paras 4.112 and 4.122, n 389 below.

[104] *Cullen v Trappell* (1980) 146 CLR 1, 21, *per* Gibbs J (High Ct).

[105] Ie, the defendant has not made steps to assess the claim, the defendant has not made an appropriate offer of settlement, or the court makes an award of damages which (excluding interest) is not less than 20% higher than the defendant's highest offer to settle the claim

only applies to loss suffered before the date of the award.[106] In both states, where interest is awarded at all, it may be awarded on damages for non-pecuniary loss, although this was precluded by legislation previously in force. In South Australia, however, no interest may be awarded on damages for "non-economic loss" in relation to motor accidents.[107]

3.29   Concern about escalating awards and the "insurance crisis" in the motor vehicle industry in particular has led a number of states to adopt restrictions (that is, thresholds and/or ceilings) upon the recovery of damages for non-pecuniary loss in personal injury claims in relation to certain types of accident, usually road accidents or accidents in the course of employment.[108] These restrictions have taken three main forms.

3.30   Under the first type of restriction, the plaintiff is only entitled to compensation if the injury was of a particular severity. Damages or statutory compensation for non-pecuniary loss can only be recovered if the injury was serious,[109] or significantly impaired the ability of the injured person to lead a normal life.[110] A second restriction has been the imposition of a financial threshold; damages for non-pecuniary loss will not be awarded if the claim for this head of damages falls below

and the court is satisfied that the defendant's offer was not reasonable with regard to the information available to the defendant when the offer was made: **NSW** Motor Accidents Act 1988, s 73, as amended by Motor Accidents (Amendment) Act 1989.

[106] **Victoria** Transport Accident Act 1986, s 93(15).

[107] **South Australia** Wrongs Act 1936, s 35a(1)(k), as amended by Wrongs Act Amendment Act 1986, s 3.

[108] See N Mullany, "A New Approach to Compensation for Non-Pecuniary Loss in Australia" (1990) 17 MULR 714, 721-727.

[109] **Victoria** Transport Accident Act 1986, s 93(2)(b) (transport accidents). Serious injury is defined as (a) serious long-term impairment or loss of a body function, permanent serious disfigurement, severe long-term mental or severe long-term behavioural disturbance or disorder, or loss of a foetus: s 93(17). The same condition is employed, again in Victoria, in the Accident Compensation Act 1985, s 135A(2), 135A(19), as introduced by the Accident Compensation (WorkCover) Act 1992, s 46 (employment accidents). In both statutes, the availability of common law damages stands alongside a statutory compensation scheme. Under the Transport Accident Act 1986, compensation may be obtained, on a no-fault basis, from the Transport Accident Commission; under the WorkCover scheme, compensation may be obtained, again on a no-fault basis, wholly or partly from the Victorian WorkCover Authority (formerly the Accident Compensation Commission) and, in some cases, partly from the injured person's employer.

[110] **NSW** Motor Accidents Act 1988, s 79(1) (road accidents); **NSW** Workers Compensation Act 1987, s 151G(1) (as introduced by the Workers Compensation (Benefits) Amendment Act 1989, Schedule 1) (employment accidents). A similar condition is imposed by the Wrongs Act 1936, s 35a(1)(a), as amended by the Wrongs Act Amendment Act 1986, s 3 (**South Australia**, relating to road accidents), where the impairment must last for at least seven days or a certain level of medical expenses must have been reasonably incurred. All these provisions relate to common law damages, although in the case of the employment accident legislation in New South Wales the employee is entitled to claim compensation from his or her employer on a no-fault basis as an alternative.

a certain level.[111] It has been argued that such a threshold is unjust because people with relatively small injuries can nonetheless suffer greatly and ought to be compensated.[112] At present the financial thresholds in New South Wales and Victoria exist alongside thresholds expressed in terms of the severity of the injury suffered: the financial thresholds are used infrequently because damages recoverable for injuries satisfying the severity criterion will generally exceed the financial threshold.[113] A third limitation has been the introduction of ceilings on awards for non-pecuniary loss.[114]

3.31   The threshold and ceiling figures are linked to an index of prices[115] or earnings.[116] In its motor accident and workers' compensation legislation New South Wales has also adopted formulae which have the effect of scaling down awards that fall in the lower part of the range between the threshold and the ceiling. For instance, under the Motor Accidents Act 1988, damages are calculated by assessing a fraction intended to represent the proportion which the injury actually suffered bears to an injury of maximum severity,[117] assuming that the assessed non-pecuniary loss fulfils the financial threshold requirement of $15,000.[118] The calculation of the award is then a mathematical task, completed by applying this proportion to the maximum

---

[111] Eg **Victoria** Transport Accident Act 1986, s 93(7)(b)(i); **Victoria** Accident Compensation Act 1985, s 135A (7)(b)(i) (as introduced by the Accident Compensation (WorkCover) Act 1992, s 46); **NSW** Motor Accidents Act 1988, s 79(4); **NSW** Workers Compensation Act 1987, s 151G(4) (as introduced by the Workers Compensation (Benefits) Amendment Act 1989, Schedule 1).

[112] Tasmanian Law Reform Commission: Compensation for Victims of Motor Vehicle Accidents (1987) Report No 52, p 37.

[113] *Southgate v Waterford* (1990) 21 NSWLR 427, 440-441 (NSW Court of Appeal).

[114] Eg **Victoria** Transport Accident Act 1986, s 93(7)(b)(ii); **Victoria** Accident Compensation Act 1985, s 135A (7)(b)(ii) (as introduced by the Accident Compensation (WorkCover) Act 1992, s 46); **NSW** Motor Accidents Act 1988, s 79(3); **NSW** Workers Compensation Act 1987, s 151G(3) (as introduced by the Workers Compensation (Benefits) Amendment Act 1989, Schedule 1); **South Australia** Wrongs Act 1936, s 35a(1)(b) and 35a(6) (road accidents). A ceiling was recommended by the Tasmanian Law Reform Commission: Compensation for Victims of Motor Vehicle Accidents (1987) Report No 52, p 37.

[115] **Victoria** Transport Accident Act 1986, s 61(2); **South Australia** Wrongs Act 1936, s 35a(6)(b) (road accidents).

[116] **NSW** Motor Accidents Act 1988, s 80(2); **NSW** Workers Compensation Act 1987, ss 79-82, 151G(7) (as introduced by the Workers Compensation (Benefits) Amendment Act 1989, Schedule 1). The figures under the Accident Compensation Act 1985 **(Victoria)** are varied annually in line with an index of average earnings in Victoria: Accident Compensation Act 1985, s 100 and Accident Compensation (Amendment) Act 1994, s 64(6).

[117] **NSW** Motor Accidents Act 1988, s 79(2).

[118] **NSW** Motor Accidents Act 1988, s 79(4).

figure set by the statute,[119] and then reducing the award by the appropriate sum as provided by section 79(5) of the Act. Awards of damages between $15,000 and $40,000 are reduced by a flat figure of $15,000: awards between $40,000 and $55,000 are also reduced, but by a figure which falls as the damages increase.[120] The motor accidents legislation in South Australia has a less complicated formula for scaling down awards. The injury is assessed on a scale from 0 to 60 and damages are awarded by multiplying the number on the scale that the court attributes to the injury by a prescribed amount, which was $1,000 initially.[121] There are different ways of defining the injury which forms the benchmark against which the actual injury is measured. In South Australia the benchmark is the worst possible loss that anyone could suffer,[122] whereas in New South Wales the loss is assessed as a proportion of *a* most extreme case, rather than *the* most extreme case.[123]

3.32   The variations between states in the threshold and ceiling figures illustrate the difficulty in fixing acceptable levels of damages for non-pecuniary loss.[124]   For example, when the Motor Accidents Act 1988 in New South Wales was first introduced, the maximum award was $180,000.[125]   The top of the scale award under the Wrongs Act 1936 in South Australia at the time of the scheme's inception in 1986 was only $60,000.[126]   The maximum recoverable under the Accident Compensation Act 1985 in Victoria was recently increased to $298,640.[127]

---

[119]   **NSW** Motor Accidents Act 1988, s 79(3) (road accidents). See also **NSW** Workers Compensation Act 1987, s 151G(2) (as introduced by the Workers Compensation (Benefits) Amendment Act 1989, Schedule 1) (employment accidents); and *Southgate v Waterford* (1990) 21 NSWLR 427, 440-441.

[120]   **NSW** Motor Accidents Act 1988, s 79(5). See also **NSW** Workers Compensation Act 1987, s 151G(5) (as introduced by the Workers Compensation (Benefits) Amendment Act 1989, Schedule 1), which reduces the amount of damages by a fixed formula for those amounts of non-economic loss that are assessed to be between $45,000 and $60,000. The formula is: Damages = [Amount assessed as loss - $45,000] multiplied by 4.

[121]   **South Australia** Wrongs Act 1936, s 35a(1)(b), 35a(6), inserted by the Wrongs Act Amendment Act 1986.

[122]   *Packer v Cameron* (1989) 54 SASR 246, 251-252, *per* Cox J; 257, *per* Duggan J (South Australia Supreme Court).

[123]   See the interpretation of the **NSW** Motor Accidents Act 1988, s 79(3) by the Court of Appeal of New South Wales in *Dell v Dalton* (1991) 23 NSWLR 528.

[124]   N Mullany, "A New Approach to Compensation for Non-Pecuniary Loss in Australia" (1990) 17 MULR 714, 725-727.

[125]   **NSW** Motor Accidents Act 1988, s 79(3) and 79(4).

[126]   **South Australia** Wrongs Act 1936, s 35a(1)(b), 35a(6), inserted by the Wrongs Act Amendment Act 1986.

[127]   **Victoria** Accident Compensation (Amendment) Act 1994, s 64(6)(d).

NEW ZEALAND

3.33 Compensation for accidents in New Zealand is effected through a statutory no-fault compensation scheme. This was first set up in 1974, under the Accident Compensation Act 1972, as amended by the Accident Compensation Amendment Act 1973. The scheme was re-enacted by the Accident Compensation Act 1982. It has now, however, been radically altered by the Accident Rehabilitation and Compensation Insurance Act 1992 ("ARCIA 1992").[128] Under the 1972 and 1982 Acts the right to damages at common law was barred where cover was provided by the scheme, and this remains the case.[129]

3.34 Under the original scheme, in addition to compensation for pecuniary loss, compensation was recoverable for non-pecuniary loss subject to a maximum amount. Section 78 of the Accident Compensation Act 1982 provided for up to $17,000 compensation for "permanent loss or impairment of any bodily function (including the loss of any part of the body)." The section operated on the basis of a schedule which set out the percentage of $17,000 payable when a particular limb or bodily part was totally lost. Section 79 provided for a further $10,000 for loss of enjoyment of life, loss from disfigurement or pain and mental suffering. There was no express provision for increasing the maximum amounts in line with inflation or the cost of living.

3.35 In 1987, amid concern about the size of awards of compensation for non-pecuniary loss, and the resultant cost to the scheme, the New Zealand Law Commission suggested that the imposition of ceilings on awards of damages for non-pecuniary loss resulted in a tendency for inappropriately high awards to be made in less serious cases because those awards were tending to move upwards towards the sums awarded in much more serious cases.[130] This problem was one among others which prompted the Commission to recommend the abolition of the two categories of lump sum compensation, for permanent loss or impairment and loss of enjoyment of life. In their place the Commission recommended the introduction of a new type of periodic payment. This would be calculated by using schedules to determine the proportion of total disability, in relation to each claimant, expressed as a percentage of total disability. The periodic payment would be calculated by applying this proportion to a maximum figure set at 80% of the average weekly income of the claimant where he or she was employed or self-employed; or at 80% of the national

---

[128] See, generally, R Mahoney, "New Zealand's Accident Compensation Scheme: A Reassessment" (1992) 40 Am J Comp L 159, 207-208; R S Miller, "An Analysis and Critique of the 1992 Changes to New Zealand's Accident Compensation Scheme" (1992) 5 Canterbury L Rev 1.

[129] ARCIA 1992, s 14.

[130] Preliminary Paper No 2: The Accident Compensation Scheme: A Discussion Paper (1987) p 12. The principle that the amount awarded in relation to a given injury should rise with inflation, subject to the statutory maximum, was later recognised judicially: *Appleby v Accident Compensation Corporation* (1989) 7 NZAR 609.

average weekly earnings where the claimant had no income.[131] The Commission recommended a threshold of five per cent disability, below which the claimant would not be entitled to any periodic payments.

3.36 ARCIA 1992 followed the Commission's recommendation in abolishing both the statutory lump sums for permanent loss and impairment, and for loss of enjoyment of life, loss from disfigurement or pain and mental suffering. They were replaced with an "independence allowance".[132] This is a relatively modest periodic sum which becomes payable not earlier than thirteen weeks after the injury occurs. The amount is based on the degree to which the claimant is disabled. The independence allowance has been described by the Minister of Labour as being intended "to enable those injured to meet the additional costs arising from a permanent disability during the remainder of their life."[133] Given that the allowance is therefore apparently intended to defray *pecuniary* loss, it is probably true to say that common law damages for non-pecuniary loss no longer have any equivalent in the New Zealand scheme.[134] The allowance has, however, been criticised on the basis that the size of the payments can be regarded as too low, or the threshold of disability too high.[135]

3.37 The Accident Compensation Scheme is again under review, this time by a Government-appointed committee. In a consultation paper[136] the committee has acknowledged criticisms of the current extent of the scheme which have been made mainly in respect of compensation for non-pecuniary loss,[137] but it has provisionally rejected the reintroduction of the common law claim for damages. The committee opposes a return to lump sum compensation, although it is in favour of arrangements under which periodic payments can be capitalised in certain circumstances.[138]

---

[131] Report No 4, Personal Injury: Prevention and Recovery: Report on the Accident Compensation Scheme (1988) pp 58, 98-99.

[132] ARCIA 1992, s 54(1) and (2).

[133] Hon W F Birch, *Accident Compensation - A Fairer Scheme* (1991) p 47.

[134] But note that, since the New Zealand scheme only applies to personal injury by *accident*, common law damages still apply to personal injuries which are inflicted intentionally, eg in claims for trespass to the person, and to personal injuries which are negligently inflicted in circumstances that do not satisfy the statutory definition of an accident.

[135] 10%, as opposed to the 5% recommended by the New Zealand Law Commission. These criticisms and others are summarised by Ken Oliphant of King's College, London in a paper given by him to the Torts Section of the Society of Public Teachers of Law on 14 September 1995.

[136] *Accident Compensation* (1995).

[137] *Ibid*, para 3.9.

[138] *Ibid*, paras 6.20-6.25.

CANADA

3.38 In three cases decided in 1978,[139] which are frequently referred to as the "trilogy", the Supreme Court of Canada analysed carefully, and changed, the approach to be applied when assessing compensation for non-pecuniary loss.

3.39 In *Andrews*, the first of these cases, the Supreme Court was explicitly influenced by a desire to avoid imposing on society the type of burdens which were perceived to have resulted from very large awards of damages for non-pecuniary loss in the United States.[140] The plaintiff had been rendered quadriplegic at the age of 21 by a car accident, although he remained fully conscious and his mental faculties were unimpaired. The award of damages for pain, suffering, loss of amenities and loss of expectation of life was reduced from $150,000 to $100,000, and the Supreme Court said that this figure should generally be regarded as the upper limit in cases of this sort. In *Thornton* the plaintiff had become quadriplegic at the age of 15 as a result of a school gymnasium accident, but, as in *Andrews*, he remained conscious and alert. General damages were reduced from $200,000 to $100,000 on appeal: the case was treated as comparable to *Andrews*. In *Teno* the plaintiff was run over by a car when she was four years old: her disabilities were such that she could walk, although with considerable difficulty. However, unlike the plaintiffs in *Andrews* and *Thornton* she had suffered significant brain damage, although not to the extent that she was unaware of her condition. It was held that, although there were clear differences between her circumstances and those of the plaintiffs in the other two cases, general damages of $100,000 were again appropriate.

3.40 In *Andrews* the court explicitly adopted the functional approach to the assessment of damages for non-pecuniary loss. The prime concern was said to be to provide adequately for the direct care of the plaintiff's injuries, and this would be achieved through the award of damages for *pecuniary* loss. Once the plaintiff was properly provided for in terms of the cost of direct care, awards of damages for non-pecuniary loss should not be excessive. Damages awarded under the head of non-pecuniary loss should be seen as providing physical arrangements to make life more endurable above and beyond the arrangements that related directly to the injuries. It was held that damages for non-pecuniary loss should in any event be moderate and subject to a rough upper limit of $100,000.

3.41 Dickson J gave the judgment of the court in these terms:

> The ... 'functional' approach ... attempts to assess the compensation required to provide the injured person 'with reasonable solace for his misfortune'. 'Solace'

---

[139] *Andrews v Grand & Toy Alberta Ltd* (1978) 83 DLR (3d) 452; *Arnold v Teno* (1978) 83 DLR (3d) 609; and *Thornton v Board of School Trustees of School District No 57* (1978) 83 DLR (3d) 480.

[140] (1978) 83 DLR (3d) 452, 476, *per* Dickson J.

in this sense is taken to mean physical arrangements which can make his life more endurable rather than 'solace' in the sense of sympathy. To my mind, this ... approach has much to commend it, as it provides a rationale as to why money is considered compensation for non-pecuniary losses such as loss of amenities, pain and suffering, and loss of expectation of life. Money is awarded because it will serve a useful function in making up for what has been lost in the only way possible, accepting that what has been lost is incapable of being replaced in any direct way ... If damages for non-pecuniary loss are viewed from a functional perspective, it is reasonable that large amounts should not be awarded once a person is properly provided for in terms of future care for his injuries and disabilities. The money for future care is to provide physical arrangements for assistance, equipment and facilities directly related to the injuries. Additional money to make life more endurable should then be seen as providing more general physical arrangements above and beyond those relating directly to the injuries. The result is a coordinated and interlocking basis for compensation, and a more rational justification for non-pecuniary loss compensation.[141]

A further point of interest that emerges from Dickson J's judgment is that he explicitly favoured the award of only one figure for all non-pecuniary loss. He said:

It is customary to set only one figure for all non-pecuniary loss, including such factors as pain and suffering, loss of amenities and loss of expectation of life. This is a sound practice. Although these elements are analytically distinct, they overlap and merge at the edges and in practice. To suffer pain is surely to lose an amenity of a happy life at that time. To lose years of one's expectation of life is to lose all amenities for the lost period, and to cause mental pain and suffering in the contemplation of this prospect. These problems, as well as the fact that these losses have the common trait of irreplaceability, favour a composite award for all non-pecuniary losses.[142]

3.42   In *Lindal v Lindal*[143] the Supreme Court took the opportunity to revisit these issues. Here the trial judge had awarded $135,000 on the ground that the case before him was an exceptional one which justified an award higher than the rough ceiling laid down in the trilogy. Although not as severely paralysed as the plaintiffs in *Andrews* and *Thornton*, Brian Lindal had suffered brain damage with resulting speech impairment, personality disorders, and consequent frustration. In upholding the British Columbia Court of Appeal's view that there was no justification for exceeding the $100,000 ceiling, the Supreme Court of Canada explained that the

---

[141]   (1978) 83 DLR (3d) 452, 476-477.

[142]   *Ibid*, 478.

[143]   (1981) 129 DLR (3d) 263. See E Veitch, "The Implications of Lindal" (1982) 28 McGill LJ 116, 117.

trial judge had incorrectly failed to apply the functional approach laid down in the trilogy. According to Dickson J:

> Fulton J appears to have misapprehended fundamentally the significance of the award of a conventional sum of $100,000 for non-pecuniary loss made by this court to the three plaintiffs in the trilogy. He seems to have assumed that the figure of $100,000 was a measure of the 'lost assets' of the plaintiffs in those cases. The issue was seen as one of quantifying and comparing the losses sustained. Once this premise is accepted, the question then becomes whether the plaintiff Lindal has lost more "assets" than did the plaintiffs in the earlier cases. If the answer to this question is in the affirmative, then it naturally follows that Brian Lindal deserves an award of over $100,000 under the head of non-pecuniary loss. The excess will represent the difference in value between what Lindal has lost and what the plaintiffs Andrews and Thornton have lost. The difficulty with this approach is with the initial premise. The award of $100,000 for non-pecuniary loss in the trilogy was not in any sense a valuation of the assets which had been lost by Andrews, Thornton and Teno. As has been emphasized, these assets do not have a money value and thus an objective valuation is impossible. The award of $100,000 was made ... in order to provide more general physical arrangements above and beyond those directly relating to the injuries, in order to make life more endurable.[144]

3.43 This clarification of the functional approach renders it hard to see how different injuries can be compared for the purpose of assessing damages for non-pecuniary loss. Indeed Dickson J expressly said that a tariff approach was impossible.[145] Yet in the *Andrews* case Dickson J had stressed the importance of uniformity and predictability and this was again emphasised in the *Lindal* case as one of the justifications for setting the $100,000 ceiling.[146] A linked difficulty with the functional approach is that, if rigidly applied, it would appear to turn the non-pecuniary loss into a pecuniary loss. On the face of it, the level of award ought to be determined on the basis of evidence as to the cost of providing amenities to make the particular plaintiff's life more bearable.[147]

---

[144] (1981) 129 DLR (3d) 263, 273-274.

[145] *Ibid*, 270.

[146] The Supreme Court recognised that the ceiling should be updated for inflation. In 1993 the ceiling was regarded as being in the region of $240,000-$250,000: see, eg: *Bailey v Rycroft* (24 February 1993; Ontario Gen Div); *Baker v Suzuki Motor Co* (13 August 1993; Alberta Ct of QB); *Stein v Sandwich West (Township)* (30 June 1993; Ontario Gen Div), all noted in the 1994 updates to *Goldsmith's Damages for Personal Injuries and Death in Canada*.

[147] B M McLachlin, "What Price Disability? A Perspective On The Law of Damages for Personal Injury" (1981) 59 Can BR 1, 48. See also G Brodsky, "A Ceiling on Damages" (1982) 40 Adv 235, 236.

3.44   In view of the difficulties posed in practice by the theoretical functional approach, it is not surprising that most Canadian judges continue to apply a comparative tariff approach as in England, albeit with the maximum award being the $100,000, uplifted for inflation, fixed by the trilogy.[148]

3.45   Indeed it is strongly arguable that the only significant practical consequence of the shift to the functional approach is that a permanently unconscious plaintiff will now be awarded no damages for non-pecuniary loss in Canada. In *Jennings v R*[149] it had been held that an unconscious plaintiff was entitled to recover substantial damages for loss of amenity. Although *Jennings* was not disapproved in the "trilogy",[150] the functional view there taken must lead to a conclusion inconsistent with the outcome in *Jennings*. This was confirmed by the majority of the British Columbia Court of Appeal in *Knutson v Farr*,[151] overturning the decision of the trial judge, who, in awarding damages for loss of amenities of $77,000, distinguished the trilogy on the basis that none of the plaintiffs in those cases had been unconscious. It was held by the majority of the Court of Appeal that had the plaintiff been permanently unconscious no damages should have been awarded. As it was, $15,000 was awarded for loss of amenity because of the existence of fresh medical evidence that suggested that the plaintiff's awareness was faintly reawakening.

3.46   The logic of the functional approach to the award of damages for non-pecuniary loss would seem to lead to the conclusion that damages for loss of expectation of life should no longer be recoverable as a head of damages distinct from pain and suffering and loss of amenities,[152] although previous decisions in which damages were awarded for loss of expectation of life[153] were not expressly disapproved or indeed referred to at all in the trilogy.[154] On the other hand the suffering caused to the plaintiff by his or her awareness of a shortened life span will clearly form part of the suffering for which compensation is intended to give solace.[155]

---

[148] In *Rau v Rau* [1993] CCL 1388, for example, although the court acknowledged that the correct approach to adopt was a functional one, it nevertheless compared the facts of the particular case to those of previous cases for similar injuries in determining damages for pain and suffering and loss of amenities of life. See also para 4.9 (v) below.

[149] (1966) 57 DLR (3d) 644.

[150] Although it was cited in relation to other issues.

[151] (1984) 12 DLR (4th) 658.

[152] See *Andrews v Grand & Toy Alberta Ltd* (1978) 83 DLR (3d) 452, 478, *per* Dickson J, who considered that, although these different heads are analytically distinct, they overlapped in practice and that therefore a "composite award for all non-pecuniary losses" was to be preferred.

[153] Eg, *Crosby v O'Reilly* (1975) 51 DLR (3d) 555 (Sup Ct).

[154] See S M Waddams, *The Law of Damages* (2nd ed 1991) para 3.67.

[155] *Andrews v Grand & Toy Alberta Ltd* (1978) 83 DLR (3d) 452, 478, *per* Dickson J.

3.47   In 1984, in its Report on Compensation for Non-Pecuniary Loss, the Law Reform Commission of British Columbia examined the "rough upper limit" of $100,000 on damages for pain, suffering and loss of amenities in personal injury actions established by the trilogy. The Commission recommended that provincial legislation be passed to override the decision of the Supreme Court and to abolish the rough upper limit on damages for non-pecuniary loss. It argued that no such limit was necessary to ensure that damages awards did not escalate beyond what was justified by inflation.[156] However, it did argue in favour of a "fair upper reference point" which it thought was represented by the trial award of $200,000 in *Thornton v Board of School Trustees of School District No 57*.[157] The Commission appeared to confirm the recommendation in its earlier Working Paper[158] that, because the award in *Thornton* had been made in 1975, the fair upper reference point should be set at $400,000 as of April 1983.[159]

3.48   In a subsequent report,[160] the Ontario Law Reform Commission questioned whether there was in fact any difference between the rough upper limit set in the trilogy and the fair upper reference point advocated by the British Columbia Law Reform Commission except that the reference point imposed the limit at a higher level. The Ontario Law Reform Commission also concluded that some sort of limit ought to be retained, for the sake of consistency, predictability and fairness, as between one award and another, and as between awards in one province and awards in another. Money could neither alleviate pain and suffering nor return to the injured person the lost years or lost amenities of life, and, given the social burdens of indulgent awards, a reasonable, moderate award was required. The Commission therefore recommended that there should be no change in the present law and practice in Canada respecting awards of damages for non-pecuniary loss.[161]

3.49   All the Canadian provinces possess statutory provisions which provide for the payment of interest on damages, including damages for non-pecuniary loss, in respect of the period before judgment.[162] These provisions vary as to whether there

---

[156] Law Reform Commission of British Columbia, Report on Compensation for Non-Pecuniary Loss, LRC 76 (1984) p 26.

[157] (1978) 83 DLR (3d) 480.

[158] Law Reform Commission of British Columbia, Compensation for Non-Pecuniary Loss, Working Paper No 43 (1983).

[159] Law Reform Commission of British Columbia, Report on Compensation for Non-Pecuniary Loss, LRC 76 (1984) pp 25-31.

[160] Ontario Law Reform Commission, Report on Compensation for Personal Injuries and Death (1987).

[161] *Ibid*, ch 3, para 7, pp 106-107.

[162] See, eg, **Alberta** Judgment Interest Act 1984, s 2; **British Columbia** Court Order Interest Act 1979, s 1; **Manitoba** Court of Queen's Bench Act 1988-89, s 80; **New Brunswick** Judicature Act 1973, s 45; **Ontario** Courts of Justice Act, RSO 1990, ss 127-128; **Prince Edward Island** Supreme Court Act 1988, ss 49-52; **Saskatchewan** Pre-

is a presumption that interest will, or will not, be awarded. In some provinces a rate of interest is set by statute or statutory instrument. The statutory rate will often represent a rate of return without an "inflationary" element,[163] and courts in some other jurisdictions will similarly exercise their discretion to set rates which seek to exclude the effects of inflation.[164]

3.50   The legislation in the different Canadian jurisdictions that provides for the survival of actions for the benefit of a deceased plaintiff's estate varies considerably in terms of the extent to which the right to claim damages for non-pecuniary loss will pass to the deceased's estate. For example, in Alberta the plaintiff's estate will only acquire the right to recover damages for "actual financial loss to the deceased or his estate,"[165] and there are express provisions confirming that the right to recover damages for disfigurement, loss of amenities, loss of expectation of life or pain and suffering will not pass. Similarly, in Saskatchewan, New Brunswick, Newfoundland, Nova Scotia, Prince Edward Island and the Yukon, only the right to claim damages for pecuniary loss will survive the plaintiff's death.[166] On the other hand, in Manitoba damages for loss of expectation of life do not survive,[167] but a claim for damages for other types of non-pecuniary loss will survive. The survival of damages for loss of expectation of life is generally very limited. The only jurisdiction in which the right to damages under this head survives in all personal injury cases is the North-West Territory, although it also survives in British Columbia and Ontario if death does not result from the injuries to which the action relates.[168]

Judgment Interest Act 1984-85-86, s 5.

[163] Eg, **Alberta** Judgment Interest Act 1984, s 4(1) sets a rate of 4%; and **Ontario** Courts of Justice Act, RSO 1990, s 128(2) (1990 reprint); Rules of Civil Procedure, r 53.10 prescribe 5%. There have been proposals for reform recommending a real rate of interest on damages for non-pecuniary loss in Manitoba (the Law Reform Commission recommended a rate of 3% in its Report on Prejudgment Compensation on Money Awards: Alternatives to Interest, No 47 (1982) p 38); in Ontario (the Law Reform Commission recommended a rate of 2.5% in its Report on Compensation for Personal Injuries and Death (1987) p 241); and in British Columbia (the Law Reform Commission recommended 3.5% in its Report on the Court Order Interest Act, LRC 90 (1987) p 96). Cf paras 2.45 above and 4.119-4.122 below.

[164] See, eg, *Leischner v West Kootenay Power & Light Co Ltd* (1986) 24 DLR (4th) 641 (British Columbia Court of Appeal); *Melnychuk v Moore* [1989] 6 WWR 367 (Manitoba Court of Appeal); see also S M Waddams, *The Law of Damages* (2nd ed 1991) pp 7-33 to 7-34. Cf *Birkett v Hayes* [1982] 1 WLR 816: see para 2.45 above.

[165] **Alberta** Survival of Actions Act 1980, s 5.

[166] **Saskatchewan** Survival of Actions Act 1990-1991, s 6(1) and (2); **New Brunswick** Survival of Actions Act 1973, s 5; **Newfoundland** Survival of Actions Act 1970, s 4; **Nova Scotia** Survival of Actions Act 1989, s 4; **Prince Edward Island** Survival of Actions Act 1988, s 5; **Yukon** Survival of Actions Act 1986, s 5.

[167] **Manitoba** Trustee Act 1987, s 53(1).

[168] **British Columbia** Estate Administration Act 1979, s 66(2)(b); **Ontario** Trustee Act 1980, s 38(1).

3.51   Trial, and therefore assessment of damages, by a jury remains generally possible in the Canadian jurisdictions in relation to personal injury claims in the higher courts,[169] although the relevant provisions differ in detail. For example, in Ontario the court has a discretion, on the application of either party, to order a jury trial.[170] In Alberta, British Columbia and Saskatchewan either party has a prima facie right to a jury trial, but the court may refuse and order trial by a judge alone if it decides that the trial would require prolonged examination of documents or accounts, or scientific or local investigations which cannot be made conveniently with a jury.[171] The Alberta and Saskatchewan legislation also requires that the party demanding jury trial, if the requisite order is made, should deposit with the court the estimated expenses of the jury.[172] In Manitoba trial will be without a jury unless the court orders otherwise.[173] In practice, jury trial is more common in British Columbia and Ontario than it is in other parts of Canada.

THE UNITED STATES

3.52   In the USA the victim of an actionable personal injury is entitled to recover damages by way of compensation for his or her pain and suffering.[174] There is no separate award for loss of expectation of life,[175] although the plaintiff's awareness that his or her life expectancy has been shortened will be taken into account in assessing the damages for suffering.[176] In some states, "loss of enjoyment of life" (equivalent to the English notion of loss of amenity)[177] is regarded as a proper separate element of damages.[178] In others, however, it is either rejected altogether

---

[169] This may be subject to a minimum sum being claimed, eg $10,000 in Alberta and Saskatchewan.

[170] **Ontario** Courts of Justice Act, s 108(1).

[171] **Alberta** Jury Act 1982, s 16; **British Columbia** Supreme Court Rules, r 39(20); **Saskatchewan** Jury Act 1981, s 16.

[172] **Alberta** Jury Act 1982, s 17; **Saskatchewan** Jury Act 1981, s 16.

[173] **Manitoba** Court of Queen's Bench Act 1988-1989, s 64.

[174] See Dan B Dobbs, *Law of Remedies* (2nd ed 1993) pp 652-656. The Second Restatement of the Law of Torts para 905 states that compensatory damages can be awarded without proof of pecuniary loss for bodily harm and emotional distress. Bodily harm is described as "any impairment of the physical condition of the body, including illness or physical pain". Past, present and future harm can be compensated: *ibid*, para 910. See also American Law Institute, *Enterprise Responsibility for Personal Injury Volume II: Approaches to Legal and Institutional Change* (1991) pp 199-200.

[175] As is now the position in England: see paras 2.6-2.9 above.

[176] See Dan B Dobbs, *Law of Remedies* (2nd ed 1993) pp 655-656.

[177] In *Huff v Tracy* the California Court of Appeal, Third District, referred to the "physical impairment which limits the plaintiff's capacity to share in the amenities of life": 129 Cal Rptr 551, 553, 57 Cal App 3d 939, 943 (1976).

[178] *Pierce v New York Central Railway Co* 409 F 2d 1392, 1399 (1969) (United States Court of Appeals, Sixth Circuit) (see also *Thompson v National Railroad Passenger Corpn* 621 F 2d 814, 824 (1980) (United States Court of Appeals, Sixth Circuit); *Andrews v Mosley Well Service* 514 So 2d 491, 498-499 (1987) (Court of Appeal of Louisiana, Third Circuit);

as being too vague or speculative or it is regarded as merely a factor in the damages for pain and suffering, so that to award both might lead to a duplication of awards.[179]

3.53   The dispute over the nature of damages for loss of enjoyment is particularly important in the case of the unconscious plaintiff, where courts which hold that loss of enjoyment damages are conceptually distinct have been less reluctant to allow the unconscious plaintiff to recover such damages. For example, in *Eyoma v Falco*[180] a court in New Jersey held that the loss of pleasure and enjoyment was not dependent on the plaintiff's ability to appreciate his or her restrictions. The court was careful to state that loss of enjoyment of life was not to be equated with the anxiety suffered as a result of being aware of that loss.[181] A contrary approach was taken by the Court of Appeals of New York in *McDougald v Garber*.[182] The judgment of the majority was given by Chief Judge Wachtler, who started from the premise that recovery for losses such as pain and suffering rested on a legal fiction that money damages can compensate for a victim's injury. This fiction was accepted because it was as close as the law could come in an effort to right the wrong done to the plaintiff. A monetary award might provide a measure of solace.[183] However, the court argued that what it viewed as an indulgence in this fiction should end when no compensatory goals were served. In such an event the damages were to be regarded as punitive, since damages awarded to a victim who was unaware of the loss had no meaning or utility. Chief Judge Wachtler accepted that it might be paradoxical that the greater the brain injury, the lower the damages, but increasing the damages had nothing to do with granting meaningful compensation.[184] In a dissenting judgment Judge Titone argued that the destruction of an individual's capacity to enjoy life as a result of a crippling injury was an

---

Kirk v Washington State University 746 P 2d 285, 292-293 (1987) (Supreme Court of Washington)). See also "Loss of Enjoyment of Life as a Distinct Element or Factor in Awarding Damages for Bodily Injury" (1984) 34 ALR 4th 293, 304-311; P J Hermes, "Loss of Enjoyment of Life - Duplication of Damages Versus Full Compensation" (1987) 63 North Dakota Law Review 561, 576-588.

[179] Eg *Hogan v Santa Fe Trail Transport Co* 85 P 2d 28, 33-34 (1938) (Supreme Court of Kansas). See P J Hermes, "Loss of Enjoyment of Life - Duplication of Damages Versus Full Compensation" (1987) 63 North Dakota Law Review 561; C R Cramer, "Loss of Enjoyment of Life as a Separate Element of Damages" (1981) 12 Pacific Law Journal 965; Dan B Dobbs, *Law of Remedies* (2nd ed 1993) p 653; "Loss of Enjoyment of Life as a Distinct Element or Factor in Awarding Damages for Bodily Injury" (1984) 34 ALR 4th 293, 300-304.

[180] 589 A 2d 653, 662 (1991) (Superior Court of New Jersey, Appellate Division).

[181] Such anxiety could only be compensated if consciously suffered: 589 A 2d 653, 662 (1991).

[182] 538 NYS 2d 937 (1989).

[183] *Ibid*, 939-940.

[184] *Ibid*, 940.

objective fact that did not differ in principle from the loss of an eye or limb.[185] This impairment existed independently of the victim's ability to apprehend it.[186]

3.54   The thesis that an award of damages for loss of enjoyment of life to an unconscious plaintiff is punitive was the main issue in *Flannery v United States*.[187] An action was brought on behalf of an accident victim against the federal government in respect of an accident caused by a federal employee on government business. The condition of the plaintiff was, at best, a permanently semi-comatose one.[188] Under the Federal Tort Claims Act 1982,[189] the United States is liable under the law of the place where the act or omission occurred. Under paragraph 2674 of the Act, however, it is not liable for punitive damages. Answering certified questions from the federal court, the state court said that damages could be awarded under West Virginian law for the loss of capacity to enjoy life.[190] It stated that the underlying function of the award of damages was to measure the degree of permanent disability to the whole person that arose from the injuries inflicted. The accident victim's subjective knowledge of the extent of the loss should not therefore be the controlling factor. The federal court held, however, that, as the accident victim could get no benefit from this award, it was punitive. The award for loss of enjoyment of life could not provide the victim with any consolation or ease any burden resting upon him. He could not spend the money on necessities or pleasure. Nor could he experience the pleasure of giving it away. The award for medical care provided all the money that would be needed for his care. If the award was compensatory to anyone, it was compensatory to the relatives who would survive the victim, and not the victim himself.[191] Circuit Judge KK Hall dissented, arguing that not only did the majority view create two different standards for damage awards in West Virginia,[192] but that the exclusion of punitive damages should only prohibit damages which were awarded solely for the purpose of punishment.[193]

---

[185]   *Ibid*, 942.

[186]   *Ibid*, 943.

[187]   297 SE 2d 433 (1982) (Supreme Court of Appeals of West Virginia); 718 F 2d 108 (1983) (United States Court of Appeals, Fourth Circuit).

[188]   "Semi-comatose" was the description given in the judgment of the Supreme Court of Appeals of West Virginia, although the judgment of the United States Court of Appeals describes him as "comatose": 718 F 2d 108, 110.

[189]   Title 28 USC 1988 ed para 1346(b).

[190]   297 SE 2d 433, 438 (1983) (Supreme Court of Appeals of West Virginia).

[191]   718 F 2d 108, 111 (1983) (United States Court of Appeals, Fourth Circuit). Douglas Laycock asks why the lost wages were not considered punitive as the accident victim could derive no benefit from them: *Modern American Remedies: Cases & Materials* (1985) p 78.

[192]   718F 2d 108, 114 (1983).

[193]   *Ibid*, 114-115 (1983), citing *Kalavity v United States* 584 F 2d 809, 811 (1978) (United States Court of Appeals, Sixth Circuit).

3.55   The correctness of this approach by the federal court must now be in doubt
        following the ruling of the Supreme Court in *Molzof v United States*.[194] The Court
        held that paragraph 2674 of the Federal Tort Claims Act prohibited awards of
        "punitive damages", not "damage awards that may have a punitive effect".[195]
        Damages for future medical expenses and loss of enjoyment of life of a permanently
        comatose accident victim are not punitive damages under the Act or at common law
        because their recoverability does not depend on proof that the defendant has
        engaged in intentional or egregious misconduct and their purpose is not to
        punish.[196]

3.56   A recent development in some states has been the introduction of "hedonic
        damages". These are intended to compensate the plaintiff for his or her loss of
        pleasure.[197] While one apparent difference between hedonic damages and loss of
        enjoyment of life damages is that the former are calculated using an economic
        formula,[198] the two terms are often used interchangeably.[199] In other states, courts
        have rejected hedonic damages on the basis that they duplicate the award in respect
        of pain and suffering.[200]

3.57   As for the survival of damages for non-pecuniary loss, some states, like New
        Jersey,[201] allow survival and others, like California,[202] do not.

[194] 116 L Ed 2d 731 (1992).

[195] *Ibid*, 739.

[196] *Ibid*, 743.

[197] "Hedonic" derives from the Greek word for pleasure. See *Sherrod v Berry* 629 F Supp 159
      (1985) (United States District Court, ND Illinois) reversed and remanded on other
      grounds 856 F 2d 802 (1988) (United States Court of Appeals, Seventh Circuit). See
      also G L Valentine, "Hedonic Damages: Emerging Issue in Personal Injury and Wrongful
      Death Claims" (1990) 10 Northern Illinois University Law Review 543; K R Crowe, "The
      Semantical Bifurcation of Noneconomic Loss: Should Hedonic Damage Be Recognized
      Independently of Pain and Suffering Damage?" (1990) 75 Iowa Law Review 1275; T M
      Tabacchi, "Hedonic Damages: A New Trend in Compensation?" (1991) 52 Ohio State
      Law Journal 331; T Webb, "Hedonic Damages: An Alternative Approach" (1992) 61
      UMKC Law Review 121.

[198] G L Valentine, "Hedonic Damages: Emerging Issue in Personal Injury and Wrongful
      Death Claims" (1990) 10 Northern Illinois University Law Review 543, 543 n 3, 547-555.

[199] Eg K R Crowe, "The Semantical Bifurcation of Noneconomic Loss: Should Hedonic
      Damage Be Recognized Independently of Pain and Suffering Damage?" (1990) 75 Iowa
      Law Review 1275, 1277 n 11. See also *Eyoma v Falco* 589 A 2d 653, 658 (1991)
      (Superior Court of New Jersey, Appellate Division). Hedonic damages have also been
      compared to the award for loss of expectation of life: *Sherrod v Berry* 629 F Supp 159, 164
      (1985) (United States District Court, ND Illinois); K R Crowe, "The Semantical
      Bifurcation of Noneconomic Loss: Should Hedonic Damage Be Recognized Independently
      of Pain and Suffering Damage?" (1990) 75 Iowa Law Review 1275, 1277 n 15. Cf Dan B
      Dobbs, *Law of Remedies* (2nd ed 1993) p 656.

[200] Eg *Leiker v Gafford* 778 P 2d 823, 834-835 (1989) (Supreme Court of Kansas).

[201] See *Eyoma v Falco* 589 A 2d 653, 658 (1991) (Superior Court of New Jersey, Appellate
      Division).

3.58   As regards the quantum of damages for non-pecuniary loss, Professor Fleming
        observes that:

> In comparison to other countries which share similar cultural values and living
> standards, American awards for non-pecuniary damages tend to be strikingly
> larger. While this disparity could arguably be seen to reflect greater sensitivity
> to psychic and other non-material values in an affluent and indulgent society, a
> more realistic explanation would be found in the twin factors of trial by jury and
> an aggressive trial bar.[203]

> Professor Fleming has also commented that consistency and uniformity, as ideals
> of equal justice, are not valued to the same degree as they are in England and
> Wales; that due to the wide discretion which juries have in assessing damages, the
> American law of tort damages for personal injuries is "surprisingly unformulated";
> and that "American law has notably devoted little attention to precisely what non-
> pecuniary damages are supposed to accomplish".[204]

3.59   The amount of damages is a question for the jury.[205] A jury must not apply the
        "golden rule" and ask what they would want in compensation if they were in the
        position of the plaintiff[206] or would want to be paid to experience the plaintiff's
        pain.[207] Nor can the jury be told of the pattern of awards in comparable cases.[208]

3.60   One method that is employed in some states to calculate the level of damages is the
        per diem approach. Each day is held to be worth a given (usually small) sum for
        pain and suffering, which is then multiplied by the number of days of pain and

---

[202] California Code of Civil Procedure, para 377-34.

[203] John G Fleming, *The American Tort Process* (1988) pp 224-225. See also pp 101-102. By
way of explanation Jeffrey O'Connell & Rita James Simon point to the rising affluence of
American society and the development, by plaintiffs' lawyers, of new and effective trial
techniques in the proof of pain and suffering, and increased awareness, among lawyers and
judges, of the large awards being made :"Payment for Pain and Suffering: Who Wants
What, When and Why?" (1972) 1 University of Illinois Law Forum 1, 101, 104.

[204] John G Fleming, *The American Tort Process* (1988) pp 123-125.

[205] Eg see the Supreme Court's approval of a jury direction in *District of Columbia v Woodbury*
136 US 450, 466, 34 L Ed 472, 478 (1890).

[206] Eg *Dunlap v Lee* 126 SE 2d 62, 65-66 (1962) (Supreme Court of North Carolina).
Douglas Laycock explains that the golden rule is an appeal to abandon neutrality: the
defendant might just as plausibly ask jurors to imagine how much they would want to pay
if they had inflicted the injuries: *Modern American Remedies: Cases & Materials* (1985) p
76.

[207] *Botta v Brunner* 138 A 2d 713, 719-722 (1958) (Supreme Court of New Jersey).

[208] American Law Institute, *Enterprise Responsibility for Personal Injury Volume II: Approaches to
Legal and Institutional Change* (1991) p 202.

suffering experienced in the past and expected to be experienced in the future.[209] With this method, seemingly inconsequential differences in value per unit time can lead to very large differences in awards,[210] and there is a noticeable disparity between juries using this method in the amounts they award.[211] It should be noted that juries assess damages with the expectation that the fees of the plaintiff's attorneys under the contingency fee system will be paid out of the non-pecuniary loss damages.[212]

3.61 Jury awards are subject to review by the appellate courts, but only in narrowly defined circumstances. For example, the Supreme Court of Washington held in *Bingaman v Grays Harbor Community Hospital*[213] that an appellate court should not disturb a jury award unless the award was outside the scope of substantial evidence, shocked the conscience of the court or appeared to have been arrived at as the result of passion or prejudice.[214] One study, however, found that 20% of jury awards were altered.[215]

3.62 As a result of deep concern over the effect of levels of damages on the insurance sector, and consequently on both industry and the professions,[216] a majority of

---

[209] See Dan B Dobbs, *Handbook on the Law of Remedies* (1973) p 545. However, some courts disapprove of such mathematical formulae: *ibid*, pp 546-548. See also J O'Connell & R J Simon, "Payment for Pain and Suffering: Who Wants What, When and Why?" (1972) 1 University of Illinois Law Forum 1, 10; *Botta v Brunner* 138 A 2d 713, 719-725 (1958) (Supreme Court of New Jersey) and *Westbrook v General Time & Rubber Co*, where the United States Court of Appeals, Fifth Circuit said that *per diem* arguments tend to produce excessive results: 754 F 2d 1233, 1240 (1985).

[210] R R Bovbjerg, F A Sloan, J F Blumstein, "Valuing Life and Limb in Tort: Scheduling 'Pain and Suffering'" (1989) 83 Northwestern University Law Review 908, 914.

[211] *Ibid*, 936-937.

[212] This is noted by Gregory A Hicks who argues that because of the maximum awards which have been introduced (see paras 3.62-3.64 below) the victorious plaintiff ought to be able to claim these fees as part of their damages: "Statutory Damage Caps are an Incomplete Reform: A Proposal for Attorney Fee Shifting in Tort Actions" (1989) 49 Louisiana Law Review 763, 771, 793. See also John G Fleming, *The American Tort Process* (1988) p 226. Under the "American Rule" each litigant bears its own costs and contingency fees are invariably used in tort litigation: *ibid*, pp 188-205.

[213] 699 P 2d 1230 (1985).

[214] The passion and prejudice must be of such manifest clarity as to be unmistakeable: *ibid*, 1233.

[215] M Shanley & M Peterson, "Posttrial Adjustments to Jury Awards" (1987), cited in R R Bovbjerg, F A Sloan, J F Blumstein, "Valuing Life and Limb in Tort: Scheduling 'Pain and Suffering'" (1989) 83 Northwestern University Law Review 908, 919 n 65.

[216] See, for example, Dan B Dobbs, *Law of Remedies* (2nd ed 1993) p 683; Douglas Laycock, *Modern American Remedies: Cases & Materials* (1987 supplement) pp 4-7; G Priest, "The Current Insurance Crisis and Modern Tort Law" (1987) 96 Yale LJ 1521. See also para 4.7 below.

states[217] have now introduced some form of tort reform legislation, the most significant of which have been maximum awards in at least some personal injury cases. These maximums, or "caps", have been applied to the total damages awarded,[218] and also to particular elements of the damages, such as non-pecuniary loss.[219] Indeed it has recently been said that "even a casual inspection of tort reform proposals reveals that compensation for pain and suffering is widely perceived as one of the tort beast's uglier heads."[220] In some states the legislation applies to all personal injury cases, and in others it applies only to certain types of case, for example medical negligence actions. The levels of these maximums vary widely.[221]

3.63 Some of the legislation imposing these caps has, however, been successfully challenged on the constitutional grounds of access to the courts,[222] equal protection,[223] due process,[224] and jury trial rights.[225] Challenges have been

[217] In 1987 one commentator cited 42 states as having enacted legislation during the previous 18 months: G Priest, "The Current Insurance Crisis and Modern Tort Law" (1987) 96 Yale LJ 1521, 1587. Some of the legislation had, or has subsequently, been challenged as being unconstitutional: see para 3.63 below.

[218] Eg the maximum placed on awards in the legislation upheld by the Supreme Court of Louisiana in *Sibley v Board of Supervisors of Louisiana* 462 So 2d 149 (1985).

[219] Eg the maximum placed on damages for non-economic loss against health care providers in para 3333.2 Californian Civil Code and upheld by the United States Court of Appeals (Ninth Circuit) in *Hoffman v United States* 767 F 2d 1431 (1985). See also S P Croley and J D Hanson, "The Non-Pecuniary Costs of Accidents: Pain-and-Suffering Damages in Tort Law" (1995) 108 Harvard L Rev 1787, 1789, n 18, indicating that federal bills have been introduced in recent Congresses that would institute caps on pain and suffering awards at the national level.

[220] S P Croley and J D Hanson, "The Non-Pecuniary Costs of Accidents: Pain-and-Suffering Damages in Tort Law" (1995) 108 Harvard L Rev 1787, 1789.

[221] At the lower end of the scale, some states (eg California and Utah) limit damages for non-pecuniary loss in medical negligence cases to $250,000; at the upper end, West Virginia has a limit of $1,000,000, again for non-pecuniary loss in medical negligence cases. See G Priest, "The Current Insurance Crisis and Modern Tort Law" (1987) 96 Yale LJ 1521, 1587 n 257. See also R R Bovbjerg, F A Sloan, J F Blumstein, "Valuing Life and Limb in Tort: Scheduling 'Pain and Suffering'" (1989) 83 Northwestern University Law Review 908, 957 and S D Sugarman, "Serious Tort Law Reform" (1987) 24 San Diego Law Review 795, 827. The general rule is that reductions for comparative fault (ie contributory negligence) are applied to the award before the court considers whether the award would, but for the statutory limit, exceed the maximum: eg *McAdory v Rogers* 215 Cal App 3d 1273; 264 Cal Rptr 71 (1989) (Court of Appeals, Second Division). For example, where there is an award of $200,000, a maximum of $100,000 and comparative fault of 50%, the plaintiff will therefore receive the maximum $100,000 rather than $50,000 in damages.

[222] Eg *Smith v Department of Insurance* 507 So 2d 1080 (1987) (Supreme Court of Florida).

[223] Eg *Wright v Central Du Page Hospital Association* 347 NE 2d 736 (1976) (Supreme Court of Illinois); *Carson v Maurer* 424 A 2d 825 (1980) (Supreme Court of New Hampshire); *Brannigan v Usitalo* 587 A 2d 1232 (1991) (Supreme Court of New Hampshire). Cf *Morris v Savoy* 576 NE 2d 765 (1991) (Supreme Court of Ohio).

[224] Eg *Morris v Savoy* 576 NE 2d 765 (1991) (Supreme Court of Ohio).

particularly successful where a particular interest group, such as health care providers, has been protected and there is no substitute compensation scheme.[226] Where there is a substitute scheme, maximums have been upheld.[227] Courts upholding such legislation have often employed the argument that the object in imposing the maximum is reasonably related to reducing the costs of medical care.[228] This *quid pro quo* argument has not been greeted with favour by courts who view the substitute remedy as clearly inadequate,[229] or who fail to see the benefits of lower insurance premiums and medical costs extending to a seriously injured plaintiff.[230] The Supreme Court of New Hampshire, for instance, when deciding that the ceiling was unconstitutional, said that it was unfair and unreasonable to impose the burden of supporting the insurance industry on those who were seriously injured and in need of compensation.[231]

3.64   The constitutional difficulties that maximum awards have posed and the continuing concern with the workings of the tort system have prompted further calls for reform. For example, the American Law Institute has recommended that pain and suffering damages should only be awarded to plaintiffs who suffer significant injuries.[232]

[225] Eg *Sofie v Fibreboard Corp* 771 P 2d 711, 780 P 2d 260 (1989) (Supreme Court of Washington); *Kansas Malpractice Victims Coalition v Bell* 757 P 2d 251 (1988) (Supreme Court of Kansas). Cf *Boyd v Bulala* 877 F 2d 1191 (1989) (United States Court of Appeals, Fourth Circuit).

[226] Eg *Lucas v United States* 757 SW 2d 687 (1988) (Supreme Court of Texas).

[227] Eg *Johnson v St Vincent Hospital, Inc* 404 NE 2d 585 (1980) (Supreme Court of Indiana).

[228] Eg *Sibley v Board of Supervisors of Louisiana* 462 So 2d 149, 158 (1985) (Supreme Court of Louisiana); *Davis v Omitowoju* F 2d 1155 (1989) (United States Court of Appeals, Third Circuit); *Peters v Saft* 597 A 2d 50 (1991) (Supreme Judicial Court of Maine), where a limit on the nonmedical damages payable by servers of alcohol was upheld as the object of the law bore a rational relationship to the health, safety and welfare of the general public. Cf *Smith v Department of Insurance* 507 So 2d 1080 (1987) (Supreme Court of Florida) where the court said that it could only speculate as to whether the legislative scheme would benefit the tort victim.

[229] *Kansas Malpractice Victims Coalition v Bell* 757 P 2d 251, 259-260 (1988) (Supreme Court of Kansas). Cf *Prendergast v Nelson* 256 NW 2d 657, 668-669, 671-672 (Supreme Court of Nebraska) where the creation of an insurance fund was held to be a *quid pro quo* for the loss of unlimited damages.

[230] *Wright v Central Du Page Hospital Association* 347 NE 2d 736, 742-743 (1976) (Supreme Court of Illinois).

[231] *Carson v Maurer* 424 A 2d 825, 837 (1980). Even when the level of the ceiling was raised, it was held unconstitutional for the same reason: *Brannigan v Usitalo* 587 A 2d 1232 (1991) (Supreme Court of New Hampshire). The American Law Institute also took this view and argued that a threshold would be fairer: *Enterprise Responsibility for Personal Injury Volume II: Approaches to Legal and Institutional Change* (1991) pp 219-221.

[232] *Enterprise Responsibility for Personal Injury Volume II: Approaches to Legal and Institutional Change* (1991) p 230. See also S D Sugarman, "Serious Tort Law Reform" (1987) 24 San Diego Law Review 795, 807, in which it is proposed that where an injury causes less than six months' disability, damages for non-pecuniary loss should only be awarded if there is a serious disfigurement or impairment.

3.65   The general rule in the United States is that interest is not payable on damages for non-pecuniary loss, or for any other damages which are not liquidated or ascertainable, in respect of the period before trial. The Second Restatement of the Law states:

> Interest is not allowed upon an amount found due for bodily harm, for emotional distress or for injury to reputation, but the time that has elapsed between the harm and the trial can be considered in determining the amount of damages.[233]

An exception to the general rule is the state of Texas, where interest is awarded, calculated at a daily rate from the date six months after the incident giving rise to the cause of action.[234]

FRANCE[235]

3.66   In France tort liability for personal injury is in general governed by *droit civil*, the principal rules of which are to be found in the French Civil Code, as supplemented by particular statutes, such as the law of 5 July 1985, relating to road accidents. Actions may be brought before the civil courts, in which case there is no jury; alternatively, if a crime has also been committed, the victim can bring a claim before the relevant criminal court in which case, if the crime is a serious one, the court may include lay jury members.

3.67   A significant number of personal injury actions are not subject to *droit civil*, however: where a tort is committed by a public authority (including public hospitals), the largely judge-made *droit administratif* applies. In these cases, the action falls within the jurisdiction of the administrative courts, which do not have juries. With respect to non-pecuniary loss, *droit administratif* was formerly more restrictive than *droit civil*; more recently, however, the administrative courts have adopted a more liberal attitude and awards are largely in line with those made by the ordinary courts.[236]

3.68   French law draws a distinction between *dommage matériel*, which embraces all forms of loss directly translatable into monetary terms (for example, property loss or damage, lost earnings or profits, medical expenses) and *dommage moral*, the equivalent of the English "non-pecuniary loss". Despite initial hesitations, the French courts now readily make awards for *dommage moral*, insisting on their duty

---

[233] American Law Institute, *Second Restatement of the Law, Torts 2d* (1977) vol 4, para 913(2). See also Dan B Dobbs, *Law of Remedies* (2nd ed 1993) p 246.

[234] See, eg, *Cavnar v Quality Control Parking, Inc* 696 SW 2d 549 (1985) (Supreme Court of Texas). See also D Laycock, *Modern American Remedies: Cases and Materials* (1985) p 195.

[235] For a comparison between English law and French law, see generally G Viney and B Markesinis, *La réparation du dommage corporel* (1985).

[236] L Neville Brown and J S Bell, *French Administrative Law* (4th ed 1993) p 191.

to give full compensation (*réparation intégrale*). Damages are awarded under this head more freely than in English law: for example, a person may claim for distress caused where a loved one (or even a loved animal) is injured or killed.

3.69 In the context of personal injury, damages for non-pecuniary loss tend to be awarded in several categories within the broad heading of *dommage moral*. These include damages for pain and suffering (*souffrances physiques et morales*) and loss of amenity (*préjudice d'agrément*). They may also include sadness and humiliation caused by disfigurement (*préjudice esthétique*) and sexual impairment (*préjudice sexuel*).[237] The assessment of damages is in general regarded as a question of fact rather than law, with the result that trial courts have a wide discretion and there are significant regional variations in the level of awards.[238] Nevertheless, although they cannot be relied on explicitly by the courts,[239] in practice considerable guidance is provided by tables, for example assigning specific amounts to different degrees of medically certified disability or impairment. With regard to quantum, French courts have been described as being generous in their awards for non-pecuniary loss,[240] although one study in 1990 estimated that the likely damages for non-pecuniary loss which would be awarded in respect of injuries inflicted on a 40-year-old man and resulting in quadriplegia would be rather smaller than they would be in England.[241]

3.70 The question of whether damages in respect of *dommage moral* are to be assessed objectively or subjectively is a vexed one in France, providing conflicting decisions in the courts. Some decisions have allowed the unconscious plaintiff to recover damages, while others have restricted awards to heads involving *dommage matériel*.[242] The difficulty of ascertaining what the plaintiff is aware of is sometimes cited as a reason for favouring an objective assessment.[243]

3.71 Where the victim of a tort dies, the deceased's right of action survives for the benefit of his or her heirs; but whether this includes claims for *dommage moral* depends on

---

[237] See D McIntosh and M Holmes, *Personal Injury Awards in EC Countries* (1990) p 78.

[238] G Viney and B Markesinis, *La réparation du dommage corporel* (1985) pp 48-49.

[239] Crim 3 November 1955, D 56, 557, n R Savatier.

[240] See P Szöllösy, "Recent Trends in the Standard of Compensation for Personal Injury in a European Context" (1991) 3 Nordisk Forsikringstidsskrift 191, 194.

[241] FF600,000 (£61,665 at the exchange rate of FF9.73 per £ sterling used by the study) as compared with £75,000 in England: see D McIntosh and M Holmes, *Personal Injury Awards in EC Countries* (1990) pp 16, 81.

[242] For a brief summary, see Carbonnier, *Droit civil*, vol 4 (1994) p 340, citing Crim 11 October 1988, *GP*, 89, 1, 440; Civ² 27 February 1991, *RT*, 91, 556 and Bordeaux, 18 April 1991, D 92, 14, n Gromb (in favour of awards for *dommage moral*); and Civ² 21 June 1989 and Civ² 1 April 1992, *RT* 90, 83 and 92, 566, n Jourdain (against). See also, more recently, Civ² 22 February 1995, Bulletin des arrêts de la Cour de Cassation, 34 (2ème chambre) (in favour).

[243] Bordeaux, 18 April 1991, D 92, 14, n Gromb.

whether *droit civil* applies or *droit administratif*.[244] As far as *droit civil* is concerned, at one time the civil and criminal courts were divided on this issue, but it is now well-established that claims for *dommage moral* are included[245] (although this position is not without its critics).[246] By contrast, the administrative courts have traditionally regarded claims for *dommage moral* as essentially personal, refusing any rights to the victim's heirs,[247] except where the deceased had already begun legal proceedings before his or her death.[248] As noted earlier, relatives may in any event have their own personal claims for *dommage moral*, in respect of distress caused to them by the death.[249]

3.72   In general, interest is assessed from the date of judgment, but the courts have the power to award interest from an earlier date if they see fit.[250] It would appear that, in exercise of this power, no distinction is drawn between *dommage matériel* and *dommage moral*; but the issue is not entirely clear, given that trial courts have considerable discretion and do not have to give reasons on this point.[251]

GERMANY[252]

3.73   Compensation for personal injury in Germany is governed by Article 847 of the German Civil Code,[253] which provides that the injured party is entitled to "fair monetary compensation". Here damages are intended to compensate the plaintiff for his or her pain and suffering, but also, apparently, to give the plaintiff some form of satisfaction for the wrong suffered.[254]

---

[244]   See Y Lambert-Faivre, "Le droit et la morale dans l'indemnisation des dommages corporels", D 92 ch 165.

[245]   Chambre mixte 30 April 1976, 2 judgements, D 77, 185, n M Contamine-Raynaud.

[246]   See, eg, Esmein, "Le commercialisation du dommage moral", D 54, ch 113; P Malaurie and L Aynès, *Les Obligations* (3rd ed 1992) p 115; and see G Viney and B Markesinis, *La réparation du dommage corporel* (1985) p 149.

[247]   Eg Cons d'Et 29 January 1971, *AJDA* 1971.279 (note) and 310 (report); but cf C adm Nantes, 22 February 1989, *AJDA* 1989.276.

[248]   Eg Cons d'Et 8 November 1968, *Rec* p 563.

[249]   See para 3.68 above.

[250]   See art 1153-1 of the *Code Civil*, as amended by the law of 5 July 1985.

[251]   Ass pl 3 July 1992, D 92, somm 404.

[252]   We gratefully acknowledge that we have relied heavily in this summary on Professor B S Markesinis's *The German Law of Torts* (3rd ed 1994).

[253]   *Bürgerliches Gesetzbuch* (BGB).

[254]   (1955) 18 BGHZ 149; see B S Markesinis, *The German Law of Torts* (3rd ed 1994) pp 920-921, 946-959. Damages for *pecuniary* loss are awarded under Article 249 I.

3.74   The pain suffered by the victim is significant in the assessment of damages.[255] Where the plaintiff is able to appreciate loss, damages will take into account mental suffering over loss of a particular pastime or hobby. Anguish caused by the realisation of a shorter life expectancy may also be taken into account when calculating the damages, although there are no damages for loss of expectation of life, as distinct from any mental suffering caused by awareness of the loss.[256] Damages for pain and suffering depend on the plaintiff's subjective experience, so that if the plaintiff does not actually experience pain, the sum awarded can be reduced, sometimes drastically.[257] As regards mentally incapacitated, as opposed to unconscious, plaintiffs, some courts have awarded such persons lower amounts as compensation for pain and suffering on the ground that these plaintiffs do not suffer to the same extent as persons of full mental capacity. These decisions have been criticised by the German Department of Justice as acts of unfair discrimination which must be eliminated.[258]

3.75   In the assessment of damages for non-pecuniary loss in personal injury cases, German law also permits courts to take account of the economic circumstances of both parties, including the existence of liability insurance coverage. A court might therefore take into account the relative financial strength of the parties so that, for example, damages awarded against a financially strong, or fully insured, defendant may be increased.[259]

3.76   Awards have been made where the victim is unconscious and is therefore incapable of suffering pain or appreciating loss. As German law does not adhere to rigid headings in its assessment of damages it could be argued that the courts in such cases were trying to compensate the victim for loss of amenity in an objective sense. However, the terms in which awards in these cases have been justified - for example, "satisfaction" or "symbolic atonement" - seem to suggest that they serve a purpose which, to some extent, goes beyond compensation.[260] In one case, for example, the court drew attention to the way in which damages for pain and suffering in Germany had its origins in the criminal law.[261] Although the primary purpose of damages for non-pecuniary loss remains compensatory, attention has been drawn to the apparent contradiction between the idea of "satisfaction" and the hostility to

---

[255] [1960] BGH VersR 401; (1955) 18 BGHZ 149; see B S Markesinis, *op cit*, p 922.

[256] B S Markesinis, *op cit*, p 923.

[257] See, eg, [1982] BGH NJW 2123.

[258] W Pfennigstorf (ed), *Personal Injury Compensation* (1993) pp 68-69.

[259] See B S Markesinis, *op cit*, p 922.

[260] B S Markesinis, *op cit*, p 922.

[261] (1955) 18 BGHZ 149: see B S Markesinis, *op cit*, pp 946-959.

punitive damages generally found in civil law jurisdictions.[262]

3.77   German law previously allowed only the injured party to claim for non-pecuniary loss. However, legislation effective from 1 July 1990 repealed the traditional rule under which claims for pain and suffering, being strictly tied to the individual, would only devolve on the injured person's estate where he or she had commenced an action while alive.[263]

3.78   Interest is payable, under Article 291 of the German Civil Code, on damages for non-pecuniary loss in respect of the period from the service of proceedings on the defendant to the date of payment of the damages.[264] This was established in a case decided in 1965.[265] It is less certain whether interest is also payable in respect of the time *before* service of proceedings, and there is no clear authority on the question.

3.79   Damages in Germany are not awarded by juries. With regard to quantum, there is evidence of an upwards tendency in the size of awards for non-pecuniary loss. A 1990 study by McIntosh and Holmes records the highest pain and suffering judgment award as DM500,000 (£172,414) and the largest known out of court settlement for pain and suffering as DM400,000 (£137,931).[266] Awards appear to have outstripped the rise in inflation in the past ten years or so.[267]

---

[262] B S Markesinis, *op cit*, p 921.

[263] Law of 14 March 1990, 1990 Bundesgesetzblatt I, p 478, repealing the second sentence of Art 847 I of the BGB.

[264] The interest is payable at a uniform rate of 4% in respect of the whole of this period.

[265] [1965] NJW 531. See also [1965] NJW 1374.

[266] D McIntosh and M Holmes, *Personal Injury Awards in EC Countries* (1990) p 10.

[267] See P Szöllösy, "Recent Trends in the Standard of Compensation for Personal Injury in a European Context" (1991) 3 Nordisk Forsikringstidsskrift 191, 205. But see W Pfennigstorf (ed), *Personal Injury Compensation* (1993) p 67.

PART IV
CONSULTATION ISSUES AND OPTIONS FOR REFORM

INTRODUCTION

4.1 The consequences of personal injury vary from person to person. This fact, together with the consideration that non-pecuniary losses have no market value, makes the assessment of damages for non-pecuniary loss particularly problematic.[1] We saw in Part II that, by adopting as their basic premise the principle that similar injuries should be compensated by similar sums, English judges have employed a tariff approach to the assessment of non-pecuniary damages, whereby a scale of values organised by reference to types of injury provides the initial range for the award. The courts then look to the plaintiff's own particular pain, mental suffering and disablement in order to reach a precise sum within the range.[2] We also saw that a notable feature of the English approach, in contrast to the position in some other jurisdictions, is that plaintiffs who are rendered permanently unconscious will receive a more than merely nominal sum of compensation for their non-pecuniary loss. A plaintiff's damages for non-pecuniary loss may therefore include compensation for the objective fact of deprivation or disablement as well as for any subjective mental suffering. The overall result is that some uniformity and consistency in awards is achieved, whilst at the same time there is scope for assessments being highly particularised and flexible. In this Part, we consider a number of different ways in which improvements might be made to the present method of assessment and to the principles which are applied.

4.2 As it is manifestly impossible to seek to achieve *exact* quantification of a non-pecuniary loss, it seems self-evident that awards for non-pecuniary loss should be standardised to some degree. If the process were entirely discretionary and wholly individualised, awards would be open to the objection that they were arbitrary and based on irrelevant criteria.[3] *Widely* varying awards to different plaintiffs for what

---

[1] It is sometimes compared with the task of sentencing in criminal cases, where the circumstances which make the defendant's offence more or less serious, or which call for greater or lesser punishment, are also multifarious; and where theories of punishment provide no precise formula by which the 'right' amount of punishment can be determined. See eg *Ward v James* [1966] 1 QB 273, 300D, *per* Lord Denning MR; and F S Levin, "Pain and Suffering Guidelines: A Cure for Damages Measurement 'Anomie'" (1989) 22 Univ Mich J Law Reform 303.

[2] There is no formal limit to the circumstances (eg age, sex, hobbies) which may be taken into account, although the courts themselves have held certain circumstances to be irrelevant. See para 2.36 above.

[3] This is a criticism of jury awards. See eg *Ward v James* [1966] 1 QB 273, 296; J G Fleming, *The American Tort Process* (1988) pp 123-124.

is essentially the same injury would almost certainly be perceived as unfair.[4] Plaintiffs would be likely to feel aggrieved by such a system;[5] and lack of uniformity and consistency hinders the negotiated settlement of personal injury actions.[6] In addition, it would be impossible for the judiciary to exercise effectively their power to review awards on appeal, in the absence of any standards by which to judge the appropriateness of a particular award.[7] Finally, but crucially, because pain, suffering and physical incapacity have no market value, comparing awards provides the most straightforward method for converting the plaintiff's loss into a sum of money.[8]

4.3   In the light of this - and in considering options for reform - we believe that the law in this area should seek to attain at least the following objectives:[9]

(i)   Fair compensation - the amount of damages must be fair to both plaintiffs and defendants and should be regarded by the public as fair.

(ii)   Consistency and uniformity - in the interests of fairness and assessability, comparable injuries should be compensated by comparable awards.[10]

---

[4]   Thus the principle that comparable injuries should be compensated by comparable sums expresses not only pragmatic concerns relating to difficulties in assessment but is based also upon it being only fair that like cases should be treated alike and unlike cases should be treated differently.

[5]   *Ward v James* [1966] 1 QB 273, 300A-B: " ... there will be great dissatisfaction in the community and much criticism of the administration of justice."

[6]   *Ibid*, 300B-C; (1971) Law Com Working Paper No 41, paras 8-9. We continue to believe that it is important to promote and encourage negotiated settlements: see also Small Personal Injury Claims: A Consultation paper on proposals for changes to the treatment of small unliquidated claims in the County Court (Lord Chancellor's Department (1993) para 11), citing the "obvious advantages" of out of court settlements. But cf Personal Injury Litigation - A Consumer Response to the Civil Justice Review, National Consumer Council (July 1986) para 5.6, arguing that, because the bargaining strengths of the defendant (invariably an insurance company) and the plaintiff are unequal, new personal injury claims procedures should "place more emphasis on court proceedings and less on negotiations." See also (1994) Law Com No 225 and earlier studies, eg Harris *et al*, *Compensation and Support for Illness and Injury* (1984), on the pressures to settle at less than the full value of a claim.

[7]   When juries assessed damages in personal injury actions with a largely unfettered discretion, appellate courts were for this reason reluctant to intervene and would do so only where the award was out of all proportion to the circumstances of the case or one which no reasonable jury could have arrived at: *Mechanical and General Inventions Co Ltd v Austin* [1935] AC 346, 377-378. It has also been argued that an essentially discretionary assessment of damages for non-pecuniary loss conflicts with the judicial duty to provide reasons for a decision: P Semmler, "ALJ Forum" (1992) 66 ALJ 748, 749, criticising the approach in *Planet Fisheries Proprietary Ltd v La Rosa* (1968) 119 CLR 118. See para 3.23 above.

[8]   Of course, choices still exist as to what precisely are the elements that are being compared.

[9]   Cf (1971) Law Com Working Paper No 41, para 49.

[10]   *West v Shephard* [1964] AC 326, 346; *Ward v James* [1966] 1 QB 273, 300A-B; (1971) Law Com Working Paper No 41, para 49(c).

(iii)   Predictability - parties should be able to predict with some measure of accuracy the sum which is likely to be awarded in a particular case.[11] In our Working Paper published in 1971,[12] we noted that the majority of claims for damages for personal injury were settled without recourse to litigation and that a tariff for the compensation of non-pecuniary loss enabled this to take place.[13] We took the view, to which we continue to adhere, that it is important to encourage settlements in order to ensure that the courts are not overwhelmed with personal injury litigation,[14] and that the method for assessing damages should therefore provide sufficient certainty to enable settlements to be negotiated.[15]

(iv)   Comprehensibility - the law relating to assessment should be easy to understand and comprehensible to the parties involved.[16]

(v)   Workability and simplicity - it is often remarked that the assessment of damages for non-pecuniary loss is one of the most difficult tasks a judge has to carry out.[17] It should be one aim of law reform to make this task[18] as easy as is consistent with the four objectives above.

4.4   We have divided our consideration of the options for reform into ten main issues:

(1)   Should damages for non-pecuniary loss be available at all?

(2)   Should English law adopt the Canadian 'functional' approach to the assessment of damages for non-pecuniary loss?

---

[11]   *Ward v James* [1966] 1 QB 273, 300B; (1971) Law Com Working Paper No 41, para 49(b).

[12]   (1971) Law Com Working Paper No 41.

[13]   *Ibid*, paras 8, 9.

[14]   A negotiated settlement may also assist the rehabilitation of the plaintiff. See Harris *et al*, *Compensation and Support for Illness and Injury* (1984) p 161.

[15]   (1971) Law Com Working Paper No 41, para 9.

[16]   *Hansard* (HL) 22 February 1994, vol 552, col 509 (the Lord Chancellor: "The purpose of the remit to the Law Commission is that it should help us to restate [the] principles [upon which damages are based] in a way that will be readily comprehensible ...").

[17]   Eg *Bird v Cocking & Sons Ltd* [1951] 2 TLR 1260, 1263; Foreword by Lord Donaldson MR to the 1st edition of the JSB *Guidelines* (1992) p vii; *Ward v James* [1966] 1 QB 273, 300C-D; *Hansard* (HC) 3 March 1989, vol 148, col 550 (Sir Nicholas Lyell QC MP). But cf (1971) Law Com Working Paper No 41, para 9, commenting that the tariff is "comparatively easily applied in most cases".

[18]   The task need not be a judicial one, although in English law the judiciary do at present conduct the assessment exercise.

(3)   Should a plaintiff who is unaware of his or her injury be entitled to damages for non-pecuniary loss?

(4)   Should there be a threshold for the recovery of damages for non-pecuniary loss?

(5)   What should be the level of damages for non-pecuniary loss?

(6)   Should any form of legislative tariff be introduced?

(7)   If a legislative tariff is not introduced, should the judiciary be assisted in fixing the amounts to be awarded for non-pecuniary loss?

(8)   Should damages be assessed by juries?

(9)   Should interest be awarded on damages for non-pecuniary loss and, if so, how much interest?

(10)   Should damages for non-pecuniary loss survive the death of the victim?

1.   SHOULD DAMAGES FOR NON-PECUNIARY LOSS BE AVAILABLE AT ALL?

4.5   We raise this question only briefly because, although some legal systems have in the past refused to award damages for this type of loss,[19] we, like the Pearson Commission before us,[20] do not now seriously question that they should be available. Instead, we acknowledge the importance of recognising, by means of an award of damages, the fact that actionable personal injury has very real *personal*, as well as financial, consequences for the individual concerned.[21] To award compensation only for the pecuniary losses which flow from personal injury would

---

[19]   Eg in the formerly Communist Eastern European jurisdictions, and in Islamic jurisdictions of the Middle East: see para 2.2, n 5 above. In the 19th century a movement prevailed in Germany which aimed at abolishing compensation for non-pecuniary loss. See H Stoll, Consequences of Liability: Remedies, Int Enc Comp Law, vol XI/2 Torts (1983) ch 8, s 36. In addition, legal systems which have implemented no-fault schemes often abandon sums in respect of non-pecuniary loss. In contrast, Professor Fleming has described damages for non-pecuniary loss as a mark of the tort system: J G Fleming, "Damages for Non-Material Losses" [1973] LSUC 1. See also Harris *et al*, *Compensation and Support for Illness and Injury* (1984) pp 86 and 237.

[20]   Pearson Report, vol 1, paras 361 and 362. See also A I Ogus, *The Law of Damages* (1973) p 194, remarking that "it has never been questioned that in English law the plaintiff should recover compensation for his non-pecuniary losses." At para 360 of its Report the Pearson Commission suggested that there were at least three functions of an award of damages for non-pecuniary loss: (i) as a palliative; (ii) to enable the purchase of alternative sources of satisfaction; and (iii) to meet hidden expenses.

[21]   Cf K M Stanton, *The Modern Law of Tort* (1994) p 252. See also (1994) Law Com No 225, especially paras 3.2, 3.3, 3.10 and 3.12.

seem to fail to accord proper significance to the fact that personal capacities (such as the ability to see, hear or run) and mental equilibrium are precisely what go to make up and affect the quality of our life as human beings. Awards of damages for non-pecuniary loss are now well established and their continuance is in keeping with the increased recognition of the significance of mental distress and other intangible interests generally.[22] It can also be argued that to abolish damages for non-pecuniary loss would be to discriminate unfairly against those (such as children, mothers who stay at home, and the unemployed) who do not suffer any, or any substantial, loss of earnings as a result of an injury.

4.6 We also take into account the views of the victims of personal injury who took part in our empirical survey: nearly all the respondents thought that they should receive compensation for non-pecuniary loss as well as for pecuniary loss.[23] Our report drew a link between the views of victims on this question and the surprisingly high number of victims (4 in 5) who were still experiencing pain at the time of the interview (2 in 5 being in constant pain). Our report said: "This widespread experience of continuing pain, even many years after the date of the injury must surely have had a significant influence on respondents' feelings about the practical and symbolic value of compensation for pain and suffering, and responses to questions about the reasons why such payments should be made reflected this depth of feeling."[24] Three of the comments made by victims as to whether damages for non-pecuniary loss should be awarded were in these terms: "If you've been fortunate enough to have good health, no money can compensate for the trauma of living with constant and severe pain - but it does sugar the pill." "Sometimes I think the pain and suffering is worse than disability. The pain and the boredom are worse than being blind." "Because it is like going to hell and back. It is the most important part of the compensation. If you hadn't had the accident you wouldn't have the pain."[25]

---

[22] See Liability for Psychiatric Illness (1995) Law Com Consultation Paper No 137. Cf also A S Burrows, *Remedies for Torts and Breach of Contract* (2nd ed 1994) p 191.

[23] (1994) Law Com No 225, p 210, para 11.6. Two main reasons were given by victims for compensating pain and suffering: (i) the impact on the quality of life (45% referred to this); and (ii) the defendant's mistake was responsible for the injury (35%). Other reasons given were that it "softened the blow", that other family members are affected, that it is difficult to measure the effect of pain, that pain affects the victim's personality and that pain is the worst effect of an accident. A survey carried out in 1972 of Illinois road accident victims who made successful tort claims found that most of those surveyed had no knowledge or expectation of receiving payment for non-pecuniary loss prior to the accident and that the receipt of such payment had little effect on feelings towards the wrongdoer (which were neutral). However, it also found that most victims wanted payment for non-pecuniary loss to be available and that they were prepared to buy it themselves if it were an optional coverage under a system of no-fault insurance. See J O'Connell and R J Simon, "Payment for Pain and Suffering: Who Wants What, When and Why?" (1972) 1 Univ of Illinois Law Forum 1.

[24] (1994) Law Com No 225, p 211, para 11.6.

[25] *Ibid*, p 212, para 11.6.

4.7 Arguments *against* the availability of damages for non-pecuniary loss include: the moral offensiveness of monetary indemnification for this type of loss; the fact that no sum can ever adequately compensate serious personal injury; the cost of compensating non-pecuniary loss; that there is a punitive element underlying damages for non-pecuniary loss; and that these damages constitute a barrier to rehabilitation. It should also be noted that, if one adopts the 'functional' approach to non-pecuniary loss (discussed in the next section) damages for so-called non-pecuniary loss are approached in terms of the cost of substitute pleasures so that, in reality, only pecuniary losses are being compensated. There is also a widely shared view amongst legal economists in the United States that damages for non-pecuniary loss are not justified because consumers would not in theory, and do not in practice, choose to insure against non-pecuniary loss.[26]

4.8 **We invite consultees to say whether they agree with our strong provisional view that the courts should continue to award damages for non-pecuniary loss.**

2. SHOULD ENGLISH LAW ADOPT THE CANADIAN 'FUNCTIONAL' APPROACH TO THE ASSESSMENT OF DAMAGES FOR NON-PECUNIARY LOSS?

4.9 We saw in Part II that there are two main theoretical approaches to non-pecuniary loss, which can be conveniently labelled the 'diminution of value' and the 'functional' approaches.[27] Our firm view, subject to the views of consultees, is that it would not be sensible for English law to abandon the former for the latter. The functional approach requires the court to think not in terms of what the plaintiff has lost, but rather in terms of the use to which the damages may be put so as to provide a solace to the plaintiff. We would reject such a change of approach for the following reasons:-

(i) The functional approach, if properly applied, would seem to transform the 'non-pecuniary' consequences of injury into a form of pecuniary loss. Damages for pain and suffering and loss of amenity would be measurable in terms of the financial cost of providing reasonable substitute pleasures to

---

[26] See, eg, G L Priest, "The Current Insurance Crisis and Modern Tort Law" (1987) 96 Yale LJ 1521, 1546-1547, 1553-1554, 1587-1588; A Schwartz, "Proposals for Products Liability Reform: A Theoretical Synthesis" (1988) 97 Yale LJ 353, 362-367. For defences of damages for non-pecuniary loss against the "insurance theory" see, eg, E Pryor, "The Tort Law Debate, Efficiency, and the Kingdom of the Ill: A Critique of the Insurance Theory of Compensation" (1993) 79 Va LR 91; S Croley and J Hanson, "The Non-Pecuniary Costs of Accidents: Pain-and-Suffering Damages in Tort Law" (1995) 108 Harvard LR 1787. See also the O'Connell and Simon article, cited at para 4.6, n 23 above; P Cane, *Atiyah's Accidents, Compensation and the Law* (5th ed 1993) pp 247-248.

[27] See para 2.3 above.

comfort the plaintiff.[28] Ultimately, therefore, the functional approach operates to extend what is awarded for 'cost of care'.[29] We consider that it would place an unacceptable burden on plaintiffs to be required to provide evidence of such pecuniary loss in order to recover for pain and suffering and loss of amenity.

(ii)   A linked point is that it is unrealistic to assume that substitute pleasures can provide full solace to a plaintiff. For example, a person who has lost her sight because of the defendant's wrong may be provided with the best hi-fi equipment and all the CDs she could possibly want: but that cannot realistically be regarded as a true substitute for restoration of her sight. Even if one thinks in terms of some of the damages being used to provide substitute pleasures, a sum would still seem to be required to make up for the loss of capacity to enjoy life that inevitably remains after 'substitutes' have been bought.

(iii)   Just as one cannot develop a tariff for 'cost of care', because it varies so much from one case to the next, so the adoption of the functional approach would seem to require the abandonment of a tariff approach for pain and suffering and loss of amenity. A comparison of the gravity of different injuries would be replaced by the plaintiff's evidence as to the cost of substitute pleasures. As Dickson J conceded in *Lindal v Lindal*,[30] once one adopts a functional approach "it will be impossible to develop a tariff. An award will vary in each case 'to meet the specific circumstances of the individual case'".[31]   Yet without a tariff it is hard to see how the court could rationally decide what would count as reasonable substitute pleasures and, as a consequence, there would be likely to be inconsistency in awards. In *Lindal v Lindal*, in the course of an explanation as to why a ceiling on damages for non-pecuniary loss was socially necessary, Dickson J said this: "[T]he claim of a severely injured plaintiff for damages for non-pecuniary loss is virtually limitless. This is particularly so if we adopt the functional approach and award damages according to the use which can be made of the money. There are an infinite number of uses which could be suggested in order to improve the lot of the crippled plaintiff. Moreover, it is difficult to determine the reasonableness of

[28]   See the Report of the Law Reform Commission of British Columbia on Compensation for Non-Pecuniary Loss (1984) at p 8: "Money alone is not solace. Solace is measured by what that money can buy. It would appear, therefore, that the functional approach is an invitation to adduce detailed evidence on what might provide the plaintiff with solace. It may represent more than an invitation to introduce such evidence. Perhaps good practice would require it".

[29]   See para 1.1, n 3 above.

[30]   (1981) 129 DLR (3d) 263. See also paras 3.42-3.43 above.

[31]   *Ibid*, 270, citing *Thornton v Board of School Trustees of School District No 57* (1978) 83 DLR (3d) 480, 490.

any of these claims. There are no accurate measures available to guide decision in this area."[32]

(iv) The functional approach would seem to dictate that no damages should be awarded in respect of pre-trial pain and suffering and loss of amenity. No substitute pleasures can act as a solace for what has already been endured. Windeyer J, while favouring the functional approach, recognised this point in *Skelton v Collins*.[33] He said, "It may be that giving damages for physical pain, that is wholly past, not continuing, and not expected to recur, is simply an anomaly, for there can be no solace for past pain".

(v) The experience in Canada, where the Supreme Court explicitly adopted the functional approach in the 'trilogy',[34] does not appear to have been a happy one. In particular, most judges have continued to apply a tariff approach to assessment; there is therefore an unfortunate inconsistency between the rationale for the award of damages for non-pecuniary loss, as authoritatively laid down by the Supreme Court, and the continued practice of many courts.[35]

4.10 For these reasons it is our view that the 'diminution of value' approach to non-pecuniary loss is to be preferred and that the 'functional' approach should be regarded, at best, as providing *supporting* reasons for conclusions principally arrived at through the traditional approach. In saying this, we are not committing ourselves to the view that plaintiffs should be awarded damages for loss of amenity even if they are unaware of their injuries: we address in the next section the question whether diminution of value should be assessed objectively (through what has been called the 'conceptual' approach) or subjectively (through what has been called the 'personal' approach). Nor do we deny that, in a loose sense, damages for non-pecuniary loss operate as a solace for the plaintiff.[36] But we do reject the view that

[32] (1981) 129 DLR (3d) 263, 271.

[33] (1966) 119 CLR 94, 132. See also para 3.22 above.

[34] See paras 3.38-3.46 above.

[35] See, eg, the Report of the Law Reform Commission of British Columbia on Compensation for Non-Pecuniary Loss (1984) pp 8-9. At p 12 the Report says: "The majority of comment we received was critical of the functional approach to assessing non-pecuniary loss. We have been advised that it presents many procedural difficulties, not the least of which is charging a jury as to the proper use of the functional approach". See also para 3.44 above.

[36] For this loose usage, see the Ontario Law Reform Commission, Report on Compensation for Personal Injuries and Death (1987) p 105: "Our endorsement of awards of damages for non-pecuniary loss applies equally to past, as well as present, pain and suffering. For some, the notion of 'solace', the purpose advanced by the Supreme Court of Canada in the trilogy as the basis of damages for non-pecuniary loss, involves the spending of the award in order to furnish some form of comfort only for anticipated on-going pain and suffering. *We believe, however, that the need for solace is not inconsistent with the memory and experience of past pain and suffering, and that it is the receipt of the award that furnishes that*

the use to which the award may be put is the key to rationalising damages for pain and suffering and loss of amenity. **We invite consultees to say whether they agree with our provisional rejection of the 'functional' approach to damages for non-pecuniary loss.**

3. SHOULD A PLAINTIFF WHO IS UNAWARE OF HIS OR HER INJURY BE ENTITLED TO DAMAGES FOR NON-PECUNIARY LOSS?

4.11 A plaintiff who is rendered permanently unconscious (for example, who is in a persistent vegetative state)[37] has suffered a serious physical and mental injury. Such a plaintiff is, however, unable to appreciate his or her condition, experiences neither pain nor mental suffering, and is incapable of personally enjoying, using or benefiting from the damages awarded as non-pecuniary compensation. He or she is already entitled to receive not only damages for loss of earnings but also damages covering the expense of all past and future care needs, in so far as they are reasonable.[38] Is English law, as laid down by the majority of the House of Lords in *West v Shephard*[39] (confirming the majority decision of the Court of Appeal in *Wise v Kaye*),[40] correct in insisting that a permanently unconscious plaintiff should receive, on top of this, a sum representing loss of amenity?

4.12 In *Lim Poh Choo v Camden and Islington AHA*[41] the House of Lords was invited to reverse *West* but it found the "formidable logic and good sense of the minority opinions ... in *Wise v Kaye* and *West v Shephard* ... matched by the equally formidable logic and good sense of the majority opinions." The question upon which opinions differed "was, in truth, as old and as obstinate as the philosopher's stone itself". A decision having been taken by the House in *West*, it should only be reversed by Parliament "within the context of a comprehensive enactment dealing with all aspects of damages for personal injury."[42]

---

solace" (emphasis added).

[37] For completely different legal problems arising from persistent vegetative state (PVS) and analogous conditions, see, eg, *Airedale NHS Trust v Bland* [1993] AC 789, especially at pp 878-879.

[38] Given the nature of the injury, this sum will be substantial (where the plaintiff's life expectancy is not greatly reduced). We will be examining the principles upon which the courts assess damages for cost of care in a forthcoming consultation paper. The principles for calculating future pecuniary loss in general were partly addressed by us in Structured Settlements and Interim and Provisional Damages (1992) Law Com Consultation Paper No 125; and (1994) Law Com No 224.

[39] [1964] AC 326. The same sort of approach was taken in Scotland in *Dalgleish v Glasgow Corpn* 1976 SC 32 (2nd Division): see para 3.5 above.

[40] [1962] 1 QB 638.

[41] [1980] AC 174.

[42] *Ibid*, 189, *per* Lord Scarman.

4.13 In *West v Shephard*, the House of Lords took the view that this type of serious injury involves grave deprivations for which the plaintiff is entitled to be compensated whether he or she is aware of them or not. English courts therefore award a substantial sum, at the top end of the scale of compensation.[43] Although this Commission endorsed this view in 1971[44] and concluded after consultation that the courts had been right to disregard the fact that the plaintiff cannot use the damages awarded,[45] the English approach has often been criticised.[46] In particular the Pearson Commission believed that damages for non-pecuniary loss ought to be awarded "only where they can serve some useful purpose" and that they "cannot do this for a permanently unconscious plaintiff". That Commission therefore recommended in 1978 that the permanently unconscious plaintiff should no longer receive any compensation for non-pecuniary loss.[47] The Canadian courts' espousal of a functional approach to non-pecuniary damages would also dictate a nil award, since someone who is and will remain wholly unaware of his or her plight is incapable of being provided with solace and cannot benefit from the damages awarded.[48] In Australia, it is recognised that a permanently unconscious plaintiff has suffered a personal loss for which he or she ought to be compensated, but more significance is attached there to the mental suffering that comes with knowing what one has lost. Thus although a permanently unconscious plaintiff will not be denied damages for loss of amenity entirely, he or she receives a low sum.[49]

4.14 While we reject the functional approach to non-pecuniary loss we are attracted by the view that non-pecuniary loss should be rationalised in terms of the mental suffering and loss of happiness caused to the plaintiff. If the plaintiff is so badly injured that he or she is incapable of suffering, then we consider it strongly arguable that, just as if the plaintiff had been instantly killed, the plaintiff should be regarded as incurring no non-pecuniary loss at all; that, in other words, all non-pecuniary loss

---

[43] Ie in the range of £105,000 to £125,000 (at June 1994). See the JSB *Guidelines*, p 6. The sum awarded will be considerably smaller where the plaintiff's life expectancy is very short.

[44] (1971) Law Com Working Paper No 41, paras 78-92.

[45] (1973) Law Com No 56, para 31.

[46] Eg *Andrews v Freeborough* [1967] 1 QB 1, 12, 18, 20 ff (in the context of a survival action); *Fletcher v Autocar and Transporters Ltd* [1968] 2 QB 322, 352-353, *per* Diplock LJ; *McGregor on Damages* (15th ed 1988) para 1525; A I Ogus, *The Law of Damages* (1973) pp 213-218; P Cane, *Atiyah's Accidents, Compensation and the Law* (5th ed 1993) pp 144-145; B S Markesinis and S F Deakin, *Tort Law* (3rd ed 1994) p 720, n 98; K M Stanton, *The Modern Law of Tort* (1994) p 255; and R A Buckley, *The Modern Law of Negligence* (2nd ed 1993) para 8.06.

[47] Pearson Report, vol 1, paras 393-398.

[48] This was confirmed by the majority of the British Columbia Court of Appeal in *Knutson v Farr* (1984) 12 DLR (4th) 658: see para 3.45 above. See also K Cooper-Stephenson & I Saunders, *Personal Injury Damages in Canada* (1981) pp 348, 376-381.

[49] See para 3.21 above. A similar approach appears to be taken in Ireland: see paras 3.12-3.13 above.

should be assessed subjectively (through the plaintiff's awareness of it) and not objectively (irrespective of the plaintiff's unawareness of it).

4.15 In his seminal article, "Damages for Lost Amenities: for a Foot, a Feeling or a Function?",[50] Professor Ogus contrasted the "functional" approach with two other approaches; the "conceptual approach", which values the plaintiff's loss objectively, irrespective of his or her awareness of it ("so much for a foot"), and the "personal approach", which values the plaintiff's loss according to his or her subjective awareness of it ("so much for a feeling"). Adopting these labels, we find attractive the "personal approach", although we recognise that it will only be in rare cases (of which the case of the unconscious plaintiff is the most obvious) that a different result will be arrived at by applying the "personal" as opposed to the "conceptual" approach. In particular, the "personal approach" does not dictate that there should be no judicial tariff or that a plaintiff who makes light of his or her injury should receive lower damages than someone who fails to come to terms with his or her injury. A flexible judicial tariff could continue to operate, with standard sums being awarded based on the loss of happiness normally associated with particular injuries, and adjustments being made in line with the plaintiff's own individual circumstances. The crucial point, however, is that in contrast to the result achieved by the "conceptual approach", application of the "personal approach" would result in a nil award for non-pecuniary loss for a permanently unconscious plaintiff.

4.16 It is sometimes suggested that a good reason for awarding damages for non-pecuniary loss to a permanently unconscious plaintiff is that we cannot know that he or she is not suffering. But while there are doctors who argue that some of those diagnosed as in a persistent vegetative state may recover feelings, there are other victims about whom there is no serious medical dispute. In other words, on present medical understanding, the law can take it as a fact that some plaintiffs are, and will remain, permanently unconscious. To argue that such plaintiffs should be awarded substantial damages for non-pecuniary loss because in the future we may discover that those in PVS do have awareness is to contradict standard approaches to proof by awarding damages on the basis of an entirely speculative possibility.

4.17 A further argument that is sometimes advanced against making a nil award for an unconscious plaintiff is that it produces the perverse result that it is cheaper to injure someone more seriously than less seriously. However, this begs the question as to what are the relevant criteria for determining the seriousness of an injury: the basis of the 'personal' approach is that the plaintiff who cannot feel anything is in a better position than someone who experiences pain and suffering. In any event, it is already the law that it may be cheaper to kill than to maim, because the victim may have no dependants, with the result that there is no-one who may have a claim under the Fatal Accidents Act 1976. In truth, there is no perversity once one

[50] (1972) 35 MLR 1.

accepts that it is compensation of the plaintiff that is in issue, not punishment of the defendant.

4.18   We have also considered whether the introduction of a nil award to unconscious plaintiffs for loss of amenity would produce a lacuna in the rights of a plaintiff's dependants. In other words, we have considered whether there is anything to be said for viewing the loss of amenity damages as compensating the dependants of the unconscious plaintiff for their non-pecuniary loss. If the victim had been killed as a result of the tort, a spouse or parent of a minor child would have a claim for bereavement damages under the Fatal Accidents Act 1976, and the suffering of the dependants where the plaintiff is rendered a 'living dead' must be similar. However, there is no evidence that the courts have ever rationalised the award of loss of amenity damages to an unconscious plaintiff as representing compensation for the dependants, and we cannot for this reason accept that a nil award would in fact produce a lacuna in the law.   Moreover, if dependants are believed to merit a remedy for their grief, this should be addressed and awarded directly and not disguised through an award to the injured plaintiff.

4.19   It is very important, however, to realise that even Diplock LJ, who dissented in *Wise v Kaye*, was willing to award some damages, albeit a small sum, for loss of amenity to an unconscious plaintiff.[51]   In other words, while he regarded the subjective personal approach as underpinning the bulk of the damages to be awarded for loss of amenity, he considered that there was a role, albeit smaller, for the objective conceptual approach; that is, loss of amenity should be largely, *but not entirely*, subjectively assessed. Diplock LJ said, "[T]he only rational basis on which [the courts can compare injuries] is by assessing ...the difference between the happiness which the victim would have enjoyed if he had not been injured and the happiness or unhappiness which he has experienced and will experience as an injured man".[52] And he earlier said, "[C]onsciousness of deprivation is, if not the sole, at least a major causative factor in the unhappiness resulting from a disabling injury...."[53]

4.20   We also acknowledge that, in our empirical survey of the victims of personal injury, a vast majority of the respondents thought that damages for non-pecuniary loss should be payable to plaintiffs even though they are unconscious.[54] The most common reasons they gave were that money should be provided for other family

---

[51]   [1962] 1 QB 638, 673-676. Diplock LJ would have awarded £1,500 rather than the £15,000 awarded by the majority for loss of amenity: ie he would have awarded one tenth of the maximum at that time for a fully conscious quadriplegic. As at June 1994 the conventional bracket for quadriplegia, as for PVS, is between £105,000 and £125,000. One tenth of this range is therefore £10,500 to £12,500.

[52]   [1962] 1 QB 638, 669.

[53]   *Ibid*, 668.

[54]   (1994) Law Com No 225, para 11.6.

members because "they suffer too" and because extra money can help families to care for victims or to provide a better standard of care. About 1 in 10 said that unconscious victims deserve the money because they were missing out on life, while another 9 per cent thought that they would have the benefit of the money if they ever recovered, and a further 9 per cent thought that an award was justified because it was impossible to establish with certainty that unconscious victims were not suffering pain. Some of these views reflect arguments that we have considered and rejected above, or indicate a confusion between damages for non-pecuniary loss and damages for the cost of the plaintiff's care. However, it may be thought significant that about 10 per cent effectively adopted the "conceptual approach", by arguing that unconscious victims deserve the money because they are missing out on life.

4.21 **We now ask consultees for their views as to the damages for non-pecuniary loss that should be awarded to plaintiffs who have been rendered permanently unconscious. In particular, should the amount of those damages be (a) nil; or (b) assessed, as at present, within a bracket that is at the top end of the judicial tariff of values;[55] or (c) a low amount (say, for example, one tenth of that awarded to a conscious quadriplegic)?[56]**

4.22 A further closely linked question is what award of damages for loss of amenity should be made to a conscious but severely brain-damaged plaintiff, who has little appreciation of his or her condition. In *West v Shephard*[57] the majority of the House of Lords, adopting the "conceptual approach" to loss of amenity, awarded £17,500 damages for non-pecuniary loss to such a plaintiff, which was at, or near, the top end of the scale of values. And under the Judicial Studies Board's *Guidelines* the bracket for very severe brain damage, where the plaintiff may be unconscious, is between £105,000 and £125,000 (at June 1994) and for moderately severe brain damage, where the plaintiff is conscious, the bracket is between £77,500 and £95,000 (at June 1994).[58] Lords Reid and Devlin, dissenting in *West v Shephard*, would have awarded a smaller sum than the majority (Lord Reid suggesting £9,000 for non-pecuniary loss made up of £5,000 for loss of amenity and £4,000 for pain and suffering). That dissenting view can be rationalised as being largely an application of the "personal approach": that is, the plaintiff with little appreciation of his or her condition does not suffer the unhappiness of a fully aware plaintiff. However, one can perhaps argue that, *even applying the personal approach*, there is a very important difference between being unconscious and being conscious, albeit with a limited understanding of one's condition; and that it is invidious to put conscious plaintiffs into very different brackets according to the extent of their

[55] See para 4.13, n 43 above.

[56] See para 4.19, n 51 above.

[57] [1964] AC 326.

[58] See the JSB *Guidelines,* p 6.

appreciation of their condition. In other words, a version of the personal approach would concur with the conceptual approach in awarding a conscious, but severely brain-damaged, plaintiff damages for non-pecuniary loss assessed at or near the top bracket of awards. The difference between the approaches would, of course, remain significant in the case of the *unconscious* plaintiff. **We invite consultees' views as to whether damages for non-pecuniary loss for a conscious, but severely brain-damaged, plaintiff who has little appreciation of his or her condition should continue to be assessed within, or near, the highest bracket of awards (at June 1994 the highest bracket for very severe brain damage was £105,000 to £125,000 and for moderately severe brain damage was between £77,500 and £95,000); or, on the contrary, whether a mid-range bracket (say, around £40,000) or an even lower sum should instead be awarded to such a plaintiff for non-pecuniary loss.**

4. SHOULD THERE BE A THRESHOLD FOR THE RECOVERY OF DAMAGES FOR NON-PECUNIARY LOSS?[59]

4.23   In England there is no threshold on the recoverability of non-pecuniary loss: that is, it is not a requirement for compensation that the personal injury should be of a particular severity or duration or that damages should exceed a certain sum. In some other jurisdictions, thresholds on the recoverability of non-pecuniary loss at common law or under compensation schemes have been introduced, with the primary aim of reducing the cost of compensation.[60] So, for example, in New South Wales statutes limit recovery in motor and industrial accident cases to where "the injured person's ability to lead a normal life is significantly impaired by the injury."[61] A monetary threshold of $15,000 in motor accidents[62] and $45,000[63] in industrial accidents is also applied. In Victoria for transport accidents the injury must be "serious" to be compensatable and a monetary threshold of $20,000 is applied.[64] Thresholds are also a common feature here of compensation schemes for personal

---

[59]   The question at the other end of the scale of whether there should be a legislative ceiling on awards is considered below, at paras 4.27 and 4.33, as part of our discussion on the level of damages. See also para 4.54(iv) below.

[60]   See generally paras 3.29-3.30 above (Australia) and paras 3.33-3.35 above (New Zealand). See also, eg, the recommendation of the American Law Institute that pain and suffering damages should only be awarded to plaintiffs who suffer significant injuries: see para 3.64 above.

[61]   **NSW** Motor Accidents Act 1988, s 79(1); Workers Compensation Act 1987, s 151G(1). See also **Ontario** Insurance Act 1990, s 266: the plaintiff must have suffered a "permanent and serious injury of an important bodily function that is physical in nature."

[62]   **NSW** Motor Accidents Act 1988, s 79(4). By s 79(5) this also operates as a deductible: ie $15,000 is deducted in full from all awards up to $40,000 and by $1,000 less than $15,000 for each $1,000 that the amount assessed exceeds $40,000.

[63]   **NSW** Workers Compensation Act 1987, s 151G(4).

[64]   **Victoria** Transport Accident Act 1986, s 93.

injury which are funded and/or administered by the state.[65] In 1978, the Pearson Commission considered whether a threshold should be introduced so as to exclude minor claims for non-pecuniary loss from the tort system. A majority of the Commission concluded that a threshold ought to be introduced and recommended that no damages should be recoverable for non-pecuniary loss suffered by a plaintiff during the first three months after the date of injury.[66] This recommendation has never been implemented.[67]

4.24   The reasons that may be put forward for imposing a threshold are usually pragmatic, rather than principled, and include the following:

(i)   *The cost of compensation*: This consideration was the principal reason underlying the Pearson Commission's recommendation.[68] The Commission considered plausible the contention that minor injuries are over-compensated,[69] with insurers tending to make excessive payments in settlement of minor cases - especially under the head of non-pecuniary loss - rather than incur the costs of defending the action.[70] It believed this to be wasteful[71] and, viewing the role of tort law as that of supplementing no-fault compensation to be provided by the state, felt that resources should instead

---

[65]   Eg the Draft Criminal Injuries Compensation Scheme, laid before Parliament on 16 November 1995 under the Criminal Injuries Compensation Act 1995, in effect imposes a threshold of £1,000 (as does the old Scheme which will continue to operate until 1 April 1996). Disablement allowance payable under the Social Security (Benefits and Contributions) Act 1992 excludes transient injuries by stipulating that no benefit is payable for the first 15 weeks after the accident. A lower limit of £250 was suggested for the proposed road accident no-fault compensation scheme in Compensation for Road Accidents: A Consultation Paper, Lord Chancellor's Department (May 1991) para 4.4.

[66]   Pearson Report, vol 1, paras 382-389. The Pearson Commission rejected a *monetary* threshold because (i) it would relate less closely than would a time threshold to the severity of the loss; (ii) it would require adjustment in line with inflation; (iii) it could encourage exaggeration of the seriousness of claims; and (iv) it would add to the uncertainties of litigation because a plaintiff would have to attempt to evaluate the claim for non-pecuniary loss before deciding whether to bring an action.

[67]   K M Stanton, *The Modern Law of Tort* (1994) p 255, reports that the proposal "attracted a great deal of criticism, chiefly on the basis that it amounted to the removal of a well recognised and vested right...".

[68]   See also P Cane, *Atiyah's Accidents, Compensation and the Law* (5th ed 1993) p 143; and Harris *et al, Compensation and Support for Illness and Injury* (1984) p 132. In Australia, statutory thresholds excluding minor injuries from compensation are often combined with statutory ceilings on the award of non-pecuniary damages which have the effect of depressing levels of non-pecuniary compensation (or at least of maintaining them at a certain level). These statutory limits have been prompted by fears concerning levels of insurance premiums: see para 3.29 above.

[69]   Pearson Report, vol 1, paras 257-258.

[70]   Pearson Report, vol 1, para 383 and vol 2, paras 519-521. Cf Harris *et al, Compensation and Support for Illness and Injury* (1984) pp 90, 318-319.

[71]   Pearson Report, vol 1, paras 310, 382-383 and 389.

be directed primarily to victims suffering serious and lasting injury,[72] whose interest in receiving compensation seems more compelling. The Pearson Commission estimated that its recommendation would result in a saving to the tort system of £44 million a year at January 1977 prices - a figure representing, at that time, about one fifth of all tort compensation for personal injury.[73] Research concerning the cost of obtaining compensation for personal injury (in terms of legal costs incurred) also suggests that the smaller the value of the claim, the higher the costs as a proportion of the claim; that, in other words, the cost of obtaining compensation for minor personal injury can be regarded as disproportionate to the amounts involved in such claims.[74] The Civil Justice Review, for instance, found that average legal costs incurred in 1984 in the High Court (where the amount awarded in 59 per cent of cases was over £3,000) were between 50 per cent and 75 per cent of the amount recovered; whereas in the County Court (where the amount awarded in 89 per cent of cases was £3,000 or less), costs were between 125 per cent and 175 per cent of the compensation awarded.[75] More recent research conducted as part of Lord Woolf's Inquiry into Civil Justice similarly found that average costs in personal injury cases under £1,000 exceeded the average amount of damages recovered.[76] The philosophy of introducing thresholds for non-pecuniary loss in order to save costs is also very clearly explained in an interim report prepared for the Australian Minister of Health in 1994.[77] It said: "The reason thresholds have been introduced in many states is to overcome the problems associated with claims from those who suffer minimal damage but who claim non-economic loss. Consideration of judgments and settlements

---

[72] *Ibid*, paras 263, 311, 362 and 384. Cf Harris *et al*, *Compensation and Support for Illness and Injury* (1984) p 336. The Home Office has described the monetary threshold which applies as part of the Criminal Injuries Compensation Scheme as "necessary to ensure that the [Criminal Injuries Compensation] Board can concentrate its resources on the more seriously injured victims and deal as quickly as possible with the heavy workload": Home Office White Paper, *Compensating Victims of Violent Crime: Changes to the Criminal Injuries Compensation Scheme*, Cm 2434 (December 1993) para 18.

[73] Pearson Report, vol 1, para 389.

[74] Harris *et al*, *Compensation and Support for Illness and Injury* (1984) pp 131-132 and figure 3.5A and B; Civil Justice Review: Report of the Review Body on Civil Justice (June 1988) Cm 394, paras 69, 90, 411-412, 425-437, 439(xii); (1994) Law Com No 225, para 11.12 and Table 1129; *Access to Justice* (1995) ch 3, paras 18-20, ch 6, paras 7-8, ch 16, para 60 and Annex III (Supreme Court Taxing Office Research on Costs in Litigation) and Annex IV (APIL Small Claims Costs Survey, December 1993).

[75] Civil Justice Review: Report of the Review Body on Civil Justice (June 1988) Cm 394, paras 417-418, 425-432. The lower figures were obtained from solicitors' questionnaires, whereas the higher ones were obtained from a sample of taxed solicitors' bills. Note that the data relate to cases started or tried at a time when the upper limit of the County Court jurisdiction was £5,000.

[76] *Access to Justice* (1995) ch 3, para 20, and Annex III. See also Annex IV.

[77] *Review of Professional Indemnity Arrangements for Health Care Professionals: Compensation and Professional Indemnity in Health Care* (Australian Government Publishing Service) (Interim Report, February 1994) para 4.56.

has shown that the overall proportion of damages associated with non-economic loss varies inversely with the seriousness of the damage suffered. Thus a person with a minor, temporary impairment may receive a judgment or settlement which consists mainly of non-economic loss. Reform in this area has been based upon the idea that this is an unnecessary cost to the system and that non-economic losses should only be payable where there is significant injury".

(ii) *Evidential problems*: Establishing the existence, extent and cause of non-pecuniary loss can give rise to considerable evidential difficulties.[78] This is especially true in the case of minor injuries, where most of the plaintiff's loss will comprise pain and suffering - 'losses' which are inherently subjective to the plaintiff - rather than physical incapacity, which is more objective. They may not necessitate any absence from work or otherwise significantly disrupt the plaintiff's life; and they may not require any (or any substantial) medical treatment. Minor injuries are perhaps, therefore, more open to fabrication and exaggeration. The introduction of a threshold for recovery might therefore be justified in so far as it "could ... serve as a demarcation between cases where there is some tangible evidence of injury and cases where there is none."[79]

(iii) *Triviality*: It is said that the imperative to provide compensation is weaker in the case of non-pecuniary loss which is minor or short-lived than in relation to more serious and lasting injury.[80] Minor or transient losses ought to be tolerated and are undeserving of compensation. This perspective is reflected, for instance, in the Pearson Commission's view that the payment of non-pecuniary damages is not justifiable where the injury is a minor one, "such as may equally be incurred through sickness or some everyday mishap."[81]

4.25 In response to the above arguments, a number of points can be made against introducing a threshold. First, it can be argued that, even if it is right that the present system is too expensive, there are better ways to proceed (in particular

---

[78] A Bell, "The Function of Non-Pecuniary Damages" (1992) para 3.2, paper delivered at the conference we organised with the Torts section of the Society of Public Teachers of Law and the Faculty of Law, University of Manchester, entitled *Compensation for Personal Injuries: Prospects for the Future*, held on 31 March - 1 April 1992.

[79] Compensation for Road Accidents: A Consultation Paper, Lord Chancellor's Department (May 1991) para 4.55. The requirement that the plaintiff sustain some actionable personal injury already provides some tangible evidence but the question is whether evidence of a very minor injury is sufficient tangible evidence.

[80] Pearson Report, vol 1, paras 263, 310, 311, 384; P Cane, *Atiyah's Accidents, Compensation and the Law* (5th ed 1993) p 146. See also A Bell, "The Function of Non-Pecuniary Damages" (1992) para 3.3, paper delivered at the Manchester conference (see n 78 above).

[81] Pearson Report, vol 1, paras 310 and 384.

through procedural reforms designed to reduce the cost of litigation)[82] than tinkering with basic common law principles. Secondly, a threshold might encourage potential plaintiffs to exaggerate or prolong their symptoms in order to ensure that they satisfy the test and obtain some compensation for the injury which, despite being minor, they have undoubtedly suffered.[83] Thirdly, since minor injuries typically involve little or no pecuniary loss, the refusal to award any non-pecuniary damages in respect of them could lead to some wrongs going completely unremedied. Fourthly, the Pearson Commission's recommendation for a threshold test should perhaps be seen against the background of its wide terms of reference (compared to ours) and of its view that the role of the tort system should be to supplement no-fault compensation provided by the state.[84] Fifthly, a number of disincentives to common law tort claims for either trivial or short-term non-pecuniary losses exist already - for example, in the form of costs.[85] Finally, an exclusion of damages for non-pecuniary loss during the first three months would, in many cases, serve only to exclude damages for the period when a victim's pain is at its most intense. For the law to be reformed in this way would fly in the face of our empirical report which indicated that the problems of pain have, if anything, been understated.[86]

4.26 **We regard the latter arguments, taken together, as persuasive. Therefore, our provisional view (given that we are not recommending and, within our terms of reference, cannot recommend a trade-off with a new no-fault compensation scheme) is that a threshold for the recovery of non-pecuniary loss should not be introduced. We ask consultees whether they agree with that provisional view. If consultees disagree, we invite them to specify the form of threshold they favour.**

---

[82] See para 1.9 above.

[83] Pearson Report, vol 1, para 385.

[84] In the description of Item II of our Fifth Programme of Law Reform (1991) Law Com No 200, we explained that we were to look only at the remedy of damages within the traditional common law system and that we would not be looking at alternative forms of compensation outside that system: see para 1.2 above. In this paper, therefore, we are not concerned with the possibility (that perhaps lay behind the Pearson Commission's thinking) of trading off a removal of awards for non-pecuniary loss in less serious cases in return for the introduction of some form of new no-fault compensation scheme (eg for road accidents).

[85] See generally Harris et al, *Compensation and Support for Illness and Injury* (1984) ch 2, pp 113-120, 317-318 and 327-328. The introduction of conditional fee arrangements may, however, remove this disincentive: see para 1.8, n 34 above. A closely linked disincentive is where one's lawyer cannot recover his or her costs from the defendant in the event of success, as under the county court small claims arbitration procedure: see para 1.8, n 32 above.

[86] (1994) Law Com No 225, para 11.6.

5. WHAT SHOULD BE THE LEVEL OF DAMAGES FOR NON-PECUNIARY LOSS?

(1) Is the present level thought to be too high or too low?

4.27 There has been much debate in recent years about the level of awards for pain and suffering and loss of amenity in personal injury actions. This has occasionally included calls for a reduction in levels of awards[87] or, at least, exhortations to be moderate.[88] The fear that levels of award may be too high is usually expressed in the context of concern about the impact which large awards will have upon insurance.[89] Although this type of argument has held little sway here,[90] it has been influential elsewhere and has led to the imposition of judicial ceilings on awards for non-pecuniary loss in, for example, Ireland[91] and Canada[92] and to the imposition of legislative ceilings on at least some awards for non-pecuniary loss in, for example, many Australian jurisdictions[93] and in many jurisdictions in the USA.[94] This difference may be a reflection of the fact that, in contrast to England, the assessment of damages by juries is, or until recently has been, commonplace in those jurisdictions.[95]

4.28 The most vociferous criticism of the current level of awards has, however, come from those - most notably, the Citizen Action Compensation Campaign

---

[87] We referred to this body of opinion in (1973) Law Com No 56, para 33.

[88] *Wise v Kaye* [1962] 1 QB 638, 670, *per* Diplock LJ; *West v Shephard* [1964] AC 326, 346, *per* Lord Morris: "awards ... must be assessed with moderation".

[89] Eg *Wise v Kaye* [1962] 1 QB 637, 669-670, *per* Diplock LJ; *Fletcher v Autocar and Transporters Ltd* [1968] 2 QB 322, 335-336, *per* Lord Denning MR; *Lim Poh Choo v Camden and Islington AHA* [1979] 1 QB 196 (CA), 217, *per* Lord Denning MR; *Hansard* (HC) 3 March 1989, vol 148, cols 515 (S Orme MP and L Cunliffe MP referring to the insurance industry's fears regarding the Citizens' Compensation Bill), 527, 528 (J Arbuthnot MP).

[90] See, eg, *Lim Poh Choo v Camden and Islington AHA* [1980] AC 174, 187E-F, *per* Lord Scarman. This Commission rejected it in (1973) Law Com No 56, paras 16, 18, 33. The Pearson Commission was equally divided on the question whether a statutory ceiling, set at five times average annual industrial earnings (about £20,000 in 1977), should be imposed on awards for non-pecuniary loss. Those against the introduction of a ceiling observed that there had been no strong demand for one in the evidence received by the Commission and considered that it would be an unnecessary complication: see the Pearson Report, vol 1, paras 390-392.

[91] See para 3.14 above.

[92] See paras 3.39-3.44 and 3.47-3.48 above. Note the Law Reform Commission of British Columbia's criticism of the Supreme Court of Canada, suggesting that its approach in the trilogy was influenced by misleading advertising circulated by American insurance interests: Report on Compensation for Non-Pecuniary Loss (1984) LRC 76, p 13.

[93] See paras 3.29-3.32 above.

[94] See paras 3.62-3.64 above.

[95] See paras 3.16, 3.26, 3.51 and 3.59-3.61 above.

("CITCOM"),[96] the National Consumer Council ("NCC") and the Association of Personal Injury Lawyers ("APIL") - who claim that levels of compensation are too low. In 1988, in the Citizens' Compensation Bill, CITCOM proposed a Compensation Advisory Board with power to recommend new levels of compensation,[97] which it hoped would lead to higher awards. Its claim that levels are presently too low was supported by three arguments. First and primarily, by reference to the views of plaintiffs themselves and, more generally, by reference to widespread public feeling about awards.[98] Secondly, by arguing that there are hidden costs of disability, for which plaintiffs at present receive no compensation.[99] And thirdly, by making unfavourable comparisons with the much higher levels of award made in defamation claims for injury to reputation.[100] CITCOM also claimed widespread support for its proposals from over 50 national legal, medical and voluntary organisations.[101]

4.29 In a paper published in September 1988 entitled *Compensation Levels for Pain, Suffering and Loss of Quality of Life*[102] the NCC supported CITCOM's call for the introduction of a Compensation Board to advise on the level of awards for pain, suffering and loss of quality of life. In support of the contention that levels of

---

[96] An organisation composed of lawyers, medical practitioners, MPs and voluntary groups providing advice or services to injured or disabled persons, and formed against a backdrop of public anger at the levels of compensation offered to claimants in the Opren case. At the launch of the campaign, its President, Lord Scarman, was quoted as saying that it was time to "put behind learned argument the strength of popular emotion": "New campaign to press for compensation advisory board" (1988) 85(20) Law Soc Gaz 4.

[97] See *Hansard* (HC) 22 June 1988, vol 135, cols 1128-1129; *Hansard* (HC) 3 March 1989, vol 148, cols 511-569; Standing Committee C (Citizens' Compensation Bill), 3 May 1989; and *Hansard* (HC) 7 July 1989, vol 156, cols 583-584 and 637-649.

[98] *Hansard* (HC) 3 March 1989, vol 148, cols 519, 520, 543, 545, 568; Standing Committee C (Citizens' Compensation Bill), 3 May 1989, cols 4, 19. See also CITCOM Bulletin (Summer 1988), referring to a Gallup poll which "showed that 88 per cent of people in Britain believed that there should be parliamentary action to raise the level of damages awarded by courts in cases like Opren." Mr Lawrence Cunliffe MP claimed that the judiciary also felt that levels of compensation were too low and would like to see them increased, but that they considered themselves bound by precedent and therefore unable to raise levels without the authority of Parliament: *Hansard* (HC) 3 March 1989, vol 148, col 514.

[99] *Hansard* (HC) 3 March 1989, vol 148, col 546 (A Morris MP).

[100] *Hansard* (HC) 3 March 1989, vol 148, cols 516, 523, and 568; Standing Committee C (Citizens' Compensation Bill), 3 May 1989, col 4. Cf also *Hansard* (HL) 9 March 1992, vol 536, cols 1167, 1168.

[101] *Hansard* (HC) 3 March 1989, vol 148, col 544; *Hansard* (HC) 7 July 1989, vol 156, col 642. It had the support of more than 200 MPs, but the majority of these were on the Opposition benches (3 March 1989, vol 148, col 521, and (1989) 133 SJ 268). Cf also Editorial, (1988) 138 NLJ 799, suggesting that "CITCOM's basic proposition, that personal injury damages for pain and suffering and loss of quality of life are too low, is supported by large numbers of personal injury lawyers with first-hand experience of the problems."

[102] Reference PD 30/88.

damages for non-pecuniary loss are too low and are out of touch with public opinion, the NCC carried out a straw poll amongst the members of the Council, its management and staff. This was designed to see to what extent the awards made by the courts reflected those of the respondents. Eight case summaries of recent cases in which the courts had awarded damages for pain, suffering and loss of amenity were given to those taking part. Their suggested figures for damages were then compared with those actually awarded by the courts. Thirty-nine responses were analysed. Although the NCC stressed that "care must be taken not to attribute any statistical authority to the findings",[103] as the sample clearly did not represent a cross-section of the population, the findings are of interest. They are summarised as follows:

In one case (case F)[104] the court award was virtually one half that of the respondents' average. In the remaining seven cases the mean NCC awards were between 3 and 5 times greater than those of the courts. Using the interquartile range[105] in case F the mean was some 30% greater than that of the court. In five cases it was more than twice the court's award and in two cases it was more than three times the court award... It is clear that the court awards of compensation for pain, suffering and loss of quality of life are lower than those felt appropriate by the majority of both the Council and staff at NCC.[106]

The NCC has repeated its call for a Compensation Advisory Board in its recent Report on Compensation Recovery; and it continues to believe "that levels of damages are too low because those who fix them do not have the expertise to take into consideration all of the factors associated with the loss. Courts rely instead on precedents which were not adequate to begin with and are rarely reviewed. Settlements are influenced by the same inadequate precedents."[107]

---

[103] *Ibid*, at para 2.1.

[104] The summary of case F, in which the court awarded £65,000, was as follows: "A man aged 23 was injured when an iron gate fell on him injuring his left leg which had to be amputated below the knee. He suffered weakness in the right foot and a 50 per cent loss of sexual functions. He could walk without a stick but could not resume his pre-accident work or take part in outdoor activities. The loss of sexual function was very serious. His chances of marriage were slender and he would never be able to have a family".

[105] The middle 20 awards of the respondents.

[106] National Consumer Council, *Compensation Levels for Pain, Suffering and Loss of Quality of Life* (1988), at para 4.2.

[107] *Compensation Recovery*, the National Consumer Council's response to the House of Commons Social Security Committee's enquiry into the Compensation Recovery Unit of the Department of Social Security (May 1995) (reference PD 16/L2/95) p 7.

4.30 The view that levels of compensation for non-pecuniary loss are too low was echoed by APIL in its preliminary submission to us,[108] although here they argued that awards had failed significantly to keep pace with inflation and that this was a major cause of the current problem.[109] The Civil Litigation Committee of the Law Society also took the view in its initial response to our Programme on Damages that "the level of damages awarded in the most serious personal injury cases [is] too low, thus adversely affecting the awards for less serious injuries."[110] Our consultation exercise in 1971 showed that many people then held the view that damages for non-pecuniary loss were inadequate,[111] and members of the judiciary have on occasion referred to the low level of awards.[112] Furthermore, although the Government, in discussions arising out of, and in the debates concerning, the Citizens' Compensation Bill, would not commit itself to the view that damages for personal injury are generally too low and remained to be persuaded that CITCOM had made out a case to this effect,[113] the Lord Chancellor has indicated that the existence of such a view was one of the reasons why he referred the whole question of personal injury damages to this Commission as one of principle, rather than by dealing piecemeal with particular cases.[114] It is therefore incumbent upon us to address the question whether damages for non-pecuniary loss in personal injury actions are too low and ought to be raised.

4.31 An important point that must always be borne in mind by anyone considering this question of levels is the relationship between damages for non-pecuniary and pecuniary loss. In principle the two are entirely distinct. In the past, however, some elements of what are now pleaded as specific items of pecuniary expense would have been regarded as covered by the damages for pain, suffering and loss

---

[108] And in its response to our consultation paper, Aggravated, Exemplary and Restitutionary Damages (1993) Consultation Paper No 132. Mr David Kemp QC, a leading authority on damages for personal injury, also believes that English courts "are not generous in their awards ... for pain and suffering and loss of amenities": D Kemp, *Damages for Personal Injury and Death* (5th ed 1993) para 5.1.

[109] APIL also pointed, however, to the feeling of most accident victims that they are badly under-compensated and, because it is of the view that "[w]hen considering the assessment of damages, the victim's interest should be paramount", appeared to regard this as a further reason for increasing the levels of awards.

[110] Initial Response to the Law Commission Programme on Damages by the Civil Litigation Committee of the Law Society (24 January 1992) reference LPD/107/37/AD, p 4. The Young Solicitors Group reported that over half the young solicitors it consulted felt that the general levels of damages for personal injury are too low; and that the remainder (43%) were divided equally between those that felt they were too high or about right.

[111] (1973) Law Com No 56, para 33.

[112] Eg *Fletcher v Autocar and Transporters Ltd* [1968] 2 QB 322, 363C-D, *per* Salmon LJ. See Pill J's speculation in *R v CICB, ex p Lazzari* [1993] PIQR P421, P424, that common law damages may have fallen out of line with statutory benefits.

[113] Standing Committee C (Citizens' Compensation Bill), 3 May 1989, cols 7, 8.

[114] *Hansard* (HL) 9 March 1992, vol 536, col 1168.

of amenity. Even today the precise line between the two is not entirely clear. In particular, a wide notion of reasonable 'medical and related' expenses might be thought to embrace the cost of substitute pleasures (for example, holidays, hi-fi equipment) that would normally be regarded as purchaseable out of the damages for pain, suffering and loss of amenity.[115] It may also be thought relevant that, once clause 6 of the Draft Damages Bill, which we proposed in our Report on Structured Settlements and Interim and Provisional Damages[116] has been fully enacted, one can expect damages for future pecuniary loss to be more accurately assessed than at present.

4.32   On a similar point, we would not wish the present controversy as to the claw-back of state benefits by the compensation recovery unit, under Part IV of the Social Security Administration Act 1992, to cloud consultees' views as to the levels of damages for non-pecuniary loss. If, as many maintain, the claw-back provisions operate unfairly, the appropriate way forward is plainly to reform the recoupment provisions.[117] It would be unacceptable to increase the levels of damages for non-pecuniary loss in an attempt to nullify possible recoupment.

4.33   Whilst one may have an intuitive sense of the extremes at which a sum of money for a particular injury is too little or too much;[118] and whilst it may be possible to say on a *relative* basis that serious injuries are under-compensated and minor injuries over-compensated, it is not immediately clear how to resolve the question whether levels of awards for non-pecuniary loss are in fact adequate. Indeed in our 1973 Report[119] this Commission expressed the view that the only helpful question is not whether the damages awarded are "right" but who ought to decide what these

---

[115] See (1971) Law Com Working Paper No 41, para 68. An important case on this question is *Cassel v Riverside Health Authority* [1992] PIQR Q168 in which Rose J's award of the cost of building a swimming pool (£32,500) as an item of pecuniary loss separate from the damages for pain, suffering and loss of amenity (assessed at £110,000) was overturned by the Court of Appeal because that item had not been established to be essential therapy for the plaintiff's injury (cerebral palsy).

[116] (1994) Law Com No 224. The Lord Chancellor announced on 22 March 1995 that the Government accepted all the recommendations in the Report. The recommendation in paras 2.9-2.15, and clause 6(2) of the Draft Bill, relating to the admissibility, as evidence, of the actuarial tables issued by the Government Actuary's Department (the Ogden Tables) has been implemented as s 10 of the Civil Evidence Act 1995. The recommendations on the tax treatment of structured settlements contained in paras 3.54-3.58 of the Report have been implemented as s 142 of the Finance Act 1995, inserting new ss 329A and 329B into the Income and Corporation Taxes Act 1988.

[117] See Fourth Report from the Social Security Committee: Compensation Recovery - Session 1994-95: HC 196; and the Reply by the Government to the Fourth Report of the Select Committee on Compensation Recovery (October 1995) Cm 2997.

[118] For instance, that for the loss of a leg £1 is too little, but £1m too much. See P Cane, *Atiyah's Accidents, Compensation and the Law* (5th ed 1993) p 140.

[119] (1973) Law Com No 56.

amounts should be.[120] **Nevertheless, we now consider that it would be useful to us to ask consultees whether they believe that the level of damages for non-pecuniary loss is too high or too low; and, if so, whether that belief rests on anything other than intuition. If consultees do think that the damages are too low we ask: (a) what would be the uplift required to render awards acceptable (for example, double or one and a half times the present levels)?; and (b) should the uplift be across the whole range of awards or confined, for example, to the most serious injuries? If, in contrast, consultees consider that the level of awards is too high, would they favour a legislative ceiling on awards for non-pecuniary loss in personal injury cases?**

(2) Have awards failed to keep pace with inflation?

4.34 One rational, rather than intuitive, basis for saying that the level of damages for non-pecuniary loss is too low would be if it were true that awards have failed to keep pace with inflation. In other words, while it may be difficult to argue rationally about the proper value of a particular injury, once the courts have adopted a modern scale of values there seems no good reason why that scale should be allowed to drop in value in real terms. Yet it has been argued, for example by APIL, that current awards are lower in real terms than they were 30 years ago.[121]

4.35 We therefore selected a few injuries of varying severity, and tried to compare the real value of the conventional sums which a plaintiff can expect to receive today as damages for non-pecuniary loss, with those which he or she could expect to receive at certain points in the past (in particular, in the late 1960s and early 1970s). We chose as examples of very serious injuries, paraplegia, quadriplegia and very severe brain injury; and, as examples of less serious injuries, total loss of one eye, effective loss of the use of one hand, various types of broken leg and total loss of taste and smell.

---

[120] *Ibid*, para 20; cf F Trindade & P Cane, *The Law of Torts in Australia* (2nd ed 1993) p 496. We do not now accept that non-pecuniary awards are wholly arbitrary amounts and that their assessment is unprincipled - although the starting figure(s) may not be susceptible of rational analysis, it *is* possible to apply principles for measuring the extent of the loss. See paras 2.10-2.38 above.

[121] APIL Preliminary Submission to the Law Commission, pp 16-17, and para 4.30 above. See also C Carling, "The decline in the value of awards of damages for pain, suffering and loss of amenities" (March 1992) BPILS Bulletin 9, p 1; C Carling, "Damages for Pain, Suffering and Loss of Amenity" [1994] JPIL 108; and the comment of the Judicial Studies Board's working party in the Introduction to its *Guidelines for the Assessment of General Damages in Personal Injury Cases* (2nd ed 1994) at pp 2-3: "[I]t seems clear that it could be argued with considerable force that the present conventional ceiling is too low for the cases in which it is applied ...."

4.36   As regards less serious injuries, the results were inconsistent: for example, while awards for total loss of one eye[122] and for total loss of taste and smell[123] did appear to have fallen slightly below the rate of inflation, the same could not be said of awards for effective loss of the use of one hand[124] and for various types of broken leg.[125] In contrast, the awards for very serious injuries appear consistently to have fallen significantly below the rate of inflation over the last 25 to 30 years: we shall now explain this point in some detail, taking in turn paraplegia, quadriplegia and very severe brain injury.

(a)   Paraplegia

4.37   In *Walker v John McLean & Sons*,[126] the Court of Appeal recognised that awards for paraplegia made by judges in the period 1973-1978 (a period of rapid inflation) had not taken sufficient account of inflation and were thus lower in real terms than awards made in the 1960s and early 1970s. Without adopting an arithmetical approach using the Retail Prices Index (RPI), the Court of Appeal indicated that a figure of £35,000 in March 1978 restored parity with sums awarded in the 1960s and early 1970s.[127]

---

[122]   In *Gardner v Dyson* [1967] 1 WLR 1497, the Court of Appeal said that the minimum that should be awarded as damages for non-pecuniary loss alone in a case of personal injury resulting in the loss of one eye was £2,750 in February 1967. The updated value of this minimum sum is £25,394 at June 1994. In comparison, the JSB *Guidelines*, p 12, suggest a minimum of £22,500 (and a maximum of £25,000) for the loss of an eye. See also C Carling, "Damages for Pain, Suffering and Loss of Amenity" [1994] JPIL 108, 109-111.

[123]   In *Kearns v Higgs & Hill Ltd* (1968) 112 SJ 252, *Kemp and Kemp*, vol 2, paras D4-018 and D4-102, the Court of Appeal said that the appropriate sum of damages for non-pecuniary loss for a combined loss of taste and smell was around £2,000 in October 1967. This sum is worth £18,293 in June 1994, contrasting with the suggested figure of £16,000 at p 15 of the JSB *Guidelines*.

[124]   In *Senior v Barker & Allen Ltd* [1965] 1 All ER 818, the Court of Appeal approved an award of £2,500 damages for non-pecuniary loss in July 1964 for the effective loss of the use of a dominant hand. The updated value of this award is £25,493 at June 1994. Depending on the severity of the injury in the particular case, a person suffering a serious hand injury such as this can actually expect to receive between £25,000 and £35,000 today (and the upper end of the bracket ought to be appropriate where the damaged hand is the dominant one), as suggested by the JSB *Guidelines*, p 30.

[125]   In *Rose v Coventry* (1965) 109 SJ 256, the Court of Appeal said that the sum of £3,000 was appropriate in November 1964 for a leg injury resulting in shortening of the leg and reduced mobility, and necessitating a special shoe and stick for walking. The updated value of this sum is £30,188 in June 1994, which compares with the range £22,500-£32,500 suggested by the JSB *Guidelines*, p 36 (category 6(K)(e)(ii)). Cf also *Adams v Park Gate Iron & Steel Co* [1966] CLY 3377. Note that hand and leg injuries are less likely to be as "self-contained" as the other injuries we examined, with consequential non-pecuniary loss varying more widely in the individual case. It is therefore more difficult to make finely-tuned comparisons in respect of these injuries.

[126]   [1979] 1 WLR 760.

[127]   Although the date of the Court of Appeal's decision was March 1979, the updated value of an award should be calculated from the date of the trial, rather than from the date of the appeal hearing (*Taylor v Bristol Omnibus Co* [1975] 1 WLR 1054, 1057D, *per* Lord Denning MR). Michael Davies J awarded the plaintiff in *Walker* £35,000 in March 1978 (see [1979] 2 All ER 965, 966); and all our updated values in this section are calculated

4.38 Using the table of monthly RPI figures in *Kemp and Kemp*,[128] the sum of £35,000 is worth **£104,165** in June 1994. The JSB *Guidelines* suggest a maximum of **£95,000** at June 1994 for paraplegia.[129] This would seem to suggest that awards for paraplegia *since* 1978 have lagged slightly behind inflation. However, the central question is whether the *Walker* guideline really did restore parity with the sums awarded in the 1960s and early 1970s.[130]

4.39 In the third edition of *Kemp and Kemp*, it was said that the average figure for paraplegia in 1967 was **£25,000**.[131] Updated to March 1978 (when *Walker* was decided), this figure is approximately **£75,874** - more than double the *Walker* guideline.[132] Updated to June 1994, it is approximately **£225,811** - again, more than double the conventional sum which a person with this injury could expect to receive as indicated by the JSB *Guidelines* figure.

4.40 Before 1970, however, general damages for personal injury were not divided into pecuniary and non-pecuniary loss and the *Kemp* figure for 1967 may have included an element representing future pecuniary loss (that is, for loss of earnings and cost of care). Indeed, it is difficult to find reports of cases during this period where the court did make a specific allocation for non-pecuniary loss and with which a more meaningful comparison can be made. In June 1963, however, a young male paraplegic with a reduced life expectancy of ten years was awarded **£16,500** as damages for non-pecuniary loss alone by Marshall J.[133] Updated to March 1978, the value of this award is **£58,429**; whilst its value in June 1994 is **£173,893**.[134] Again, in July 1971 the Court of Appeal affirmed an award of **£20,000** damages for non-pecuniary loss alone, made by Forbes J to a paraplegic with unusual and serious

from the date of the trial.

[128] Vol 1, para 0-111. This is the table upon which all our updating calculations above and below are based. An example of how to make the appropriate calculation can be found at vol 1, para 0-107 of *Kemp and Kemp*.

[129] See p 5.

[130] When making comparisons in the paragraphs below, we have tried to avoid using awards made in the period 1973-1978, for the reasons given by the Court of Appeal in *Walker*.

[131] *The Quantum of Damages: Personal Injury Claims* (3rd ed 1967) vol 1, p xii.

[132] We used the RPI figure for the month of December in 1967 when carrying out the updating calculation.

[133] *Forrest v Sharp* [1963] CLY 957; (1963) 107 SJ 536.

[134] Marshall J also awarded the plaintiff £400 as the *Benham v Gambling* conventional sum for loss of expectation of life. Including this sum, the updated figures are £59,845 and £178,109 respectively.

elements in his condition.[135] The comparable sums in March 1978 and June 1994 are £47,411 and £141,102 respectively.[136]

4.41 Subject to the reservations to which we draw consultees' attention below,[137] it therefore seems that the Court of Appeal's guideline figure for paraplegia in *Walker* actually *decreased* the conventional sum for this type of injury - in this sense, awards today have failed to keep pace with inflation and are not comparable with those made in the late 1960s and early 1970s.[138]

(b) Quadriplegia

4.42 In *Housecroft v Burnett*,[139] the Court of Appeal was faced with the argument that the "going rate" for quadriplegia in 1983 was too low because, if one applied the inflation factor to comparable awards in the late 1960s and early 1970s, this demonstrated that a **six-figure award** was required.[140] The Court took the view, however, that, firstly, the 1969 to 1970 awards did not offer a true comparison because the sums awarded for "pain, suffering and loss of amenity" in this period in fact included sums to cover items which would now be claimed separately as items of pecuniary loss: for example, items such as motoring expenses so as to provide outdoor mobility, future expenses covering holidays, heat and the services of a gardener, the provision of therapeutic equipment, a telephone and future physiotherapy.[141] Secondly, that the 1973 to 1978 awards did not offer a true comparison either, for the reasons given in *Walker*.[142] The Court of Appeal was therefore of the opinion that the more recent awards were a better guide. After examining some of them and indicating that "the time has come for a fresh start", it concluded that as a guideline in April 1985 a figure of **£75,000** should be used for an average case of quadriplegia.[143]

---

[135] *Dougan v British Steel Corpn* (unreported) 14 July 1971, referred to in *Daish v Wauton* [1972] 1 All ER 25, 34g-h (CA). Since this is an indication by the Court of Appeal of the appropriate sum to be awarded, it is a more reliable guide for our purposes than the award made by Marshall J. See para 2.24 above.

[136] These values are updated from the date of the hearing in the Court of Appeal rather than from the date of Forbes J's assessment.

[137] See para 4.50 below.

[138] Note the ambiguity in the fact that in *Walker* [1979] 1 WLR 760, 765C-E, Cumming-Bruce LJ, giving the judgment of the Court of Appeal, admitted that "the award ... [of £35,000] ... may be regarded as an award ... *on a rather lower level* than the scale generally awarded in the most serious class of case between 1950 and 1973" (emphasis added), and yet he then went on to state that "by his award of £35,000 ... the judge restores a consistency with awards made before 1973".

[139] [1986] 1 All ER 332.

[140] *Ibid*, 334d. The trial judge had awarded £80,000 in July 1983.

[141] *Housecroft v Burnett* [1986] 1 All ER 332, 337d-j, 338b-c.

[142] *Ibid*, 338b-c.

[143] *Ibid*, 338a-340b.

4.43 Updating this sum to June 1994, its value is **£114,502**. The JSB *Guidelines* suggest a range of **£105,000 to £125,000** at June 1994 for quadriplegia.[144] This suggests that awards for quadriplegia since 1985 have actually kept pace with inflation.[145] But, in comparison with awards made in the 1960s and 1970s, did the *Housecroft* guideline figure actually decrease the conventional sum for this injury?

4.44 In the third edition of *Kemp and Kemp*, it was said that the average sum for quadriplegia in 1967 was **£35,000**.[146] Updated to April 1985, this figure is approximately **£207,072** - almost three times the *Housecroft* figure.[147] Updated to June 1994, it is approximately **£316,136** - more than double the JSB *Guidelines* figure. But for the reasons given above,[148] the *Kemp* sum may not be a proper basis for comparison. We have therefore turned to some of the specific awards for "non-pecuniary loss" approved by the Court of Appeal before 1973.[149] In February 1970, the Court of Appeal indicated that **£25,000** non-pecuniary damages for "a dreadful case" of quadriplegia was "high" but "not unfair as being immoderately high".[150] The value of this sum is **£131,639** at April 1985 and **£200,972** at June 1994.[151] In November 1970, the Court of Appeal said that **£20,000** damages for non-pecuniary loss awarded to a young quadriplegic with a life expectancy of ten years was "not excessive either in comparison with other modern awards or when considered in isolation."[152] The updated values for April 1985 and June 1994 are **£99,611** and **£152,076**.[153] Finally, in *Wise v Kaye*, Diplock LJ expressed the view that "after loss of earnings and expenses of future care and nursing have been provided for", a figure of the order of **£15,000 or even £20,000** represented the maximum non-pecuniary award at that time (December 1961) for a fully aware quadriplegic.[154] The

---

[144] See p 5.

[145] Assuming that the average case is not the worst case, the mid-point of the JSB range is £115,000, which compares favourably with the updated *Housecroft* figure.

[146] *The Quantum of Damages: Personal Injury Claims* (3rd ed 1967) vol 1, p xii.

[147] Again, we have used the RPI figure for the month of December in 1967 when carrying out the updating calculation.

[148] See para 4.40 above.

[149] We have ignored awards made in the period 1973-1978, for the reasons given by the Court of Appeal in *Walker*.

[150] *Fowler v Grace* (1970) 114 SJ 193. But see *Housecroft v Burnett* [1986] 1 All ER 332, 337f-j, 338b-c.

[151] The updated sums are calculated from the date of the Court of Appeal's, rather than Shaw J's, judgment.

[152] *Agar v Elliott* (1970) 114 SJ 887.

[153] These sums are calculated from the date of the Court of Appeal's decision.

[154] [1962] 1 QB 638, 674. Although Diplock LJ dissented on the principles to be applied in the assessment of damages for non-pecuniary loss, this does not affect his opinion as to the sum representing the top end of the conventional scale in 1962.

updated equivalent is a range of £107,950 to £143,933 in April 1985 and a range of £164,806 to £219,742 in June 1994. All these updated values are significantly higher than either the *Housecroft,* or the JSB *Guidelines,* figure.[155]

4.45 Ignoring, for the moment, the Court of Appeal's criticism in *Housecroft* of awards made between 1969 and 1970,[156] it would therefore seem that the guideline figure for quadriplegia established by *Housecroft* and heralding "a fresh start", actually *decreased* the conventional sum for this type of injury,[157] although awards have kept pace with inflation since then.

(c) Very severe brain injury

4.46 The JSB *Guidelines* suggest a range of **£105,000 to £125,000** at June 1994 for very severe brain damage including permanent unconsciousness or a persisting vegetative state.[158] How does this compare in real terms with the sums which a plaintiff suffering this type of injury could have expected to receive in the past?[159]

4.47 The leading English cases on the principles to be applied in the assessment of damages for non-pecuniary loss were in fact, as we have seen, cases which involved plaintiffs with very severe brain injury.[160] In *Wise v Kaye*,[161] the Court of Appeal approved an award of £15,000 damages for non-pecuniary loss made by Finnemore J in February 1961 to a young woman rendered permanently unconscious and

---

[155] See also *Kitcat v Murphy* (1969) 113 SJ 385; and *Povey v Rydal School* [1970] 1 All ER 841.

[156] See paras 4.42 above and 4.50 below.

[157] This view is expressed by David Kemp QC, a leading authority on the subject of the assessment of damages for personal injury, in *Kemp and Kemp*, vol 1, para 1-004/3 and in a letter to the Law Commission dated 18 May 1994.

[158] (2nd ed 1994) p 6. This is the same range as that suggested for quadriplegia (p 5), although lack of insight and a greatly reduced life expectancy will in practice often mean that the very severely brain-injured person receives less than the fully aware quadriplegic. Further, these are important variables which mean that the range for this type of injury is probably much wider than the range for, eg quadriplegia, where the variables are more limited. A recent settlement, approved by the Court of Protection and the High Court in the case of a middle-aged plaintiff in a persistent vegetative state and with a life expectancy of between 10 and 25 years, was structured on the basis of a sum which included £100,000 for non-pecuniary loss: *John Smith v Redland plc* (1994) vol 10 No 6 PMILL 47. See similarly *Thorpe v Hooper* [1995] 9 CL 185. The highest reported award for non-pecuniary loss of which we are aware is £130,000, made in February 1994 to a young woman suffering multiple injuries, including a severe closed head injury resulting in confinement to a wheelchair, loss of the ability to cry, laugh or speak and complete dependency on others but who was fully conscious and aware of her situation: *Whiteside v Howes*, 11 February 1994 (Hidden J), *Kemp and Kemp*, vol 2, para B2-001.

[159] See also C Carling, "The decline in the value of awards of damages for pain, suffering and loss of amenities" (March 1992) BPILS Bulletin 9, p 1; and "Damages for Pain, Suffering and Loss of Amenity" [1994] JPIL 108.

[160] See paras 2.16-2.18 above.

[161] [1962] 1 QB 638.

completely unaware of her surroundings.[162] Updated to June 1994, this sum would be £171,853. In *West v Shephard*,[163] the House of Lords upheld an award of £17,500 damages for non-pecuniary loss made in May 1962 to a woman severely disabled, physically and mentally, as the result of brain injury but who had some limited appreciation of her condition.[164] The value of this sum in June 1994 is £187,435 - greater than current awards made for this injury, as suggested by the JSB *Guidelines*.

4.48 In *Lim Poh Choo v Camden and Islington AHA*,[165] the House of Lords was once again called upon to review an assessment of damages for non-pecuniary loss in a similar case involving this type of injury.[166] Bristow J had awarded the plaintiff £20,000 in December 1977. The values of the sums awarded in *Wise* and *West*, updated to December 1977, are £56,722 and £61,865 respectively. It was therefore argued on a cross-appeal by the plaintiff in *Lim Poh Choo* that, bearing in mind the depreciation in the value of money, Bristow J's award was too low and "quite out of touch" with the sums awarded in earlier comparable cases.[167] The cross-appeal was dismissed. Rejecting an exact, mathematical approach to the issue of inflation, Lord Scarman (with whom the other law lords agreed) insisted that an award for pain, suffering and loss of amenities is dependent only in the most general way upon the movement in money values - provided that the sum awarded is a substantial sum in the context of current money values, the updating requirement is met.[168] He refused to interfere with the award of £20,000 because, in his view, this was "even today, a substantial sum."[169] Updated to June 1994, the value of this sum is £60,595 - approximately half the amount which a plaintiff with similar injuries could expect to receive today.[170]

---

[162] It was unclear to what extent the plaintiff's life expectancy had been affected, although it was accepted that it was reduced. In addition to the £15,000 she was therefore awarded £400 as the now defunct conventional sum for loss of expectation of life.

[163] [1964] AC 326.

[164] Her life expectancy was much reduced - to approximately 7 years from the date of the accident. In addition to the £17,500, she was therefore awarded £500 as the now defunct conventional sum for loss of expectation of life.

[165] [1980] AC 174.

[166] The plaintiff in *Lim Poh Choo* was a woman of 36 who had suffered severe brain damage leaving her sentient but completely dependent on others and unable to appreciate her condition. Her life expectancy remained substantially the same as it had been before the accident.

[167] [1980] AC 174, 178, 180D-F, 185F, 189E (HL).

[168] *Ibid*, 189G-190A.

[169] *Ibid*, 190A.

[170] Severely brain-injured plaintiffs whose life expectancy is very substantially reduced will receive much smaller sums than those suggested here because the period of their loss is short. But Dr Lim's life expectation after her injury remained much the same and the period over which her loss had to be measured was therefore fairly lengthy.

4.49 In summary, the value of the proper award for pain, suffering and loss of amenity in cases of very severe brain injury today is much greater, in real terms, than the value of the specific sum impliedly regarded as appropriate by the House of Lords in 1977. However, it remains significantly less than the value of awards which were considered appropriate by the courts in the 1960s, and to this extent awards of damages for non-pecuniary loss for this serious injury have also failed to keep pace with inflation.

(d) Conclusion

4.50 In respect of very serious injuries, the results of this (admittedly very limited) comparative exercise would appear to support the view that damages for pain, suffering and loss of amenity have indeed failed to keep pace sufficiently with inflation and are significantly lower in real terms than the sums which the courts were awarding in respect of the same injuries 25 to 30 years ago. However, we are most anxious to emphasise that the comparison of awards in paragraphs 4.36 to 4.49 above must be regarded as a very rough one. Before 1970 (when *Jefford v Gee*[171] was decided) it was not the practice of the courts to itemise the award of general damages in personal injury cases, so that it is difficult to isolate the sum awarded for non-pecuniary loss from that awarded for future pecuniary loss (for example, for loss of future earnings and medical expenses). And while we have tried to rely on decisions where that distinction has been drawn, they are so few and far between that it is not clear that they can be safely regarded as being truly representative of the "going rate" for the particular injury at that time (although indications by the appellate courts of the appropriate award clearly provide a more reliable basis for comparison). Even more importantly, sums which are now pleaded as specific items of future pecuniary expense (for example, for hiring taxis or purchasing mobility aids) would in the past have been covered, if at all, as part of the award for loss of amenity.[172] It is conceivable therefore that the sums taken for non-pecuniary loss in the 1960s are misleadingly high. However, unless expressly referred to, it seems unlikely that the courts were attaching much weight to such unquantified expenses, especially given the ethos pre-1970 to the effect that fair and reasonable compensation, rather than full compensation, of pecuniary loss was to be aimed at. In any event, even if one were to discount the awards for the very serious injuries used above by 15 per cent,[173] one still ends up with a picture whereby awards from the late 1960s and early 1970s have failed to keep up with the rate of inflation.

4.51 **We ask consultees whether they agree with our provisional conclusion that the above exercise does provide some support for the view that, at least in**

---

[171] [1970] 2 QB 130.

[172] *Housecroft v Burnett* [1986] 1 All ER 332, 337, *per* O'Connor LJ.

[173] Indeed, with the exception of *Agar v Elliott,* the discount can be 25%.

respect of very serious injuries, damages for non-pecuniary loss have failed to keep pace with inflation when compared with awards 25 to 30 years ago. We also ask consultees whether they have any other evidence either to support or contradict the view that awards for non-pecuniary loss have failed to keep up with inflation.

(3) **If damages for non-pecuniary loss are too low, what should be done to raise them?**

4.52   *If* damages for non-pecuniary loss are too low, the question arises as to what should be done to rectify the position. The possible ways forward tie in closely with the next two sections (on legislative tariffs and methods of assisting the judiciary in assessing damages) albeit that those sections address concerns that go beyond any problem of levels being too low. **At the risk of an overlap with answers to be given to questions posed in the next two sections, we now ask consultees: if damages for non-pecuniary loss are too low, what should be done to rectify the position?**

6.   SHOULD ANY FORM OF LEGISLATIVE TARIFF BE INTRODUCED?

4.53   As we have already observed,[174] damages for non-pecuniary loss in personal injury actions are currently assessed in English law by reference to an informal, flexible tariff. Although the plaintiff's particular circumstances will be taken into account, the basic tariff figure for any particular injury is to be found in precedent, by looking at previous awards. It is therefore *the judiciary* who, by their decisions, have set the levels of awards for non-pecuniary loss and have devised the scale, ranking injuries according to their own perceptions of which of them are the most 'severe' and thus deserving of the highest awards.

4.54   The principal justification for turning to a legislative tariff in preference to the present method of assessment might be one or more of the following:[175]

(i)   **To reflect society's views as to the level of awards.** It is arguable that levels of damages for non-pecuniary loss are essentially a matter for society as a whole rather than a matter of law for the judiciary.

(ii)   **To regulate judicial discretion and promote standardisation.** Depending on the extent to which a judge's discretion is reduced or structured, a legislative tariff might increase certainty, uniformity and

---

[174] See paras 2.21-2.37 above.

[175] The onus is on those proposing radical change in the method of assessment to demonstrate that it will represent a significant improvement to the present system - ie that it is positively better. See the Government's objections to proposals for the introduction of a Compensation Advisory Board: *Hansard* (HC) 3 March 1989, vol 148, cols 548, 549, 553-554; and Standing Committee C (Citizens' Compensation Bill), 3 May 1989, cols 7, 8. The relevant proposals are discussed at paras 4.28 and 4.30 above and 4.68-4.70 below.

predictability by further standardising awards. It would, in turn, enable practitioners to advise their clients more quickly and easily than under the present system where past cases, collected in, for example, *Kemp and Kemp*, must be consulted.

(iii)   **To reset the levels of awards**. A legislative tariff could raise (or lower) the levels of awards for non-pecuniary loss on the ground that they are currently too low (or too high).

(iv)   **To set a ceiling to awards**. Most forms of legislative tariff (that is, whether composed of fixed sums, upper and lower limits, or maximum sums) would effectively set a ceiling on awards for non-pecuniary loss. However, if one's concern is purely to set an overall ceiling on awards for all injuries, rather than a ceiling for particular injuries, this could be achieved directly, without a legislative tariff, by a legislative ceiling on awards.[176]

(v)   **To reconstruct the scale**. A legislative tariff might reflect a view (for example, of the public generally or of informed medical opinion) about the relative seriousness of injuries - and hence about the ranking of injuries on the scale - which differs from that of the judiciary.

4.55   If it is thought that a legislative tariff is desirable, this could take a number of forms. It might be a tariff of fixed sums, upper and lower limits, maximum sums, minimum sums or average sums. These differ according to the amount of discretion they leave to judges in selecting a *precise* sum for the injury before them.

4.56   A fixed sum tariff allocates to each category of injury a *single* figure,[177] from which the judge is not permitted to depart. Once the injury has been placed within the category which best describes it, the amount to be awarded is thus automatic and clear. Although modern legal systems in general avoid completely standardised awards of non-pecuniary damages,[178] there are some precedents for them. The

---

[176] See paras 4.27 and 4.33 above.

[177] At its most extreme, injuries might not even be compared at all, with all plaintiffs in personal injury actions receiving the same token lump sum to represent their non-pecuniary loss.

[178] H Stoll, Consequences of Liability: Remedies, Int Enc Comp L, vol XI/2 Torts, ch 8, s 46. But whilst this method of "compensation" may be unusual in terms of the quantification of tort *damages*, it is a basis upon which state *benefits* are commonly paid. For example, for disablement benefit (a social security benefit for non-pecuniary loss payable to the victims of industrial injury under the Social Security Contributions and Benefits Act 1992), the degree of disablement resulting from the injury is assessed, in many instances, according to tariffs which allocate a fixed percentage degree of total disablement to specified types of faculty (eg 60% for loss of a hand). The tariffs are found in regulations having effect under the Act, eg SI 1982 No 1408, reg 11 and Sched 2. Note, however, that the prescribed percentages may be departed from where, having regard to general principles for assessment laid down in Sched 6 of the 1992 Act, they do

system of set payments of *bót*,[179] which operated in England up until the end of the 12th century,[180] was a primitive and crude form of fixed sum tariff. In Denmark, awards of tort damages for "permanent disability" are assessed by multiplying the percentage of medical disability (determined according to medical disability schedules) by a fixed amount.[181] In recent changes made to the way in which victims of criminal injury are compensated under the Criminal Injuries Compensation Scheme the Secretary of State has been given the power to substitute a tariff of fixed payments for the common law method of assessing damages.[182] Comparison might also be made with the former *Benham v Gambling* award for loss of expectation of life, a standard award to represent the value of life;[183] and with the current award for bereavement under section 1A of the Fatal Accidents Act 1976,[184] a fixed sum of £7,500.[185]

4.57   A fixed sum tariff is therefore the least discretionary and most certain form of tariff, removing the opportunity to make an individual assessment in each case. Although the categories of injury may be narrowly drawn,[186] once the plaintiff's injury has been allocated to a category there is no room for reflecting - in the size of the award - any variations which may exist in the particular circumstances of different plaintiffs who suffer the same category of injury.[187] The only scope for judicial discretion is

not provide a reasonable assessment of the extent of disablement resulting. For further discussion, see P Cane, *Atiyah's Accidents, Compensation and the Law* (5th ed 1993) pp 284-287, 292-296. Cf B Cregan, "Ireland - A Case Study", 1st International Personal Injury Compensation Awards Conference (17 March 1992) p 17.

[179] Eg Laws of Ethelbert, c 600 AD 34: "If there be an exposure of the bone, let *bót* be made with III shillings".

[180] At which time the system was supplemented by damages determined by a tribunal according to the facts of the particular case: F Pollock & F Maitland, *The History of English Law*, vol II, pp 458-459, 523.

[181] See B von Eyben, "Standardised or Individual Assessment of Damages for Personal Injury and for Loss of Supporter: Some Reflections on the Danish Tort Liability Act, 1984" (1985) 29 Scand Studies in Law 51, 73-75.

[182] See the Criminal Injuries Compensation Act 1995 and the Draft Criminal Injuries Compensation Scheme, which requires Parliamentary approval before it can be brought into force on 1 April 1996; *Criminal Injuries Compensation: Proposals for a Tariff Based Scheme*, 11 May 1995, Home Office; *Hansard* (HC) 23 May 1995, vol 260, cols 734-811 (Second Reading); *Hansard* (HC) 29 June 1995, vol 262, cols 1093-1136 (Report and Third Reading).

[183] [1941] AC 157. See paras 2.6-2.9 above.

[184] Inserted by s 3 of the Administration of Justice Act 1982.

[185] The Damages for Bereavement (Variation of Sum) (England and Wales) Order 1990, SI 1990 No 2575.

[186] And in this way attempt to capture many of the possible variations in the personal consequences which injury can have for different plaintiffs.

[187] Hence a single (fixed) tariff figure is most appropriate with respect to those injuries where, in the nature of things, the variables are very limited. Cf *Housecroft v Burnett* [1986] 1 All ER 332, 337c-d. An example might be plaintiffs in a persistent vegetative state (the

therefore in the determination of the category to which the plaintiff's injury properly belongs.[188] This makes the judicial task fairly mechanical and more akin to an administrative one.[189] It does, however, make the process of "assessment" a simple, relatively speedy and inexpensive one. Hence, a fixed tariff may appear to represent the best means of attaining the objectives of consistency, predictability and simplicity,[190] which we have identified as desirable in this context;[191] but it manifestly fails to be sensitive to the plaintiff's particular circumstances.

4.58　A tariff of upper and lower limits effectively establishes a range or band for each category of injury. Within that range, the judge has discretion to select the figure which is most appropriate to the particular plaintiff's circumstances.[192] But the judge will not be permitted to depart from it. This form of tariff is similar to the current system for assessing non-pecuniary damages, except that the ranges used at present

permanently unconscious plaintiff), whose medical condition will be almost identical.

[188] Eg the tariff might include a category for "disfigurement" and another for "serious disfigurement". In a difficult case, placing a plaintiff in one rather than the other may require the exercise of considerable judgment. Cf the draft CICS tariff, containing three categories for facial scarring which are distinguished according to whether the scarring involves "minor disfigurement" (£1,500), "significant disfigurement" (£3,500) or "serious disfigurement" (£7,500): Draft Criminal Injuries Compensation Scheme, laid before Parliament on 16 November 1995 under s 11(1) of the Criminal Injuries Compensation Act 1995 (obtainable from the Criminal Injuries Compensation Authority and containing the "Tariff of Injuries"). Note also that the original proposals for a tariff scheme specifically contemplated appeals against awards on the ground that the applicant's injury had been wrongly classified: Compensating Victims of Violent Crime: Changes to the Criminal Injuries Compensation Scheme, Home Office White Paper, Cm 2434, December 1993, para 32.

[189] Under the original proposals for a tariff scheme, it was intended that responsibility for the running of the new CICS would belong to a non-departmental public body, replacing the CICB, since "the introduction of a straightforward tariff scheme ... means that the specialised skills of senior lawyers with experience of personal injury casework will no longer be needed and that cases can be decided administratively." Accordingly, it was intended that the grade mix of the administrative staff would be changed in order to reflect the fact that staff would be taking decisions themselves rather than processing papers for consideration by CICB members. See Compensating Victims of Violent Crime: Changes to the Criminal Injuries Compensation Scheme, Home Office White Paper, Cm 2434 (December 1993), paras 28, 30. It seems from the new tariff scheme laid before Parliament on 16 November 1995 under s 11(1) of the Criminal Injuries Compensation Act 1995, and accompanying statements, that the administration of the new scheme will be similar to that originally proposed.

[190] Possibly also comprehensibility, although if the system is widely perceived to be unfair, it may in turn be regarded as incomprehensible.

[191] See para 4.3 above.

[192] The exercise of this discretion will be structured by principles of assessment for identifying and measuring the extent of the recoverable loss. The legislative scheme may prescribe these principles of assessment for reaching a precise sum within the range; or it may be left to the common law. If the former, the legislative scheme represents a whole method of assessment; if the latter, it merely sets out quantum ranges and would resemble, for example, the Judicial Studies Board's Guidelines.

have been established by the judiciary and are more flexible in that they are not regarded as absolutely fixed.[193]

4.59　A further possible legislative tariff is one that takes the form of maximum sums (or upper limits) for each category of injury. Alternatively, it might take the form of minimum sums (or lower limits). Each kind of tariff sets a limit on the non-pecuniary award for the particular category of injury, but confers an unfettered discretion upon the judge to award any sum below the limit (in the case of maximum sums) or above it (in the case of minimum sums).

4.60　A tariff of average sums specifies a single figure for each category of injury, representing the appropriate non-pecuniary award for the average plaintiff in a typical (ordinary) case of that injury. It therefore contemplates permitting an unfettered judicial discretion to make an award above or below the average sum, giving the judge a generous rein in the decision whether to depart from the tariff figure and by how much.[194] It could perhaps be said that, where the Court of Appeal sets a guideline figure in the way contemplated by Lord Diplock in *Wright v British Railways Board*,[195] it is indicating the average sum for the injury in question;[196] and that the informal tariff which judges currently employ therefore involves some quite definite average sums, around which floating ranges develop. Indeed, it seems inevitable that informal ranges would eventually emerge from the case law around the figures specified in any legislative tariff of average sums.

4.61　This is a reflection of the wide discretion which this form of tariff grants to judges - it is the most discretionary of those discussed. Like a tariff of upper and lower limits, it achieves a similar balance between uniformity and a very individualised assessment of loss to that which we have now. By affording so much scope for an individualised assessment, it recognises that one cannot capture in a rigid legislative formula all the variations in the non-pecuniary consequences which personal injury can have for plaintiffs. But, significantly, at the same time it removes the initial choice about the proper levels of compensation and the relative severity of different

[193] But see Lord Diplock's warning in *Wright v British Railways Board* [1983] 2 AC 773, 785C-D, to the effect that, although these (judicial) ranges set no binding precedent, neither should they be altered too frequently as this would deprive "them of their usefulness in providing a reasonable degree of predictability in the litigious process and so facilitating settlement of claims without going to trial."

[194] But the circumstances which the judge may take into account in reaching the sum actually awarded will be dependent upon what the legislative scheme provides - eg it may set out an *exhaustive* list of relevant circumstances, which structures the process of assessment to some extent. The current common law principles could also be prescribed in the legislation and govern the judicial discretion in using the average sums.

[195] [1983] 2 AC 773, 785A-F.

[196] See *Housecroft v Burnett* [1986] 1 All ER 332, 339j-340b, where the Court of Appeal indicated that "as a guideline in April 1985 a figure of £75,000 should be used *for an average case of tetraplegia*" (emphasis added).

injuries from the judiciary, and declares what those levels are, making them more accessible. In our Working Paper on Personal Injury Litigation in 1971 the provisional view was taken that, if it were decided to have a legislative tariff, it should contain average figures.[197] One legal commentator who favours a legislative scheme for the compensation of non-pecuniary loss also believes that the correct balance between uniformity and evaluation of the individual case is achieved by a tariff of average sums.[198]

4.62   In our Working Paper in 1971 we tentatively suggested that it is at least arguable that society, through the legislature, rather than the courts, ought to fix the sums payable as compensation for non-pecuniary loss;[199] that if it was really felt that levels of award were too low then a legislative tariff was one way of raising them;[200] and that this method for assessing non-pecuniary damages was the best alternative to unguided judicial discretion.[201] In the Report on the subject, however, we concluded that a legislative tariff ought not to be introduced.[202] We were unable to devise any legislative guidelines which we believed would assist the courts and, in the absence of any real enthusiasm on the part of consultees for the reform, we did not feel that we ought to recommend it.[203] The Pearson Commission also addressed the same question and came to a similar conclusion.[204] It did not appear to think that a legislative scale would improve the present system,[205] and saw as one of the latter's benefits the fact that the judge is able to take an overall view of the interrelated losses of pain and suffering, loss of amenity, and "loss of faculty".[206]

[197]   (1971) Law Com Working Paper No 41, para 102.

[198]   N Mullany, "A New Approach to Compensation for Non-Pecuniary Loss in Australia" (1990) 17 MULR 714, 730. It appears to be the case that those with legal expertise in this area are anxious that judicial discretion should be preserved. Cf (1973) Law Com No 56, para 34, referring to the view expressed at the time by the Bar Council; and *Hansard* (HC) 3 March 1989, vol 148, cols 529 (J Arbuthnot MP), 533 (W Menzies Campbell QC MP), 539 (K Barron MP), 549 (Sir Nicholas Lyell QC MP), 550 (W Menzies Campbell QC MP and Sir Nicholas Lyell QC MP), 553-554 (Sir Nicholas Lyell QC MP) and 563 (F Doran MP). In 1989, the Lord Chancellor stated to CITCOM that "the Government do not wish to impose too much on judges, who have wide discretionary powers to assess cases", Standing Committee C (Citizens' Compensation Bill), 3 May 1989, col 3.

[199]   (1971) Law Com Working Paper No 41, para 98.

[200]   *Ibid*, paras 104, 208, 212. See also (1973) Law Com No 56, para 33.

[201]   (1971) Law Com Working Paper No 41, para 104.

[202]   (1973) Law Com No 56, paras 20, 31-35.

[203]   *Ibid*, paras 31, 35.

[204]   Pearson Report, vol 1, paras 377-380; recommendation 7.

[205]   Since part of its argument, *ibid* at para 379, was that "[t]he introduction of a scale of damages for loss of faculty would not eliminate the arbitrariness of pecuniary awards for non-pecuniary loss; nor would it avoid the problem that similar awards for similar losses of faculty represent greater compensation for a poor man than for a rich man."

[206]   *Ibid*, para 379. It appears that the Pearson Commission largely had in mind a legislative scale for loss of faculty only.

4.63   Two further reasons for not moving from a judicial tariff may be suggested in the light of developments since those reports. The first is that the judicial tariff has been rendered more accessible in recent years by the publication of the Judicial Studies Board's *Guidelines for the Assessment of General Damages in Personal Injury Cases*.[207] The second is that, given the widespread criticism of the reform, by the imposition of a fixed sum tariff, of the Criminal Injuries Compensation Scheme, the public may be suspicious that any legislative tariff constitutes an attempt to reduce sums payable to victims.[208] Moreover lawyers who have expressed their opposition to a tariff approach to ex gratia state compensation, as being too inflexible, can be expected to oppose even more strongly a tariff approach to the assessment of common law damages.

4.64   We believe that, if a legislative tariff were to be introduced, the real choice as to the form of that tariff lies between a tariff of fixed sums and one of upper and lower limits. It is only these forms of tariff which control and regulate judicial discretion in a way which would justify abandoning the present system for assessing non-pecuniary damages. They each ensure that the legislative scale will itself remain intact, by providing limits beyond which the judge is not permitted to transgress. Consequently also, they promote more uniformity and consistency in awards. In contrast, there appears to be no significant difference between a tariff of either maximum sums, minimum sums or average sums and the informal judicial tariff which we currently have.[209] Further, these carry a real danger, because of the breadth of the ranges of award that they permit, that a new judicial tariff will emerge to undermine the statutory sums.

4.65   A fixed sum tariff eliminates judicial discretion altogether.[210] We consider it to be unacceptable because it prevents the judge from taking into account the individual

---

[207] See para 1.5 above.

[208] See para 4.56 above. A tariff scheme was brought into effect by the Home Secretary, amid much criticism, on 1 April 1994 but in *R v Home Secretary, ex p Fire Brigades Union* [1995] 2 All ER 244 the House of Lords ruled that the scheme had been unlawfully introduced. The 1994 tariff scheme was criticised on wider grounds than its mode of introduction, however, including that a tariff of fixed sums for specified injuries is unfair to victims because it is inflexible and precludes an individual assessment. See, eg, *Hansard* (HL) 16 June 1994, vol 555, cols 1828-1851; and Lord Carlisle, "Compensating the Compensators: Why the Government Should Re-think its Proposed Revisions to the Criminal Injuries Compensation Scheme" (8 July 1994) 4/94 Quantum 6. This criticism has been reiterated in relation to the new, revised tariff scheme which will be introduced in April 1996 under the Criminal Injuries Compensation Act 1995: see, eg, A Dismore, "Home Office Proposals for Compensating Victims of Crime" (July 1995) 11/6 PMILL 44; and C Dixon, "New-look injuries Bill 'still unfair'" *The Lawyer*, 1 August 1995, p 1.

[209] The purpose of adopting any one of these would be (i) to reset levels of awards, at least initially; (ii) to locate (primary) information on levels of awards in statute, rather than in practitioners' texts like *Kemp and Kemp*.

[210] Subject to what we say at para 4.57 above concerning the choice of category to which the injury belongs.

circumstances of the plaintiff's case. A high level of uniformity is achieved at the expense of sensitivity to the particular consequences which an injury may have had for the plaintiff and we believe that this sets the balance between uniformity and an individualised assessment in the wrong place. Accordingly, if a legislative tariff were to be introduced, we would provisionally favour one which involved upper and lower limits (ranges or brackets),[211] coupled with a non-exhaustive list of relevant factors which may legitimately affect the level of award within the range, as guidance for the judge.

4.66 If such a legislative tariff were to be introduced, it might largely resemble, in statutory form, the Judicial Studies Board's *Guidelines for the Assessment of General Damages in Personal Injury Cases*. But rather than reproducing those exact figures, the opportunity would be open to reassess both the levels of award and the relative severity of the injuries. In fixing such a legislative tariff, advice could be widely sought from, for example, medical experts and lay people as well as lawyers. Moreover, the tariff could be reviewed periodically by an advisory body so as to ensure that it would not fall out of line with "society's" values.[212] In any event, we would think it essential that such a legislative tariff be automatically updated for inflation. The opportunity might also be taken to spell out in greater detail than in the JSB *Guidelines* the relevant discretionary factors for determining the precise award within the range; and to cover in a more comprehensive and detailed way the range of injuries (the *Guidelines* contain fairly wide categories of injury and ranges, and not all injuries are covered).

4.67 **We invite consultees to say whether or not they agree with our provisional view that, *if there is to be a legislative tariff*, its form should follow that of the present judicial tariff by fixing upper and lower limits and by laying down a non-exhaustive list of relevant discretionary factors for determining the precise award: and we invite the views of consultees as to whether there should be such a legislative tariff.**

7. IF A LEGISLATIVE TARIFF IS NOT INTRODUCED, SHOULD THE JUDICIARY BE ASSISTED IN FIXING THE AMOUNTS TO BE AWARDED FOR NON-PECUNIARY LOSS?[213]

---

[211] We are supported in this view by the content of the CITCOM proposals.

[212] Cf the proposal for a Compensation Advisory Board to advise *the judiciary*, discussed in paras 4.68-72 below.

[213] We do not favour, and do not consider it worth putting out to consultation, the possibility of personal injury cases being heard by a new "damages tribunal" rather than the judiciary in normal court proceedings. This proposal was considered and rejected by the Winn Committee, Report of the Committee on Personal Injuries Litigation (1968) Cmnd 3691, paras 401-406; by the Pearson Commission in its Report, vol 1, para 736; and by this Commission in (1973) Law Com No 56, paras 44-45. In our own consultation exercise in 1973 all but two of the responses were opposed to the introduction of any new type of tribunal. Similarly we reject, and are not consulting on, the suggestion that expert

(1) A Compensation Advisory Board

4.68 The setting up of a "Compensation Advisory Board" was proposed in the Citizens' Compensation Bill in 1988.[214] The starting point for CITCOM - the pressure group behind the Bill[215] - was its belief that general levels of damages for pain, suffering and loss of amenity, as set by judges, are too low and that there should be more public input in the determination of what constitutes appropriate non-pecuniary compensation for personal injury.[216] To achieve this end, it proposed the establishment of an independent body composed of specialists informed in, and with relevant experience of, matters affecting injured persons.[217] Its duty would be to recommend new (higher) levels of non-pecuniary compensation appropriate to

assessors should sit with, and assist, the judges. We rejected this idea in (1973) Law Com No 56, para 46 for two reasons: (i) it is unsatisfactory that decisions should be taken upon or influenced by opinions or advice given elsewhere than in open court; (ii) decisions arrived at in this way cannot be readily checked, thereby undermining the controlling jurisdiction of the Court of Appeal. The Winn Committee and the Pearson Commission reached similar conclusions. We are also not consulting on the suggestion at para 294 of (1973) Law Com No 56, that one might set up Judges' Conferences on the Assessment of Damages following the model of Judges' Conferences on Sentencing in criminal cases. This is because, since that suggestion was made, the Judicial Studies Board has been established and has assumed the task of educating judges who hear personal injury cases (albeit that there may be more scope in this area for the Board to consider the educative role of non-lawyers such as doctors and care workers and to hold short specialist seminars on personal injury cases more frequently). We would like to take this opportunity to emphasise the great importance that we attach to the continuing education of the judiciary in the sphere of claims for personal injury. See also Structured Settlements and Interim and Provisional Damages (1994) Law Com No 224, para 2.29, for our hope that mandatory training will be arranged for all judges who are appointed to hear personal injury cases in relation to the purpose and use of the Ogden Tables and the use of Index-Linked Government Securities in calculating damages awards.

[214] A similar type of body has been proposed in the USA by W Zelermyer, "Damages for Pain and Suffering" (1954) 6 Syracuse L Rev 27, 41-42; and by F S Levin, "Pain and Suffering Guidelines: A Cure for Damages Measurement 'Anomie'" (1989) 22 Univ Mich J Law Reform 303. The NCC has recently repeated its support for a Compensation Advisory Board: see para 4.29 above.

[215] See para 4.28, n 96 above.

[216] *Hansard* (HC) 3 March 1989, vol 148, cols 515, 516, 517, 553 (L Cunliffe MP), 531 (R Litherland MP), 546 (A Morris MP), and 549 (K Barron MP). The campaign had other objectives also, but its overriding aim was "to enable citizens harmed by the actions or products of others to obtain fair and prompt compensation at reasonable cost".

[217] Including at least one medically qualified person specialising in the rehabilitation of injured persons; one clinical psychologist specialising in the counselling of injured persons; one solicitor and one barrister experienced in personal injury litigation; and four persons appointed after consultation with voluntary organisations providing advice or services to injured or disabled persons. The Board was to be chaired by a High Court judge. See cls 1(2) and (4)(a), (b), (c) and (d) of the Citizens' Compensation Bill. At the Standing Committee stage, it was sought to amend cl 1 by inserting a further requirement that the Board should also include insurance and employer interests, but agreement could not be reached on the entire clause and by the third reading of the Bill Mr Lawrence Cunliffe MP was forced, in the face of Government intransigence and in order to ensure the passage of the Bill's provisions on bereavement, to abandon the proposal for a Compensation Advisory Board altogether. See also para 1.4 above.

specific categories of injury,[218] after consultation with carers and voluntary organisations providing advice or services to persons having the injury in question.[219] The composition of the Board and its duty to consult were therefore specifically intended to ensure that public feeling about non-pecuniary awards would be reflected in the levels it eventually recommended. These levels, which were to be advisory only and not mandatory,[220] would then be reviewed from time to time.[221]

4.69 The CITCOM proposals specifically envisaged a body which largely reflected the interests of plaintiffs. It would seem more appropriate (in legitimising the recommended levels of award) for such a body to embrace a wider spectrum of interests and expertise and, in particular, to include representatives of insurers and employers: on the other hand, a wider range of representation might present a risk that the Board would be unable to reach a consensus view.

4.70 Although it maintained that it welcomed the Citizens' Compensation Bill and was agreed in seeking to achieve the object of fair compensation for victims of personal injury,[222] the Government remained sceptical of CITCOM's proposals for a Compensation Advisory Board,[223] which had to be abandoned eventually by the Bill's promoter. The Government was unconvinced that the case for increasing levels of compensation, on the ground that they are presently too low, had been made out;[224] or that the establishment of a Board would improve the assessment of

---

[218] Clause 2(2)(a) of the Bill.

[219] Clause 2(3) of the Bill.

[220] The Bill imposed a duty upon the judge to "have regard to" the published compensation levels: cl 3(1). The promoters of the Bill seemed concerned to reassure its opponents that judicial discretion in the assessment of non-pecuniary damages would be preserved.

[221] Clause 2(2)(d) and (6) of the Bill. CITCOM, at the inception of its campaign, envisaged that the Board would disband once initial guidelines were set, but that it would meet periodically to update figures in line with inflation and reconvene in response to certification by the court of a "new" or previously unencountered injury requiring assessment (see *News from CITCOM* (Summer 1988) p 2, and cl 4 of the Bill). However, Mr Lawrence Cunliffe MP, when promoting the Bill, emphasised that the Board would "not be a permanent quango" and seemed to contemplate a lifespan of only two years at most for it: *Hansard* (HC) 3 March 1989, vol 148, col 553; Standing Committee C (Citizens' Compensation Bill), 3 May 1989, col 4.

[222] *Hansard* (HC) 3 March 1989, vol 148, col 547 (Sir Nicholas Lyell QC MP).

[223] Standing Committee C (Citizens' Compensation Bill), 3 May 1989, col 7 ("The Government remain unconvinced that the case for a compensation board has been made, for practical and not obstructive reasons."); *Hansard* (HC) 7 July 1989, vol 156, col 642 ("It was never suggested that there was agreement on the compensation board") *per* Sir Nicholas Lyell QC MP. Cf col 644 ("At one stage we were told, in essence, that the Government would steamroller the Bill if the compensation advisory board was kept intact") *per* L Cunliffe MP.

[224] Standing Committee C (Citizens' Compensation Bill), 3 May 1989, cols 7 and 8 (Sir Nicholas Lyell QC MP).

non-pecuniary damages.[225] It also appeared to oppose the proposals because it was not well disposed towards the creation of another quango,[226] and was concerned at both the costs[227] and possible hindrance to the speedy resolution of claims which it believed this might involve.[228] A further point made by the Bill's opponents was that the whole reason for proposing a Board in the first place was to *increase* levels of award and yet, in the absence of a statutory duty to that effect, increases were not guaranteed merely by establishing a body with power to recommend new levels.[229]

4.71   We provisionally consider that, if a Compensation Advisory Board were to be established:-

(i)   Its composition should be wider than that proposed by CITCOM and should include, in addition to members of the medical and legal professions and bodies providing advice or services to injured or disabled persons: a representative of insurers, a representative of employers, a representative of trade union organisations and some lay representation.[230] The Board should be chaired by a High Court judge with experience of personal injury litigation.

(ii)   The Board should have a duty to recommend to the judiciary levels of damages for non-pecuniary loss that it considers fair, but not excessive, compensation. It should recommend levels of damages for, at least, the categories of injury which are set out in the JSB *Guidelines*;[231] but the Board

---

[225] *Hansard* (HC) 3 March 1989, vol 148, cols 529 (J Arbuthnot MP), 548, 549, 553-554, 558, 560 (Sir Nicholas Lyell QC MP); Standing Committee C (Citizens' Compensation Bill), 3 May 1989, cols 7, 8 (Sir Nicholas Lyell QC MP).

[226] *Hansard* (HC) 3 March 1989, vol 148, cols 552-553; Standing Committee C (Citizens' Compensation Bill), 3 May 1989, col 6. It was his awareness of this antipathy which perhaps led Mr Cunliffe to emphasise that the Board was *not* a quango and would not exist in perpetuity: see n 221 to para 4.68 above.

[227] *Hansard* (HC) 3 March 1989, vol 148, cols 552-553; Standing Committee C (Citizens' Compensation Bill), 3 May 1989, col 5. *Contra* L Cunliffe MP, who claimed that the Board would cost less than 15% or 20% of the cost of the CICB; and CITCOM, which estimated that the implementation of new compensation guidelines by the Board would perhaps lead to a saving to the civil justice system of approximately £100 million: "New campaign to press for compensation advisory board" (1988) 85 (20) Law Soc Gaz 4.

[228] *Hansard* (HC) 3 March 1989, vol 148, cols 557 and 560; Standing Committee C (Citizens' Compensation Bill), 3 May 1989, cols 5 and 8. *Contra* J Garrett MP, *Hansard* (HC) 3 March 1989, vol 148, col 536.

[229] *Hansard* (HC) 3 March 1989, vol 148, col 529; Standing Committee C (Citizens' Compensation Bill), 3 May 1989, col 6 (J Arbuthnot MP). Cf M Arnheim, "Personal injury compensation: identifying the real problem" (1988) 132 SJ 1546, 1547.

[230] This is similar to the range of people who we thought ought to participate in a Damages Conference. See (1973) Law Com No 56, para 294.

[231] The injuries for which CITCOM proposed its Compensation Advisory Board should have the power to recommend new levels of damages for non-pecuniary loss were listed in Sched 2 to the Bill. In our view, the JSB *Guidelines* now provide a convenient (and more comprehensive) model for this purpose.

should also have the power to devise its own categorisation of injuries. The Board would have the power to recommend either fixed sums or brackets[232] representing fair compensation for the pain, suffering and loss of amenity usually associated with the particular injury concerned.

(iii)   The recommendations of the Board would be advisory only. That is, while the judiciary would be placed under a duty to have regard to the recommendations of the Board, a judge could depart from them for good reason, which he or she would be under a duty to articulate. Where appropriate, an appellate court might hold that the judge had failed to take proper account of the Board's recommended levels.[233]

(iv)   While this is ultimately dependent on consultees' responses to the question posed at paragraph 4.33 above, we would at this stage envisage that for most, if not all, injuries the Board would have a duty to recommend levels of damages for non-pecuniary loss that are not lower than current levels. The Board would be required to take into account evidence that awards have failed to keep pace with inflation when compared with awards made 25 to 30 years ago.[234]

(v)   The Board would in the first instance be required to produce a report, containing its recommended levels, within one year of its creation. Subject to a power in the Lord Chancellor to provide otherwise by regulations, it should then meet annually for the first two years after reporting and thereafter once every three years, in order to review its recommendations.

(vi)   The sums recommended by the Board would be automatically updated for inflation on an annual basis, by reference to the Retail Prices Index.

4.72   **We invite consultees: (a) to consider the desirability, in the absence of a legislative tariff, of establishing a Compensation Advisory Board,[235] for the purpose of setting new levels of compensation which better reflect the value which society places upon the non-pecuniary consequences of personal injury; and (b) to indicate whether they disagree with, or can foresee problems regarding, any elements of the model for a Board which we have outlined at paragraph 4.71 above.**

---

[232]   Cf paras 4.56-4.58 and 4.64-4.66 above, where we examine the forms (fixed sum/brackets/maximum sums/minimum sums) which a *legislative* tariff might take.

[233]   See *Hansard* (HC) 3 March 1989, vol 148, cols 533-534 (W Menzies Campbell QC MP).

[234]   See paras 4.34-4.51 above.

[235]   Note that the values comprised in a legislative tariff (see paras 4.53-4.67 above) could be determined by a Compensation Advisory Board.

(2) Guinea-pig jury trials

4.73 It was suggested to us by APIL that, occasionally, personal injury cases should be tried by a jury as a means of providing sample awards for the judicial assessment of non-pecuniary loss.[236] Cases could perhaps be selected for jury trial either at random by court officials, so that, say, one in fifty trials were heard by a jury;[237] or alternatively a judge appointed for the purpose could decide which cases should be referred to a jury, in order to ensure a suitably wide range of cases (subject to submissions by the parties).[238] APIL saw sample jury awards as a means of redressing the problem of what it believes to be inadequate levels of non-pecuniary damages.

4.74 We are strongly opposed to this suggestion. We argue below that the assessment of compensatory damages for personal injury should never be left to a jury and it would therefore plainly contradict our thinking to *extend* the present limited power to order jury trial in this sphere.[239] Our basic objection to jury assessment is that it is unpredictable and inconsistent; and yet, given the difficulty of articulating clear principles for the assessment of non-pecuniary loss, the comparability of awards is crucial. In our view, even occasional awards by juries would suffer the same defect and would not provide a consistent guide for the judiciary.

4.75 In *Hennell v Ranaboldo*,[240] the Court of Appeal held that it was wrong for a judge to exercise the discretion to order jury trial under RSC, Ord 36, r 1[241] for the purpose of providing an example of the damages a jury would award.[242] We agree.

---

[236] APIL Preliminary Submission, pp 17 and 22.

[237] But it is difficult to see how random selection could give rise (except perhaps after the system had operated for a very long time) to a body of sample awards which would provide judges with a complete or useful tariff.

[238] It would need to be asked whether the power to order jury trial could be exercised where one or both of the parties to the action objects. In *Hennell v Ranaboldo* [1963] 1 WLR 1391, 1394, Diplock LJ remarked that, even if it were the case that it would be useful to have a few "guinea-pig" cases of this kind where both parties are willing, it was quite plain that if either of the parties to a particular case objected to being made the "guinea-pig" then the judge ought not to pick on the case simply because of the general desirability that a "guinea-pig" case should occasionally be taken to a jury.

[239] See paras 4.82ff below.

[240] [1963] 1 WLR 1391.

[241] See now RSC, Ord 33, r 5(1) and s 69(3) of the Supreme Court Act 1981, which contains a presumption against trial with a jury in personal injury actions. See also para 4.82 below.

[242] The Court of Appeal invoked the general objection to jury trial, namely that it impedes the attainment of uniformity and that the assessment of non-pecuniary damages has to be made according to a conventional scale, which judges know and maintain. The case was decided prior to the decision in *Ward v James* [1966] 1 QB 273, where the full Court of Appeal held that for these reasons a judge ought not, in a personal injury case, to order trial by jury save in exceptional circumstances.

We are further supported in this view by the fact that only two of those who responded to Working Paper No 41 were in favour of extending jury trial.[243]

4.76 Do consultees agree with our provisional view that trial by jury should not be used as a means of providing sample awards for the judicial assessment of non-pecuniary loss?

(3) Greater reliance on medical "scores"

4.77 It has been suggested - albeit with particular reference to the criminal injuries compensation scheme - that a medical model for determining the severity of a plaintiff's injury could form the basis of the assessment of damages for non-pecuniary loss.[244] Under this approach the plaintiff's physical and psychological injury will be scored according to recognised medical scoring systems.[245] Tariff values could then be assigned (by the judiciary or by a Compensation Advisory Board)[246] corresponding to scores of injury severity. The possible benefit of adopting such a model would be in providing a scientific and rational way of *comparing* injuries: that is, while medical scores cannot assist in fixing the general level of damages they could assist in rationalising the different amounts awarded for different injuries. It can also be argued that the scientific basis of the comparison would make the assessment process more straightforward to administer and easier for non-lawyers to understand.[247] On the other hand, it would appear that the medical scoring systems do not take account of the particular characteristics of those injured (for example that the plaintiff who has lost the tip of a finger was a pianist); and, moreover, that they score the injury at the time of the injury and do not therefore take into account the fact that the recovery rate and problems associated with the same injury can vary considerably between individuals (for example, one plaintiff may make a complete recovery from a severely broken wrist while another,

---

[243] (1973) Law Com No 56, para 42.

[244] J Shepherd, P Richmond and D Miers, "Assessing general damages: a medical model" (1994) 144 NLJ 162.

[245] Eg the Glasgow Outcome Score, the Abbreviated Injury Score (AIS), the Injury Severity Score (ISS), the Structured Clinical Interview for PTSD (SCID) and the Clinician Administered PTSD scale (CAPS). See also P Pysent, J Fairbank, A Carr (eds), *Outcome Measures in Orthopaedics* (1993) chapters 5, 12; P Pysent, J Fairbank, A Carr (eds), *Outcome Measures in Trauma* (1994) chapters 2, 3, 10, 24 and 25: we are grateful to Mr A H R W Simpson, Honorary Consultant Orthopaedic Surgeon and Clinical Reader, Oxford University, who was a contributor to the latter book, for his assistance. It should be noted that the use of medical scores for evaluating the extent of a plaintiff's non-pecuniary loss is already the norm for certain types of injury: eg the more common cases of lung disease all have to be related to the Medical Research Council grading system and the appropriate grade, both at trial and for the future, must be established by agreement or ruling. See the JSB *Guidelines*, p 17.

[246] If a legislative tariff were to be introduced, medical scoring could be used to compare awards in fixing the tariff: see para 4.66 above.

[247] J Shepherd, P Richmond and D Miers, "Assessing general damages: a medical model" (1994) 144 NLJ 162.

with exactly the same injury, may continue to suffer pain and disability). A further problem is that some injuries (such as disfigurement or injury to reproductive organs) may be minor in purely medical terms, yet severe when one takes account of their effect on the plaintiff's social relationships (which, under the present law, will be reflected in the damages awarded for suffering and loss of amenity). We are also aware that, while increasingly commonly used by the medical profession, there remains some doubt within that profession as to the validity of at least some of the various scoring systems.

4.78   Even if it is felt that existing scoring systems cannot directly assist the judiciary, we wonder whether it would be possible for a special medical scoring system to be devised for use in assessing damages for personal injury. In other words, just as special actuarial tables were devised specifically to meet the needs of personal injury litigation in the assessment of future pecuniary loss,[248] so it might be possible for existing medical scoring systems to be adapted for use in assessing damages for non-pecuniary loss.

4.79   **We ask consultees, particularly those with the appropriate medical expertise, for their views as to whether greater reliance should be placed on medical scoring systems in comparing awards for non-pecuniary loss. In particular, would it be possible and sensible to devise a special medical scoring system for use in assessing damages for non-pecuniary loss in personal injury cases?**

(4)   Computerised assistance

4.80   One suggestion which could give more help to judges is the use of computers in assessing non-pecuniary loss. Lord Ross has suggested that judges could use computers as an aid to more consistent sentencing in criminal cases.[249] Before passing sentence, judges would be able to see a wide range of information, processed into readily usable statistical form, relating to sentencing and other relevant aspects of trials for similar crimes over the previous five years. A study by the University of Strathclyde into the scheme's feasibility has recently been completed.[250] A similar scheme, giving judges easy access to information on past awards, could be introduced in civil cases, and would tie in with the increasing interest in the use of information technology as a tool serving the administration of justice. An important current example of this interest has been the project, known as Project JUDITH, which the Court Service Development Division of the Lord

---

[248] *Actuarial Tables for Use in Personal Injury and Fatal Accident Cases* (2nd ed 1994) HMSO. See also Structured Settlements and Interim and Provisional Damages (1994) Law Com No 224, paras 2.9-2.23; and para 4.31, n 116 above.

[249] See *The Times*, 18 October 1993.

[250] We understand that the report is to be published shortly.

Chancellor's Department[251] undertook in 1992, in consultation with the Judicial Standing Committee on Information Technology (JSCIT).[252] This involved the investigation of the possibilities available to the judiciary through increased use of computers, and has highlighted the potential for information technology in several areas, including access to reference materials such as precedents. Following these findings, the Lord Chancellor's Department announced that computers would be made available to judges[253] and 300 computers have now been allocated. Lord Woolf, in his review of the civil litigation system, has enthusiastically welcomed the growing role of information technology in the courtroom, particularly in case management.[254] Similar advances have been made in some other jurisdictions.[255] **We ask consultees for their views as to whether greater use could be made of computers as an aid to the more consistent assessment by judges of damages for non-pecuniary loss and, if so, in what precise ways do they envisage computers being used?**

(5) Other ways of assisting the judiciary

4.81 **In addition to the specific questions posed in this section, we ask consultees generally whether there are any other ways, that we have not mentioned, in which (on the assumption that a legislative tariff is not introduced) the judiciary might be assisted in fixing the amounts to be awarded for non-pecuniary loss.**

---

[251] Now the Information Systems Division of the Court Service.

[252] JSCIT was chaired by Neill LJ at the inception of Project JUDITH, and is now chaired by Saville LJ. The project followed a report, *Information Technology for the Judiciary*, produced by MBA Consultants in April 1992.

[253] See *The Daily Telegraph*, 24 March 1994.

[254] *Access to Justice* (1995).

[255] See, eg, the reports of the Colloquies on the Use of Computers in the Administration of Justice, held under the auspices of the Council of Europe.

8. SHOULD DAMAGES BE ASSESSED BY JURIES?

(1) Should the assessment of compensatory damages for personal injury be taken away from juries in all cases?

4.82   We noted in Part II that under section 69 of the Supreme Court Act 1981 a plaintiff has the right to jury trial in claims for libel, slander, malicious prosecution or false imprisonment or where there is a charge of fraud: in all other cases trial must be by judge alone unless the court, in its discretion, orders trial by jury.[256] In *Ward v James*[257] the Court of Appeal said that the court's discretion should almost always be exercised against jury trial in personal injury cases because jury assessment of damages fails to achieve the desirable aims of accessibility, uniformity and predictability. In *H v Ministry of Defence*[258] this proposition was confirmed and strengthened: "Trial by jury is normally inappropriate for any personal injury action in so far as the jury is required to assess compensatory damages, because the assessment of such damages must be based upon or have regard to conventional scales of damages".[259] Indeed the Court of Appeal could not think of a personal injury case in which only compensatory damages were sought where jury trial might be appropriate.

4.83   We agree with these two decisions. Indeed we go further. Given the difficulty of assessing damages for non-pecuniary loss in personal injury cases and the judicial tariff that has been developed to ensure a measure of consistency and uniformity, we consider it unsatisfactory that juries might ever be called upon to assess compensatory damages for personal injury. Juries do not have the benefit of knowledge of the scale of values that has been developed and the inevitable consequence is unacceptable inconsistency with awards in other cases. It is sometimes suggested that a mid-position would be for juries to be provided with the scale of values, while leaving them to fix the precise figure within the tariff. But we see no need in this context for a 'half-way house'. Moreover, in this context we tend to agree with the Court of Appeal's objection to the citing of figures in *Ward v James*.[260] Lord Denning MR said:

---

[256] See para 2.2, n 7 above. For county courts, see s 66 of the County Courts Act 1984.

[257] [1966] 1 QB 273.

[258] [1991] 2 QB 103.

[259] *Ibid*, 112, *per* Lord Donaldson MR giving the judgment of the Court of Appeal, which reversed a decision by Hutchison J who had ordered trial by jury in a case where a major part of the plaintiff's penis had been amputated. *Ward v James* was decided under s 6 of the Administration of Justice (Miscellaneous Provisions) Act 1933 under which there was simply a discretion whether to order jury trial or not. *H v Ministry of Defence* was decided under s 69 of the Supreme Court Act 1981 under which there is a prima facie presumption against jury trial. In the Court of Appeal's view, the change in statutory wording strengthened the presumption against jury trial. See also, generally, *Hendry v Chief Constable of Lancashire Constabulary*, 7 December 1993 (unreported) CA.

[260] [1966] 1 QB 273, 302-303.

Another suggestion is that the jury should be told of the conventional figures in this way, that the judge should be at liberty in his discretion to indicate to the jury the upper and lower limits of the sum which in his view it would be reasonable to award. Thus in the case of the loss of a leg, he might indicate that the conventional figure is between £4,000 and £6,000. This proposal has many attractions. It would give the jury the guidance which they at present lack. But ... we come up against a serious objection. If the judge can mention figures to the jury, then counsel must also be able to mention figures to them ... Each counsel would, in duty bound, pitch the figures as high or as low as he dared. Then the judge would give his views on the rival figures. The proceedings would be in danger of developing into an auction. The objections are so great that both counsel before us agreed that counsel ought not to be at liberty to mention figures to the jury. If this be so, I think that the judge should not do so either.

Apart from this, it seems to me that if the judge were at liberty to mention the upper and lower limits, then in order to be of any real guidance, they would have to be somewhat narrow limits. It would be no use his telling the jury (as judges have done in the past) for the loss of a leg: 'Do be reasonable. Don't give as much as £100,000, or as little as £100.' The judge would have to come nearer home and say: 'The conventional figure in such a case as this is between £4,000 and £6,000.' But if he can give them narrow limits of that kind, there is little point in having a jury at all. You might as well let the judge assess the figure himself.

4.84 It will be a rare case where a personal injury claim is now heard by a jury. Nevertheless, we think it sensible at the outset to state our view that where there is an existing right to trial by jury (for example, where the victim of a false imprisonment also alleges battery) the assessment of damages for personal injury (that is, for a physical injury, disease or illness; or for a recognised psychiatric illness) should be made by the judge and not the jury; and in all other cases where there is at present a discretion to order trial by jury and a jury trial is (exceptionally) ordered, the assessment of damages for personal injury should again be made by the judge and not the jury. So, while the jury can be left free to determine, for example, the appropriate percentage reduction for any contributory negligence, once the jury has found that the plaintiff has suffered the actionable personal injury alleged, the quantum of damages for that injury should be determined by the judge alone. Having said that, we have had some concern whether, in a case where aggravated or exemplary damages are available (for example, where the plaintiff brings a claim for trespass to the person against the police), it might create difficulties to 'hive off' to the judge the assessment of damages for the non-pecuniary and pecuniary loss consequent on the personal injury while leaving the jury to assess aggravated or exemplary damages.[261] But while, in formulating new directions to juries, care will be needed to ensure that the jury is told how much the judge is to award as compensation for the personal injury before it considers aggravated or exemplary damages, we see no insurmountable practical difficulties in taking away the assessment of damages for personal injury from juries. We believe that this is to do nothing more than to recognise that, while in the past the assessment of damages could be regarded as a matter of fact, the development of principles and a scale of values in this field means that it is nowadays better viewed as largely a matter of law.

4.85 **We are therefore of the provisional view that the assessment of compensatory damages for personal injuries should always be a matter for the judge and should never be left to a jury. We ask consultees to say whether they agree with that provisional view.**

(2) Should the assessment of damages in defamation cases be taken away from juries?

4.86 We consider it crucial to this paper to consider the assessment of damages by juries in defamation cases because it is a cause of dissatisfaction with the general level of awards for non-pecuniary loss in personal injury actions that comparatively high levels of damages are awarded for injury to reputation by juries in defamation actions.[262] For instance, a person who loses a leg through amputation can expect a judge in a personal injury action to award a sum in the region of £35,000 to £50,000 as damages for the past and prospective pain, suffering and deprivation such an injury entails;[263] and even the most severe personal injuries, involving permanent paralysis and lifelong dependency on others, will only attract damages for non-pecuniary loss up to a rough maximum of £125,000.[264]

4.87 In contrast, six figure sums far in excess of this are frequently reported by the media as having been awarded by juries to plaintiffs in defamation actions, for injury to feelings and damaged reputation.[265] In May 1989 a jury awarded Sonia Sutcliffe

---

[261] The question of whether exemplary and aggravated damages should be retained and, if so, whether exemplary damages should always be assessed by a judge not a jury was considered in Aggravated, Exemplary and Restitutionary Damages (1993) Law Com Consultation Paper No 132 and will be addressed further in our Report on that subject.

[262] See para 4.28 above.

[263] See, eg, the JSB *Guidelines*, p 35; *White v Estate of Constantino*, 25 October 1989 (CA), *Kemp and Kemp*, vol 3, para I2-206 (£32,500 for a below knee amputation - £44,700 updated to September 1995 for inflation).

[264] Eg the JSB *Guidelines*, pp 5, 6; *Housecroft v Burnett* [1986] 1 All ER 332 (£75,000 for quadriplegia - £119,200 updated to September 1995 for inflation).

[265] See generally Julie Scott-Bayfield, "Libel: Bonanza or Burst Bubble?" (1993) 137 SJ 45; "Back To Basics - Is Libel On The Decline?" (1994) 138 SJ 95; and "Defamation Update" (1995) 139 SJ 189. We are aware that juries often do award lesser sums and that the following awards are not necessarily typical. They are, however, useful illustrations of

£600,000 damages in her action against the publishers of *Private Eye* magazine. In July 1989, a jury awarded two plaintiffs in *Tobias v Association Newspapers*[266] £250,000 and £200,000 respectively. In November 1989 Lord Aldington was awarded damages of a record £1,500,000 against the historian Count Tolstoy and his publisher Nigel Watts.[267] A jury awarded Teresa Gorman MP the sum of £150,000 in July 1991.[268] The plaintiff in *Smith v Houston* (unreported) was awarded damages for slander of £150,000 by a jury in October 1991.[269] In December 1991 the jury awarded broadcaster Esther Rantzen £250,000 in her libel action against Mirror Group Newspapers.[270] In March 1992, the jury awarded the plaintiff in *Telnikoff v Matusevich* (unreported) £240,000. In April 1992 actor and singer Jason Donovan was awarded libel damages of £200,000 against *The Face* magazine. In May 1992 the jury awarded the plaintiff in *Said v Baki* (unreported) £400,000 libel damages. In November 1993 a jury awarded singer Elton John £75,000 compensatory damages (plus £275,000 exemplary damages)[271] in his libel action against *The Sunday Mirror*. In July 1994 a jury awarded one of the plaintiffs in *Walker and Wingsail Systems v Yachting World and IPC Magazines* (unreported) £450,000 in damages.[272] In June 1995 a jury awarded football manager Graham Souness damages of £750,000 against Mirror Group Newspapers.[273]

the sums that juries are *capable* of awarding. A climate of high awards may also serve to encourage high settlements: eg in December 1988, Elton John settled a number of libel actions against *The Sun* newspaper in the sum of £1 million (including costs).

[266] 28 July 1989 (unreported). The plaintiffs were directors of a third plaintiff, a sales trading company, which was awarded £20,000.

[267] The case came before the European Court of Human Rights in *Tolstoy Miloslavsky v United Kingdom* [1995] 20 EHRR 442. The Court found unanimously that, having regard to the size of the award in conjunction with the state of English law at the relevant time, there had been a violation of Count Tolstoy's right to freedom of expression under Article 10 of the European Convention on Human Rights. Note that at the relevant time, the Court of Appeal had no power to substitute its own award for that of the jury; it now has that power under s 8(2) of the Courts and Legal Services Act 1990 (see para 4.91 below).

[268] *Gorman v Mudd* (unreported). This sum was reduced on appeal in October 1992 to £50,000.

[269] This sum was reduced on appeal to £50,000 on 16 December 1993. See para 4.91, n 290 below.

[270] This sum was reduced on appeal in March 1993 to £110,000: *Rantzen v Mirror Group Newspapers Ltd* [1994] QB 670. See para 4.91 below.

[271] To the best of our knowledge, this is the highest ever award of exemplary damages in this country. We understand that an appeal on quantum is pending.

[272] See *The Times*, 9 July 1994, page 1, column e. Damages were comprised as follows: £450,000 and £35,000 respectively to John Walker and Jean Walker, the directors of Wingsail Systems, and £1 million to the company. We understand that, the defendants having appealed, the parties have now settled in the sum of £260,000 including undisclosed costs (see *The Guardian*, 14 November 1995, s 2, p 13). We do not know how the balance of the settlement was apportioned between the plaintiffs.

[273] *The Times*, 16 June 1995, page 1, and see para 4.92(i) below. Mirror Group Newspapers appealed on quantum and the parties settled in the sum of £100,000: see *The Daily Telegraph*, 8 November 1995, page 2.

4.88   Although it is possible that, in some of the above cases, the juries were including awards for a pecuniary loss suffered by the plaintiff (or that damages were exemplary and not compensatory)[274] we consider that, in the absence of proof of pecuniary loss and in the absence of reference by the judge to pecuniary loss (or to exemplary damages), one is entitled to regard the above awards as essentially being made for loss of reputation (and injury to feelings) as a non-pecuniary loss. They can therefore be legitimately contrasted with the lower awards made for non-pecuniary loss in personal injury cases. The disparity between the sums of compensation awarded offends the proper relationship which ought to exist between pain, suffering and loss of amenity on the one hand and loss of reputation and injury to feelings on the other. A "wrong scale of values" is being applied. As Diplock LJ said in *McCarey v Associated Newspapers Ltd (No 2)*:[275]

> In putting a money value on these kinds of injury, as the law requires damage-awarding tribunals to do, they are being required to attempt to equate the incommensurable. As in the case of damages for physical injuries, it is impossible to say that any answer looked at in isolation is right, or that any answer is wrong. But justice is not justice if it is arbitrary or whimsical, if what is awarded to one plaintiff for an injury bears no relation at all to what is awarded to another plaintiff for an injury of the same kind, or, I would add, if what is awarded for one kind of injury shows a wrong scale of values when compared with what is awarded for injuries of a different kind which are also incommensurable with pounds, shillings and pence.

This line of reasoning led Diplock LJ to conclude that:

> It is, I think, legitimate as an aid to considering whether the award of damages by a jury is so large that no reasonable jury could have arrived at that figure if they had applied proper principles, to bear in mind the kind of figures which are proper, and have been held to be proper, in cases of disabling physical injury.[276]

This is also the view now taken by the High Court of Australia. Mason CJ and Deane J, in their dissenting judgment in *Coyne v Citizen Finance Ltd*, said:[277]

---

[274] However, we understand that in none of the above cases was there a claim for pecuniary loss or (with the exception of the Elton John and Teresa Gorman cases) exemplary damages. In Teresa Gorman's case the jury declined to award exemplary damages.

[275] [1965] 2 QB 86, 108C-E. See also *Groom v Crocker* [1939] 1 KB 194, 231, *per* MacKinnon LJ (contrasting the "frequent niggardliness of verdicts in cases of personal injury" with the "invariable profuseness in claims for defamation").

[276] *McCarey v Associated Newspapers Ltd (No 2)* [1965] 2 QB 86, 109G-110A.

[277] (1991) 172 CLR 211, 221.

... it would be quite wrong for an appellate court, entrusted with hearing appeals in both defamation and personal injury cases, to be indifferent to the need to ensure that there was a rational relationship between the scale of values applied in the two classes of case.

This approach was then approved by a bare majority of the High Court of Australia (including Mason CJ and Deane J)[278] in *Carson v John Fairfax & Sons Ltd.*[279] Moreover, the majority did not confine its comments to appellate courts but went on to say:

...we see no significant danger in permitting trial judges to provide to the jury an indication of the ordinary level of the general damages component of personal injury awards for comparative purposes, nor in counsel being permitted to make a similar reference.[280]

Similarly in *Broome v Cassell*[281] Lord Diplock commented that "an evanescent sense of grievance at the defendant's conduct is often grossly over-valued in comparison with a lifelong deprivation due to physical injuries caused by negligence." The same criticism has been made by politicians and others,[282] and it has also led the victims of personal injury themselves[283] and those representing their interests[284] to argue

---

[278] The other two judges in the majority were Dawson and Gaudron JJ: Brennan, Toohey and McHugh JJ dissented.

[279] (1993) 178 CLR 44.

[280] *Ibid*, 59. However, on the rehearing of the case (which was limited to the question of damages) the trial judge, Levine J, refused to apply this dictum: see *Carson v John Fairfax & Sons Ltd* (1994) 34 NSWLR 72. From 1 January 1995 legislation in New South Wales lays down that the trial judge and not the jury should determine the amount of damages in a defamation case and the trial judge, in assessing such damages, is required to take account of the general range of damages for non-pecuniary loss in personal injury awards in New South Wales: see ss 7A and 46A of the Defamation Act 1984 (NSW) as inserted by the Defamation (Amendment) Act 1994 (NSW). See also the New South Wales Law Reform Commission, Report 75, Defamation (1995), paras 1.10-1.12, 3.1-3.34, 7.1-7.18.

[281] [1972] AC 1027, 1130H.

[282] Eg *Hansard* (HL) 9 March 1992, vol 536, cols 1167 (Lord Irvine of Lairg) and 1167-1168 (Baroness Phillips); P Gegan, "Publish - and be not damned" (1994) 144 NLJ 983; Initial Response to Item 11 by the Civil Litigation Committee of the Law Society; and numerous newspaper editorials criticising large defamation awards, eg, *The Daily Mail*, 5 November 1993, p 8. See also *Hansard* (HL) 22 February 1994, vol 552, col 510.

[283] See, eg, (1994) Law Com No 225, para 11.4, p 207.

[284] Eg CITCOM and the promoters of the Citizens' Compensation Bill 1989: *Hansard* (HC) 3 March 1989, vol 148, col 516 (L Cunliffe MP). During the Second Reading of the Bill, Sir Hal Miller MP referred to the existence of "a widespread feeling" that damages for personal injury simply do not match those awarded in libel cases, whilst Mr John Evans MP said that "most people are outraged by" this disparity: *ibid*, cols 523, 568-569. But note that the contrast between awards for defamation and personal injury is usually referred to unfavourably *by judges* in order to suggest that awards for defamation are too high, rather than to suggest that awards for personal injury are too low.

with some force that the general level of awards for non-pecuniary loss in personal injury actions is, by comparison to that in defamation cases, too low.

4.89 On the other hand, the prevailing English judicial approach is that a valid comparison cannot be made between personal injury awards and damages for defamation and it is impermissible for juries in defamation cases to be referred to awards made for personal injury.[285] It has been emphasised, for example, that defamation awards include a vindicatory element: the plaintiff "must be able to point to a sum ... sufficient to convince a by-stander of the baselessness of the charge".[286] Furthermore, damages for defamation may be (and often are) aggravated, and hence increased, because of the defendant's conduct, which typically involves a repetition of the libel complained of, a renewed attack upon the plaintiff's character, or an exacerbation of the injury by, for example, robust cross-examination at trial. In contrast, aggravated damages cannot be awarded in a standard personal injury action based on negligence.[287] Thus, although it is true that both types of action involve losses which cannot be calculated precisely by reference to the market, it can be argued that the basis and measure of compensation is fundamentally different.

4.90 However, we do not believe that such counter-arguments can explain entirely, or indeed justify, a practice "whereby a plaintiff in an action for libel may recover a much larger sum by way of damages for an injury to his reputation, which may

---

[285] *Broome v Cassell* [1972] AC 1027, 1070G-1071F; *Blackshaw v Lord* [1984] 1 QB 1, 31, 39, 43; *Sutcliffe v Pressdram Ltd* [1991] 1 QB 153, 175D-F, 186A-C, 189; *Rantzen v Mirror Group Newspapers Ltd* [1994] QB 670, 694C-695H; Supreme Court Procedure Committee's *Report on Practice and Procedure in Defamation* (the Neill Committee), July 1991, para XXIII 9. See also Lord Donaldson's comments in *The Legal Executive Journal*, December 1992, p 19. Non-compensatory exemplary damages may also be awarded for defamation in certain circumstances. Even where they are not strictly available, the notion of deterrence may yet have more significance in defamation actions if it is felt that the availability of only small sums of compensation would enable wealthy newspapers to publish defamatory statements with impunity: see *Hansard* (HL) 9 March 1992, vol 536, col 1167 (Lord Rawlinson). Note that defamation actions very rarely include a claim for pecuniary loss. Professor Street, *Principles of the Law of Damages* (1962) p 4, has suggested that it may therefore be considered less important that awards for non-pecuniary loss are kept to a minimum.

[286] *Broome v Cassell* [1972] AC 1027, 1070G-1071F, *per* Lord Hailsham. We doubt whether the need for a "vindicatory element" requires more than that the plaintiff is fairly compensated for his or her loss of reputation. Moreover, an award for pecuniary loss will tend to distort any vindicatory role played by the non-pecuniary damages. In any event, if vindication is really thought crucial, a form of declaratory relief would appear to afford a more flexible and precise way of achieving that vindication.

[287] *Kralj v McGrath* [1986] 1 All ER 54, 61E-G (cited with approval by Stuart-Smith LJ in *AB v South West Water Services Ltd* [1993] QB 507, 527H-528E). But a plaintiff suffering personal injury may be awarded aggravated damages where the defendant's conduct is such as to amount to some other nominate tort, for instance battery or false imprisonment, eg *W v Meah* [1986] 1 All ER 935. See further, Aggravated, Exemplary and Restitutionary Damages (1993) Law Com Consultation Paper No 132, paras 3.4, 3.12-3.14, 3.30 and 6.53.

prove transient in its effect, than the damages awarded for pain and suffering to the victim of an industrial accident who has lost an eye or the use of one or more of his limbs."[288] We find it understandable that members of the public should make this comparison and we accept the force of the criticism that it is wrong for the law to appear to convey the message that reputations are valued more highly than are lives and limbs. We also think it fair to assume that, even if the principles for assessing compensation are different, a judge is still more likely to make lower awards for defamation than is a jury.[289] It is difficult to explain some of the very large sums awarded by juries in defamation actions even as aggravated compensatory damages. Moreover, we are concerned that the continuation of the present system of assessment of damages by juries in defamation actions will undermine any steps taken to raise the levels of damages for pain, suffering and loss of amenity; even if, for example, one were to uplift personal injury damages at a stroke, higher and unpredictable levels of damages awarded by juries in defamation cases will continue to lead to unfavourable comparisons being drawn and, in time, will inevitably lead to the assertion (again) that personal injury damages are too low.

4.91   Two fairly recent developments are of importance on this issue. First, under section 8 of the Courts and Legal Services Act 1990 the Court of Appeal has been given the power to substitute its own sum for that awarded by a jury.[290] In the past, unless both parties consented, the Court of Appeal was restricted to ordering a new trial where the damages awarded by the jury were excessive. Secondly, the Court of Appeal in *Rantzen v Mirror Group Newspapers Ltd*[291] held that the threshold for interfering with jury awards should be lowered from that traditionally insisted on so as properly to protect freedom of expression as required by Article 10 of the European Convention on Human Rights.[292] The Court envisaged that awards made by it, in exercising its new power under section 8 of the 1990 Act, could be regarded as establishing the prescribed norm to which the jury could be referred in

---

[288] *Rantzen v Mirror Group Newspapers Ltd* [1994] QB 670, 695F, *per* Neill LJ, delivering the judgment of the Court of Appeal.

[289] Note that one of the reasons why the Court of Appeal refuses to look at sums awarded in personal injury actions when reviewing damages for defamation is that the former are assessed by a judge, the latter by a jury: *Sutcliffe v Pressdram Ltd* [1991] 1 QB 153, 175F-176A, 181F-186C, 189H-190E.

[290] RSC, Ord 59, r 11(4), made under s 8 of the Courts and Legal Services Act 1990, provides that "[i]n any case where the Court of Appeal has power to order a new trial on the ground that damages awarded by a jury are excessive or inadequate, the court may, instead of ordering a new trial, substitute for the sum awarded by the jury such sum as appears to the court to be proper ...." The Court of Appeal has on several occasions exercised this new power: for example, the award of £250,000 to Esther Rantzen was reduced to £110,000 in March 1993; and in December 1993 the award in *Smith v Houston* (unreported) was reduced from £150,000 to £50,000 (see para 4.87 above).

[291] [1994] QB 670.

[292] The courts must "subject large awards of damages to a more searching scrutiny than has been customary in the past. It follows that what has been regarded as the barrier against intervention should be lowered...": *ibid*, 692G.

subsequent defamation cases, thereby enabling a tariff to be developed. Until such a corpus has been established, the jury should be directed to consider the purchasing power of any award and asked to ensure that any award is proportionate to the harm to the plaintiff and is a sum which it is necessary to award in order to provide adequate compensation and to vindicate his or her reputation.[293]

4.92   It may be that, in time, the approach in *Rantzen* will stop excessive awards by juries. But three problems with that approach suggest themselves to us:

(i)   No substantial corpus of Court of Appeal decisions, and therefore no tariff, has yet been established. We doubt whether, in the meantime, the directions set out in the preceding paragraph are sufficient to curb excessive awards, for experience shows that the tendency of juries to award large sums of libel damages continues unabated: the awards of £450,000 to one of the plaintiffs in *Walker and Wingsail Systems v Yachting World and IPC Magazines* (unreported) in July 1994[294] and £750,000 to Graham Souness in June 1995[295] post-dated section 8 of the Courts and Legal Services Act 1990 and the *Rantzen* decision.

(ii)   It will not be easy to develop a tariff in the context of defamation because of the widely differing fact situations involved. The tariff will need to take account of, for example, the scale of publication, the conduct of the defendant and the nature of the libel. Indeed to expect the Court of Appeal (without the assistance of the decisions of judges at first instance) to develop a helpful tariff from the limited number of cases it hears may be too optimistic.

(iii)   We have doubts whether the establishment of such a tariff will in any event inhibit excessive awards, for juries will not be bound by the tariff, which will be merely for their guidance. It is true that any award in excess of the prescribed norm will be liable to be reduced on appeal, but we believe that defendants ought not as a matter of course to be put to the additional expense of an appeal in order to secure a just adjudication. This view was shared by the Irish Law Commission in its Report on the Civil Law of Defamation,[296] where it said:

>   ...it seems to us unsatisfactory in principle to defend the present law under which disproportionate awards are made with a significant degree of

---

[293]   *Ibid*, 694-696.

[294]   See para 4.87 above.

[295]   See para 4.87 above.

[296]   (December 1991) para 10.3.

frequency on the ground that the resulting injustice can always be remedied on appeal.

We therefore conclude that the Court of Appeal's decision in the *Rantzen* case has not yet had and is unlikely to have the desired effect of curbing excessive awards by juries in cases of defamation.

4.93 It remains to be seen what effect, if any, the Lord Chancellor's proposals for the reform of defamation proceedings[297] may have upon reducing levels of damages for defamation and hence the objectionable disparity with personal injury awards. We note that the Draft Defamation Bill does not address directly the issues of trial by jury and jury determination of awards.[298] But, if the proposed summary procedure (for less serious cases) and offer of amends defence operate effectively, the incidence of jury trial in defamation actions may be significantly reduced.

4.94 Irrespective of our particular concern about the disparity between damages for defamation and personal injury damages, we believe that it is important for us to consider more general arguments as to whether juries should assess damages in defamation cases. The Faulks Committee[299] recommended that damages should be assessed by the judge in all defamation actions.[300] It identified eleven arguments against the trial of defamation actions by jury.[301] Confining ourselves here to the *assessment of damages* by juries, the following five of the eleven arguments of the Faulks Committee seem to us to be relevant and valid:

(i) *A jury is more likely than a judge to be influenced by irrelevancies and to give disproportionate weight to emotional factors.* For example, in cases where exemplary damages have not been sought, commentators frequently identify what they perceive to be a punitive element in jury awards.

---

[297] *Reforming Defamation Law and Procedure*, Consultation on Draft Bill, Lord Chancellor's Dept (July 1995).

[298] Although the Consultation Paper envisages at para 3.5 that assessment of damages where the defendant has made an offer of amends will always be a matter for the judge alone. See also cl 3(7) of the Draft Bill.

[299] *Report of the Committee on Defamation* (March 1975) Cmnd 5909, ch 17.

[300] *Ibid,* para 457. The Faulks Committee thought that, where a defamation case was tried by jury, the jury's function in the assessment of quantum should be limited to stipulating whether damages should be substantial, moderate, nominal or contemptuous: *ibid,* para 513. Note that although the question of juries was outside its terms of reference, the Supreme Court Procedure Committee's *Report on Practice and Procedure in Defamation* (the Neill Committee, July 1991) nevertheless recommended (at para XXIII.7) that the assessment of damages for *financial* loss should be reserved to the judge rather than the jury. In New South Wales, the trial judge and not the jury now determines, in defamation cases, whether any defence was established and the amount of damages: see para 4.88, n 280 above.

[301] (1975) Cmnd 5909, para 454.

(ii)   *(a) The parties benefit from the reasoned judgment of a judge, since it is easier for
        an unsuccessful party to decide whether to appeal. (b) The public benefits from the
        reporting of judicial reasoning, which makes for greater certainty.* We agree with
        argument (a), while acknowledging that it perhaps holds less weight following
        the lowering of the threshold for allowing an appeal against an excessive award
        in the *Rantzen* case. We agree with argument (b). Reasoned judgments at
        first instance would facilitate the development of a corpus of law relating to
        the assessment of quantum, akin to publications such as *Kemp and Kemp* in
        the field of damages for personal injury. A greater measure of certainty will
        encourage reasonable out-of-court settlements, especially where liability is not
        in issue.

(iii)   *The unpredictability of jury awards results in plaintiffs with weak cases being
        advised that they have a better prospect of success with a jury than with a judge
        sitting alone. Lawyers recommend negotiation with a view to settlement. This
        climate encourages gold-digging and blackmail.* While we doubt whether any
        legal adviser would encourage a client to proceed with a claim knowing it to
        be without merit, we acknowledge that the above considerations do indeed
        motivate a certain type of litigant in bringing the action in the first instance.
        In such cases, proceedings having commenced, positions may become
        entrenched and a negotiated settlement unachievable. We consider that this
        argument applies with equal force in so far as the jury's unpredictability *in
        assessing quantum* is concerned.

(iv)   *A jury's award of damages is likely to be excessive or unpredictably higher than the
        award of a judge, who has a wide knowledge of the previous awards of juries and
        of judges sitting alone.* We agree. Although the jury can now be referred to
        previous decisions of the Court of Appeal,[302] the Court of Appeal's guidance
        is of merely persuasive authority. Nor can the jury be referred to the
        decisions of other juries in libel cases[303] or to the tariff of awards in personal
        injury cases.[304]

(v)   *The routine trial of defamation cases by judges sitting alone would quickly build up
        a body of precedent forming a generally reliable scale of damages.* Although the
        widely differing fact situations mean that the development of a tariff will not
        be straightforward, we consider that a workable tariff is likely to develop from
        a combination of the decisions of judges at first instance and guidelines set out
        by the Court of Appeal.

---

[302] *Rantzen v Mirror Group Newspapers Ltd* [1994] QB 670. See para 4.91 above.

[303] *Sutcliffe v Pressdram Ltd* [1991] 1 QB 153, 178C-179D, 186E-F; *Rantzen v Mirror Group
      Newspapers Ltd* [1994] QB 670, 694C-696G.

[304] *Sutcliffe v Pressdram Ltd* [1991] 1 QB 153, 178C-179D, 186A-C; *Rantzen v Mirror Group
      Newspapers Ltd* [1994] QB 670, 694C-695G.

Of the remaining six arguments identified by the Faulks Committee as militating against juries in defamation actions, four seem inapplicable to the assessment of quantum,[305] a fifth is unpersuasive,[306] while the sixth has been addressed by section 8 of the Courts and Legal Services Act 1990 and the *Rantzen* case.[307]

4.95 Arguments (i) to (x) of the eleven arguments identified by the Faulks Committee *in favour of* the retention of the jury in defamation actions[308] appear to us either to carry no real force or to have force only in relation to the determination of liability. We have considered but, for the reason to be stated, reject the remaining argument:

> *Damages awarded by a jury are more likely to be adequate compensation than the award of a judge.* They are also more likely to be excessive.

4.96 However, whatever the strength of the arguments against the assessment of damages by juries, it must be seriously questioned whether the Faulks Committee's proposal[309] to separate the respective roles of the jury (which would decide liability) and judge (who would decide quantum) is workable in the sphere of defamation. In response to the objection that it would be invidious to allow the possibility of a jury deciding for liability purposes that the loss of reputation was slight, while the

---

[305] *Viz:* (a) the selection of jury members cannot be relied upon to produce sufficiently sophisticated juries; (b) a jury can easily assume that admitted antagonism is evidence of malice; (c) other things being equal, jury trial is more expensive than trial by a judge sitting alone; and (d) the right (subject to s 69 of the Supreme Court Act 1981) of either party to insist on a jury is an unreasonable imposition on the jury. See (1975) Cmnd 5909, para 454 B, sub-paras (i), (iii), (vi), (x) and (xi).

[306] *Viz*: the increasing number of cases where both parties have agreed upon trial by judge alone suggests a large measure of confidence in this forum.

[307] *Viz:* the Court of Appeal could only set aside a jury's verdict in very limited circumstances, whereas a judge's verdict was more easily susceptible to variation on appeal. See (1975) Cmnd 5909, para 454 B, sub-para (vii).

[308] (1975) Cmnd 5909, para 454 A: (i) juries drawn from different walks of life are more likely than a judge to arrive at a true appreciation of the facts; (ii) a jury is better equipped than a judge to assess the meaning of allegedly defamatory words; (iii) a jury is a more reliable instrument than a judge to assess the merits of matters in issue affecting the honour and integrity of an individual and a majority verdict affords greater flexibility in marginal cases; (iv) the public lacks confidence in the opinions of judges, who are assumed to be out of touch; (v) jury service associates the public with the administration of justice, so that a jury's verdict carries greater weight than that of a judge; (vi) a jury's verdict is a verdict of the public and not of the establishment; (vii) a jury's verdict is anonymous, while a judge's verdict is attributed to him personally; (viii) the power of the press and broadcast media is so overwhelming that only juries can redress the balance in favour of the small man; (ix) judges should always appear to be detached from political or religious issues, such as may arise unexpectedly in defamation cases; and (x) a losing party more willingly accepts a jury's verdict than that of a judge and the fact that a jury does not give reasons normally makes its verdict conclusive.

[309] See para 4.94 above.

judge for quantum purposes takes the view that the loss of reputation was serious,[310] the Faulks Committee recommended that the jury should have the power to state whether damages should be substantial, moderate, nominal or contemptuous.[311] An initial question is whether those four categories are satisfactory. This was discussed by the Irish Law Commission.[312] Having recommended that the function of assessing damages should be transferred from juries to judges,[313] that Commission reconsidered its provisional recommendation that the jury should continue to determine whether damages should be nominal, compensatory or exemplary, on the ground that the distinction between the categories is not easy to draw. It detected a punitive element in many cases where, strictly speaking, exemplary damages should not have been awarded. It also thought that complications could arise where appeals were taken both from the jury's categorisation and the judge's assessment.[314] It therefore recommended that the jury should have the power merely to indicate that the case is an appropriate one for nominal (that is, contemptuous) damages.[315]

4.97   It has to be doubted, however, whether these kinds of categories can make much sense unless the jury can put figures on what it understands by, for example, a 'nominal' or 'moderate' award. And that, of course, would tend to defeat the whole point of the split in function.

4.98   Several libel lawyers have further impressed upon us that there is an even more serious problem in attempting to split liability and quantum in the context of defamation. Two leading libel silks put it to us in this way:

> It is not possible to divorce the issue of liability from that of quantum because a defendant who unsuccessfully pleads justification is nonetheless entitled to rely on matters adduced in support of his plea of justification in order to mitigate the amount of the damages: *Pamplin v Express Newspapers Ltd*.[316] This principle (which arises in a large proportion of contested libel actions) strongly suggests that the same tribunal should decide both quantum and liability. If the judge has to decide damages but not liability, how is he expected to know how much, if any, of the plea of justification was accepted by the jury as the tribunal dealing with liability?

[310] See the *Report of the Committee on Defamation* (the Faulks Committee) (March 1975) Cmnd 5909, para 512.

[311] *Ibid*, paras 455(c), 457, 512 and 513; and see para 4.94, n 300 above.

[312] *Report on the Civil Law of Defamation* (December 1991).

[313] *Ibid*, para 10.3.

[314] *Ibid*, para 10.4.

[315] *Ibid*, paras 10.4, 10.6(2).

[316] [1988] 1 WLR 116.

4.99   It may be thought that one way forward would be for the judge to ask the jury
         questions framed so as to elicit the jury's findings of fact in relation to the libel.
         However, in our preliminary conversations with leading practitioners, one recurring
         observation was that such an exercise would be akin to setting the jury an "exam
         paper", which in some cases could only be answered by an "essay" which could take
         days for the jury to draft. Moreover, judges' questions may not correspond to the
         way in which juries actually arrive at their verdicts. The jury's conclusion may be
         impressionistic and determined by factors which are difficult for it to articulate:
         juries tend to 'fudge' the issues. In any event, the jury is *entitled* to bring in a
         general verdict. We were told that the task of answering the judge's questions
         would not only be time-consuming but would tend to reveal contradictions and
         inconsistencies between jurors' views and therefore to undermine their decision.

4.100   **In the light of these problems - and subject to the views of consultees - we
         have reluctantly reached the provisional view that the Faulks Committee's
         recommendation to split the determination of liability and damages between
         jury and judge in defamation cases is unworkable. Nevertheless, we would
         welcome views, particularly from lawyers with relevant practical experience,
         as to whether there is any solution to the difficulties that we have referred
         to in splitting the determination of liability and damages between jury and
         judge in defamation cases.**

4.101   The question that is then posed is whether there is anything that we can recommend
         in this project to avoid the unsatisfactory disparity between personal injury awards
         and awards in defamation cases. Clearly the radical solution would be to remove
         altogether the right to jury trial in defamation cases (which was a further
         recommendation of the Faulks Committee).[317] But that raises fundamental and
         wide-ranging questions, including constitutional ones relating to free speech, that
         we cannot sensibly and properly address within this project which is concerned with
         damages, not liability.

4.102   One reform, which we provisionally believe would help matters, would be for juries
         to be informed of the levels of award for non-pecuniary loss in personal injury cases.
         Although, as we have seen,[318] the contrary view has often been taken, we believe
         that justice requires that a relationship of proportionality ought to exist between
         awards for non-pecuniary loss in different causes of action. This relationship ought
         to be determined by reference to the relative seriousness of the respective types of
         injury. If for example juries were told that the highest award for non-pecuniary loss
         in the most serious and tragic personal injury case is, say, £125,000, we believe that
         this would have some 'chilling effect' on their awards for defamation. Indeed

---

[317] *Report of the Committee on Defamation* (March 1975) Cmnd 5909, paras 455, 456, 516(a).

[318] See para 4.89 above.

reference to personal injury awards has five advantages over the Court of Appeal's approach in the *Rantzen* case, whereby the tariff developed by the Court of Appeal in defamation cases, once established, will be cited to juries:

(i)   The tariff for non-pecuniary loss in personal injury cases is already in place and well-established.

(ii) The information necessary for the judge to direct the jury on the personal injury tariff is now easily accessible to a judge through the Judicial Studies Board's *Guidelines for the Assessment of General Damages in Personal Injury Cases*.

(iii) As one is not *precisely* comparing like with like, it will not matter much which precise personal injuries are chosen by the judge, although we would envisage that the brackets for a broad range of injuries would be given to the jury. In contrast, one can expect serious difficulties and disputes in applying the defamation tariff, as to where on the tariff the particular case falls.

(iv) A jury is more likely to be cautious once it is made aware of the awards that have been given in personal injury cases because, at least at the top end of the personal injury tariff, one is dealing with cases that indisputably justify higher compensation than cases concerned merely with loss of reputation.

(v)   This reform would precisely meet our central aim of ensuring a sense of proportion between damages for defamation and damages for non-pecuniary loss in personal injury cases, so that the former does not distort the latter.

Of course a jury will be free to ignore the personal injury tariff irrespective of the judge's direction: but we consider that this reform is likely to have some beneficial effect in moderating awards for defamation made by juries.

4.103 **Our provisional view, therefore, is that a judge in directing the jury in relation to the assessment of damages in a defamation case should inform the jury of the range of awards for non-pecuniary loss in personal injury cases as is conveniently set out in the Judicial Studies Board's *Guidelines for the Assessment of General Damages in Personal Injury Cases*. Indeed, we think that the same approach should be applied in any other (non-defamation) case where a jury is required to assess damages for non-pecuniary loss (for example, for malicious prosecution or false imprisonment). We would welcome the views of consultees as to whether they agree with this proposed reform.**

4.104 A further suggestion that has been made to us by a leading libel silk is that there should be a statutory ceiling on awards for non-pecuniary loss in defamation cases.

The maximum sum could be automatically up-dated annually for inflation and/or made subject to periodic review by the Lord Chancellor. Even if, contrary to our provisional opinion, one prefers the view that it is misleading to cite the range of personal injury awards to a jury in a defamation case, one may support the introduction of a statutory ceiling. An advantage of a statutory ceiling, over merely citing personal injury scales to the jury, is that the jury could not then exceed the limit set. As against that, it might be thought difficult to fix an acceptable limit (although, if one believes, as we do, in there being a valid comparison to be made between non-pecuniary loss in personal injury and defamation cases, one obvious possibility would be to take the highest award for non-pecuniary loss in personal injury cases which, as at June 1994, was around £125,000). **We would welcome views as to whether there should be a statutory ceiling on awards for non-pecuniary loss in defamation cases and, if so, what the appropriate maximum sum should be and how it should be kept up-to-date.**

9. SHOULD INTEREST BE AWARDED ON DAMAGES FOR NON-PECUNIARY LOSS AND, IF SO, HOW MUCH INTEREST?

4.105 Once damages have been assessed, there remains the question of the principles which ought to govern the award of interest upon them. We noted above[319] that the award of interest upon damages for personal injury is compulsory, unless there are special reasons to the contrary, but that the court is given a discretion as to what part(s) of the total award should carry interest, in respect of what period and at what rate. In relation to that part of the plaintiff's damages which represents non-pecuniary loss, the present guideline developed by the courts for the exercise of this discretion is that interest should be awarded on the whole sum at a rate of 2 per cent from the date of service of the writ until the date of trial.[320] The issues which arise for consideration, and which are to some degree interdependent, are:

(1) **Should interest be awarded on damages for non-pecuniary loss at all?**

(2) **If so, should interest be awarded only on that part of the damages which represents the plaintiff's pre-trial non-pecuniary loss?**

(3) **Should the date of service of the writ be the date from which interest is payable?**

(4) **Is the current rate of 2 per cent satisfactory?**

---

[319] See para 2.41 above.

[320] See para 2.47 above.

(1) Should interest be awarded on damages for non-pecuniary loss at all?

4.106   Section 35A of the Supreme Court Act 1981 confers a discretion on the High Court as to *what part* of the plaintiff's damages for personal injury should carry interest.[321] That interest should be given on pre-trial pecuniary loss has never seriously been questioned in recent years. But the award of interest on the non-pecuniary part of personal injury damages is more controversial. In Ireland, for instance, the relevant statutory provisions preclude the award of interest on damages for non-pecuniary loss.[322] In 1973, this Commission recommended that no interest should be awarded in respect of non-pecuniary loss and,[323] on the basis of our reasoning, the Court of Appeal in *Cookson v Knowles*[324] adopted a rule of practice to this effect. The rationale was that, since damages for non-pecuniary loss are already adjusted for inflation, an award of interest on them allowed the plaintiff to gain twice and was therefore unfair to the defendant.

4.107   This argument based on inflation has been exposed as fallacious by the Pearson Commission[325] and the House of Lords in *Pickett v British Rail Engineering Ltd*.[326] Nevertheless, the Pearson Commission was still able to come to the conclusion that interest should not be awarded.[327] It did so on two grounds. First, in times of high inflation an investor cannot generally expect to do much more than maintain the real value of his or her investment, once inflation and tax are taken into account. As damages for non-pecuniary loss are assessed according to values at the time of trial, to award no interest on non-pecuniary damages might be at least as favourable as the award of interest at a market rate on damages for past pecuniary loss. Secondly, to apply detailed financial calculations to what the Commission regarded as essentially arbitrary figures for non-pecuniary loss was regarded as inappropriate. In any case, allowance would have to be made for inflation in selecting the appropriate interest rate and in principle this should then be applied only to pre-trial non-pecuniary loss, which would be difficult and highly artificial. It has similarly been argued by Harvey McGregor QC that the award for pain and suffering and loss of amenities must be in the nature of a conventional sum and to award interest upon such a conventional sum becomes supererogatory.[328]

---

[321]   Section 69 of the County Courts Act 1984 confers the same discretion on the county court.

[322]   Section 22(2)(i) and (ii) of the Courts Act 1981. See para 3.18 above. See also para 3.27 above (Western Australia) and para 3.65 above (United States).

[323]   (1973) Law Com No 56, paras 273-277, 286. See para 2.43 above.

[324]   [1977] QB 913.

[325]   Pearson Report, vol 1, para 746.

[326]   [1980] AC 136. See para 2.44 above.

[327]   Pearson Report, vol 1, paras 747-748.

[328]   *McGregor on Damages* (15th ed 1988) para 597. This point was also put to us by Dr McGregor in 1971: see (1973) Law Com No 56, para 274.

4.108　The Pearson Commission's first argument, concerning the effect of inflation upon interest rates, can be addressed by lowering the *rate* of interest which is payable upon the plaintiff's non-pecuniary damages,[329] rather than by excluding interest altogether. Indeed, this is the basis of the Court of Appeal's decision in *Birkett v Hayes*[330] (subsequently approved by the House of Lords in *Wright v British Railways Board*).[331] Moreover, the defendant has still had the use of the plaintiff's money.[332]

4.109　In relation to the second point, Professor Waddams has argued that the conventional nature of a sum of damages does not seem in itself sufficient reason for depriving the plaintiff of interest when the sum is not paid:

> Conventional though the sum may be, the plaintiff was still entitled to have it paid promptly; the plaintiff suffers a loss and the defendant reaps a gain from its unjust retention. Indeed, it seems to add insult to injury to say to a plaintiff: 'The law recognises that this conventional sum is quite inadequate compensation for serious bodily injury; and for that reason you are not even entitled to interest on it if it is wrongfully withheld.'[333]

4.110　Once one accepts that a plaintiff in a personal injury action is entitled to damages for the non-pecuniary, as well as for the pecuniary, loss suffered then the compensatory principle and the rationale for the award of interest[334] apply just as much to these damages as they do to the damages representing pecuniary loss, and the plaintiff ought to receive interest on at least that part of the damages which represent the pre-trial non-pecuniary loss. To award no interest at all would be to *under*compensate him or her.[335] There is also the important pragmatic point that an award of interest is one of the few incentives given to defendants either to settle the action or to make efforts to bring the proceedings to trial as quickly as possible.[336]

---

[329] Ie by excluding the counter-inflationary element from the interest rate and giving a plaintiff the "real" interest rate only.

[330] [1982] 1 WLR 816. See para 2.45 above.

[331] [1983] 2 AC 773. See para 2.46 above.

[332] Indeed, since in most cases it is really the defendant's insurer who has had the use of the money, it is likely that better returns have been made on it than the rate of interest awarded to the plaintiff.

[333] S Waddams, *The Law of Damages* (2nd ed 1991) para 7.720.

[334] See para 2.42 above.

[335] Cf S Waddams, *The Law of Damages* (2nd ed 1991) para 7.700; and P Cane, *Atiyah's Accidents, Compensation and the Law* (5th ed 1993) p 123, pointing out that the award of pre-judgment interest gives effect to the principle of full compensation.

[336] Eg the Winn Committee, Report of the Committee on Personal Injuries Litigation (1968) Cmnd 3691, section 12, paras 322-325; P Cane, *Atiyah's Accidents, Compensation and the Law* (5th ed 1993) pp 124, 226 and 234; H Luntz, *Assessment of Damages for Personal Injury and Death* (3rd ed 1990) para 11.3.4. Note also Lord Woolf's proposals, discussed at para 4.124 below, for awarding interest at an enhanced rate in order to encourage the

Although the delays that occur in personal injury litigation suggest that this has little impact in practice,[337] it would seem inappropriate, at a time when there is such concern over the issue of delay, to remove this *possible* incentive for defendants to resolve personal injury claims at an early stage. Whilst in the 1970s we, and the Pearson Commission, recommended that interest ought not to be awarded upon damages for non-pecuniary loss, we find it difficult to accept today that the award of interest on these damages (especially if it continues to be awarded at a low rate of 2 per cent) is unfair to defendants. **Our provisional view therefore is that interest should continue to be awarded on damages for non-pecuniary loss in personal injury actions. We invite consultees to say whether they agree.**

(2) Should interest be awarded only on pre-trial non-pecuniary loss?

4.111   In principle, it would seem that interest should only be awarded on that part of the plaintiff's non-pecuniary damages which represents the pre-trial pain and suffering and loss of amenity, because the defendant cannot be said to have kept the plaintiff out of money representing losses which have not yet occurred.[338] This is accepted in the case of pecuniary loss, where the rule is that a plaintiff will only receive interest on the actual pecuniary loss suffered up to the date of trial, and not at all on future pecuniary losses.[339] In contrast, as far as damages for non-pecuniary loss are concerned, the English courts have always awarded interest on the whole sum and have never attempted to segregate the damages into sums representing past and future loss. The explanation given for this practice is that non-pecuniary loss is by its nature indivisible and therefore impossible to separate into past and future loss.[340] This approach was endorsed by us in 1973[341] and again by the Pearson Commission.[342] In arguing that no interest at all ought to be awarded on damages for non-pecuniary loss both Commissions took the view that it would be too difficult and very artificial to try to separate the plaintiff's pain and suffering and loss of amenity into that endured in the past and that to be endured in the future and that this ought not therefore to be attempted.

early settlement of proceedings. See, however, the doubts expressed in (1973) Law Com No 56, para 271.

[337] See para 2.41, n 160 above.

[338] See para 2.42 above.

[339] *Jefford v Gee* [1970] 2 QB 130. The rule has subsequently been applied also to damages for dependency awarded under the Fatal Accidents Act, which must now be separated into pre-trial and future loss, with interest allowed only on the former: *Cookson v Knowles* [1979] AC 556 (HL).

[340] *Jefford v Gee* [1970] 2 QB 130, 147F.

[341] (1973) Law Com No 56, para 273.

[342] Pearson Report, vol 1, para 747.

4.112 Despite such difficulties, it has been maintained that, if interest is to be awarded, both principle and fairness alike require that the plaintiff's damages for non-pecuniary loss should be divided into those which, very broadly, represent past loss on the one hand and those which represent future loss on the other, with interest being permitted only on the former.[343] Nor would it actually seem impossible - provided it is done on a very broad basis - to make such a separation, given that this is the established practice of the courts in, for example, some Australian jurisdictions and in Scotland.[344] In Australia, for instance, where such a dissection is undertaken, it is carried out on broad lines, without any "nice apportionment" being necessary.[345] Similarly, in Scotland the courts take a broad and flexible approach to the division. It should be noted, however, that in these jurisdictions the courts also apply a higher rate of interest than in England[346] and the interest tends to run from a date earlier than the date of service of the writ.[347]

4.113 **We ask consultees for their views on whether the English practice should be changed so that a division is made between past and future non-pecuniary loss with interest being allowed only on the former. If it is considered that such a change should be made we ask consultees (after reading the following two subsections) to say whether this change should be combined with the application of a higher rate of interest than the current 2 per cent rate and, if so, why; and/or whether the date of the accident should then be taken as the date from which interest runs and, if so, why.**

(3) Should the date of service of the writ be the date from which interest is payable?

4.114 In principle the date from which interest should be payable is the date at which the loss occurred. At the earliest this is the date of the accident, when the plaintiff's cause of action arose.[348] Where the loss is continuing or does not all occur at this moment, as is generally true in the case of personal injury, it would be difficult and time-consuming to adhere strictly to principle by attempting to make detailed and

---

[343] *McGregor on Damages* (15th ed 1988) para 597.

[344] See paras 3.7 and 3.27 above.

[345] *Fire & All Risks Insurance Co Ltd v Callinan* (1978) 140 CLR 427. It is apparently the convention in New South Wales to apportion damages for pain and suffering 50:50 in respect of the periods before and after trial. This practice has been justified on the ground that, although the period before trial is likely to be shorter than the period thereafter, the intensity of the pain before trial is likely to be greater (*Moran v McMahon* (1985) 3 NSWLR 700, 706E). Where, however, most of the pain and suffering and loss of amenity clearly occurs before trial, a different apportionment ought to take place: D I Cassidy, "Interest at Common Law" (1982) 56 ALJ 213, 218.

[346] See para 4.122, n 389 below.

[347] See paras 3.7 and 3.27 above.

[348] *BP Exploration Co (Libya) Ltd v Hunt (No 2)* [1979] 1 WLR 783, *per* Robert Goff J; *McGregor on Damages* (15th ed 1988) para 601.

144

separate calculations in respect of each item of loss as it occurs, for example in respect of weekly wage loss or each individual item of medical expense. Hence for pre-trial pecuniary loss, interest is awarded from the date of the accident, but the appropriate rate is then halved in order to reflect the fact that not all the relevant losses will have occurred at this time. In Scotland and all save two of the Australian jurisdictions the date of the accident is similarly taken as the date from which interest should be awarded on damages for non-pecuniary loss.[349] In *Jefford v Gee*, however, the English Court of Appeal selected the date of service of the writ, in preference to the date of the accident, as the starting point of the period for which interest should be awarded on these damages. It also indicated in that case that it might be appropriate to select an even shorter period where there had been delay on the part of the plaintiff in bringing the action to trial.[350]

4.115   The Court of Appeal justified the adoption of this later date by reference to three considerations, restated with approval by Lord Diplock in *Wright v British Railways Board*.[351] First, attention was drawn to the fact that non-pecuniary loss is by its nature continuing and does not all occur at the date of the accident: instead, it may spread indefinitely into the future.[352] Nor can it be quantified easily at this point in time,[353] especially where the injury is serious and the plaintiff's condition may not have stabilised.[354] Secondly, the plaintiff can only be said to have been kept out of his or her money from the time at which the defendant ought to have paid it, and this was thought by the Court of Appeal to be the date when the action was brought, namely the date of service of the writ.[355] Until that date, when the demand is made, the defendant could hardly be described as "wrongfully withholding" a sum of money to which the plaintiff is entitled.[356] Thirdly, there was the important practical consideration that choosing the date of service of the writ as the appropriate starting point from which interest ought to run "should stimulate the

---

[349] See paras 3.7 and 3.27 above.

[350] [1970] 2 QB 130, 147E-H, 151B-C, F. See para 2.42 above.

[351] [1983] 2 AC 773, 778H-779H. However, this aspect of the guideline had not been questioned by the appellant in *Wright*.

[352] *Jefford v Gee* [1970] 2 QB 130, 147E-F.

[353] *Ibid*, 147F.

[354] *Wright v British Railways Board* [1983] 2 AC 773, 779D-E. Uncertainty regarding the exact sum to which the plaintiff is entitled, particularly where the plaintiff's medical condition is unstable, also formed part of the justification for applying to non-pecuniary damages a rate of interest which is lower than the full appropriate rate. See paras 2.45 above and 4.119 ff below.

[355] *Jefford v Gee* [1970] 2 QB 130, 147F-H.

[356] *Wright v British Railways Board* [1983] 2 AC 773, 779E-F.

plaintiff's advisers to issue and serve the writ without delay - which is much to be desired."[357]

4.116   The choice of a date later than the date of the accident has been questioned. In Australia, for instance, it has been held that the fact that the defendant may not know how much to pay is not a good reason for not awarding interest from the earliest time permitted by the relevant statutory provisions, since the defendant has had the use of the money meanwhile.[358] For the same reason Professor Luntz has argued that delay by the plaintiff should not affect the question of interest.[359] Harvey McGregor QC has described the principle upon which the English rule is based as "dubious" and Lord Diplock's restatement of the justifications for it as unconvincing.[360] In *Slater v Hughes*,[361] Davies LJ conceded that there was a certain illogicality in allowing interest on the non-pecuniary damages to run only from the date of service of the writ while allowing interest on the special damages from the date of the accident. Similarly, in its Preliminary Submission to us, APIL argued that "[t]here is no logic to limiting interest from the date of service of the writ, as the plaintiff's loss commences from the date of the accident, not from any artificial date coincidental with the writ." APIL therefore submitted that a plaintiff should be entitled to interest (at the full special account rate) from the date of the accident.[362]

4.117   In 1973, we doubted whether apprehension about the effect of delay on interest had in fact produced any significant increase in the expedition with which plaintiffs commenced proceedings.[363] More recent experience tends to support the point.[364] In any event, it might be considered harsh to penalise plaintiffs simply in order to encourage a speedy issue of the writ.[365] We also note that when the Court of

---

[357] *Jefford v Gee* [1970] 2 QB 130, 147H, *per* Lord Denning MR.

[358] *Parker v Guardian Fire Sprinkler Co (Qld) Pty Ltd* [1982] Qd R 709; *Andrews v Armitt* (1978) 80 LSJS 424; *Pacini v Cooper* (1982) 101 LSJS 166. For jurisdictions other than Victoria and South Australia, the earliest time permitted is the date when the cause of action arose. D I Cassidy, "Interest at Common Law" (1982) 56 ALJ 213, 216, comments that a general rule to the effect that interest should only be awarded from the date of service of the writ would place a gloss on the words of the Australian statutes which they cannot easily bear.

[359] H Luntz, *Assessment of Damages for Personal Injury and Death* (3rd ed 1990) para 11.3.18.

[360] *McGregor on Damages* (15th ed 1988) para 601.

[361] [1971] 1 WLR 1438.

[362] See also para 4.122 below.

[363] (1973) Law Com No 56, para 271.

[364] See para 2.41 above.

[365] R Bowles, "Interest on Damages for Non-Economic Loss" (1984) 100 LQR 192, 196, who also points out that such a penalty will be reflected in out of court negotiations and settlements because total awards expected in court will be reduced. P Cane, *Atiyah's Accidents, Compensation and the Law* (5th ed 1993) pp 226-227, and 234, states that, on

Appeal in *Jefford v Gee* chose the date of the service of the writ as the point from which interest on damages for non-pecuniary loss should be payable it at the same time held that interest should be payable at the *full* short term investment account rate.[366] Whether by accident or design, the relatively short period over which interest was calculated can be regarded as having had the effect of mitigating some of the "overcompensation" resulting from calculating interest at the full rate on sums which already took account of inflation.[367] The choice of a date later than the date of the accident is perhaps more difficult to justify, even on pragmatic grounds, when the plaintiff is entitled only to a low rate of interest of 2 per cent.[368]

4.118 **We invite consultees' views as to whether interest on damages for non-pecuniary loss should be payable from the date of the accident rather than from the date of the service of the writ.**

(4) Is the current 2 per cent rate satisfactory?

4.119 The third aspect of the courts' discretion is the rate at which interest should be payable.[369] For pre-trial pecuniary loss, it is assumed that a market rate ought to apply and for this purpose the rate payable on money in court which is placed in the High Court special account[370] is taken as the most reliable guide.[371] Since 1 February 1993, this has stood at 8 per cent.[372] The rate is then normally halved to reflect the fact that interest runs from the date of the accident and yet the losses have not all been incurred at that time. In *Jefford v Gee*, the Court of Appeal assumed that the short term investment (now, special) account rate should apply also to the damages representing non-pecuniary loss;[373] and there was no suggestion that that rate should be halved, presumably because the interest was to run from the date of the writ rather than from the date of the accident. However, twelve years

---

the whole, defendants and insurers have less to lose by delay than plaintiffs.

[366] Admittedly, when approving the low, 2% rate of interest in *Wright v British Railways Board*, Lord Diplock also seemed to endorse the selection of the earlier date. He did, however, observe that this part of the *Jefford v Gee* guideline "has not been questioned in the instant appeal": [1983] 2 AC 773, 778H-779H.

[367] R Bowles, "Interest on Damages for Non-Economic Loss" (1984) 100 LQR 192, 196.

[368] *Ibid.* See also counsel's argument in *Wright v British Railways Board* [1983] 2 AC 773, 774H-775A.

[369] See paras 2.45-2.46 above.

[370] Prior to 1987 this was called the short term investment account. Changes in the rate are effected by Lord Chancellor's Direction.

[371] Since bank rates fluctuate too much: *Jefford v Gee* [1970] 2 QB 130, 148F-H.

[372] Lord Chancellor's Direction 27 January 1993. See the Supreme Court Practice (1995) vol 2, Pt 5, para 1262.

[373] [1970] 2 QB 130, 148-149, 151. At the time *Jefford v Gee* was decided, this was about 6% (taking the average rate over the period for which interest was being awarded).

later, in *Birkett v Hayes*,[374] it revised this guideline and applied a low interest rate of 2 per cent instead, primarily on the ground that a plaintiff can reasonably expect to receive no more than a net "real" rate of interest.[375] This low interest rate, and the reasoning upon which it was based, was soon after approved by the House of Lords in *Wright v British Railways Board* and has been applied ever since.[376]

4.120   In *Wright v British Railways Board*, Lord Diplock recognised that the choice of 2 per cent as an appropriate indication of the real interest rate, net of tax, depends on the assumption that current commercial interest rates contain a large counter-inflationary element. He therefore conceded that the guideline might need to be reviewed and the rate raised from 2 per cent, if and when economic conditions changed to such an extent that this assumption ceased to hold good.[377] No expert evidence was given in *Wright v British Railways Board* but the evidence in *Birkett v Hayes* was that for the period in question there (namely, between May 1976 and July 1981 when inflation was "rampant"), no better return than 2 per cent in excess of the rate of inflation could be expected as the real reward for foregoing the use of money.[378] In the absence of evidence to the contrary and whilst it was unknown what the long term future of inflation would be, Lord Diplock thought that this guideline ought to be followed for the time being. He warned that the predictability which facilitates the settlement of claims would be undermined if the guideline were to be revised too often, on the basis of merely temporary shifts in the trend of inflation.[379] Instead, the 2 per cent rate "should continue to be followed ... until the long term trend of future inflation has become predictable with much more confidence."[380]

[374] [1982] 1 WLR 816.

[375] See para 2.45 above for the precise way in which the Court of Appeal reached the figure of 2%, as representing the net real rate of return.

[376] [1983] 2 AC 773. See para 2.46 above. The argument in favour of applying only a real rate of interest to damages for non-pecuniary loss has been recognised in Canada: see para 3.49 above.

[377] [1983] 2 AC 773, 784B, 785G-786B. See Appendix A of Structured Settlements and Interim and Provisional Damages (1992) Law Com Consultation Paper No 125, which shows how real interest rates over the last 20 years were considerably higher in the 1980s compared to the 1970s when an inflationary climate was triggered by oil prices and monetary policy.

[378] *Wright v British Railways Board* [1983] 2 AC 773, 783C-784A.

[379] *Ibid*, 785C-D, G-786A. In addition he drew attention to the expense which would be involved in regularly calling economic evidence at trials of personal injury actions in order to establish the net real reward for foregoing the use of money.

[380] *Ibid*, 785H-786A.

4.121　At the time when the 2 per cent guideline was introduced it was close to the net return obtainable on index-linked government securities ("ILGS"),[381] although in 1983 (when *Wright v British Railways Board* was decided in the House of Lords) ILGS were of recent origin and comparatively rare. They are now an established feature of the market,[382] providing an up-to-date and reliable indication of real interest rates. In our Report on Structured Settlements and Interim and Provisional Damages in 1994, we recommended that, for the purpose of determining the expected return on damages for future pecuniary loss and thus for determining the appropriate rate of discount to be applied when assessing those damages, legislation should be introduced requiring the courts to take account of the net rate of return upon an index-linked government security.[383] We took the view that "ILGS now constitute the best evidence of the real return on any investment where the risk element is minimal".[384] Although our recommendations concerning the use of ILGS rates were made in the context of discounting damages for future pecuniary loss, it is arguable that the question raised here is the same: what provides the best indication of the net real rate of return on a low-risk investment?[385] While it would be possible to establish this net real rate by taking the net rate on other low-risk investments (for example, the special account rate) and then deducting the actual inflation rate over the period up to trial, it may be thought more convenient simply to take the net ILGS rates (which are already index-linked).[386] And if in practice the choice is between a "fixed"[387] 2 per cent rate or a more accurate,[388] fluctuating rate,

---

[381] *Birkett v Hayes* [1982] 1 WLR 816, 824H-825A; *Wright v British Railways Board* [1983] 2 AC 773, 784A-B. See also n 388 below.

[382] Structured Settlements and Interim and Provisional Damages (1992) Law Com Consultation Paper No 125, para 2.24.

[383] (1994) Law Com No 224, paras 1.12, 2.24-2.36 and 6.2-6.4. The Lord Chancellor announced on 22 March 1995 that the Government accepted all the recommendations in the Report. See para 4.31, n 116 above.

[384] (1994) Law Com No 224, para 2.28. It seems reasonable to assume that the injured plaintiff is naturally risk-averse and should have to face only a low level of risk (such as that found in ILGS), rather than the high level of risk found, for example, in equities. See *ibid*, paras 2.29-2.30; B Braithwaite, C Cooper & C Illidge, "New Ogden Tables Fuel Debate on Multiplier Interest Rates" (1994) 6/94 Quantum 1, 3. (1994) Law Com No 225, para 10.2, shows that a large number of recipients of damages for personal injury tend to place their awards in low-risk investments, such as a building society account or bank account.

[385] See D Kemp, "Discounting Compensation for Future Loss" (1985) 101 LQR 556, 561-562; B Braithwaite, C Cooper & C Illidge, "New Ogden Tables Fuel Debate on Multiplier Interest Rates" (1994) 6/4 Quantum 1, 2; Ontario Law Reform Commission, Report on Compensation for Personal Injuries and Death (1987) p 209.

[386] ILGS rates are already published in *Kemp and Kemp* and the Law Society's Gazette. In Structured Settlements and Interim and Provisional Damages (1994) Law Com No 224, paras 2.33 and 6.3, we recommended that they should be published also in the Supreme Court and County Court Practices and regularly updated, in order to enhance their accessibility to practitioners and the judiciary.

[387] It is, of course, within the discretion of the court whether to apply a rate of interest of 2% or some other rate; but in practice the 2% rate is invariably applied. We recognise the practical advantages (eg savings in court time and costs) in applying a conventional or

then the convenience and accuracy of the ILGS rates renders them particularly attractive.

4.122   However, not everyone accepts that it is appropriate to apply a net real rate of interest to damages for non-pecuniary loss in personal injury cases.[389] A real rate of interest assumes that all non-pecuniary awards have in fact been adjusted properly for inflation,[390] whereas it is argued by some, as we have seen above, that the courts are not always taking inflation into account.[391] In its Preliminary Submission to us APIL therefore argued that

> If damages had kept pace with inflation, then the [2 per cent] interest rate for general damages is less of a problem, but ... this has not been the case, and in the absence of any radical reform to up-rate general damages, a plaintiff should

"fixed" rate without evidence being called on the point.

[388] B Braithwaite, C Cooper and C Illidge, "New Ogden Tables Fuel Debate on Multiplier Interest Rates" (1994) 6/4 Quantum 1, 2 and 3, found that the return on ILGS was 2.84% after tax at 25%, and 2.27% after tax at 40%. They also found that the net real rate of return on a capital sum invested entirely in ILGS would be: 2.5% for a sum of £1,000,000; 2.7% for a sum of £700,000; and 2.9% for a sum of £300,000. Due to higher rates of taxation, the return decreases as the size of the fund increases. Since the current unofficial maximum which may be awarded as damages for non-pecuniary loss is approximately £130,000 (see para 2.40, n 158 above), this would suggest that a 2% rate of interest is in fact rather low as a reflection of the net real rate of return. Cf also *Thomas v Brighton Health Authority*, *The Times* 10 November 1995, in which in the context of determining the appropriate discount to be applied when calculating future pecuniary loss and the rate of interest to be applied to accommodation costs, Collins J observed that in 1983 when *Wright v British Railways Board* was decided ILGS were producing 2% but that the rate has now settled at about 3%.

[389] The High Court of Australia has held that the full commercial rate of interest should apply to the non-pecuniary element of personal injury damages, just as it does to the pecuniary element (*Cullen v Trappell* (1980) 146 CLR 1, 21-2), although in South Australia the courts apply a real rate of interest of 4% (*Wheeler v Page and Harris* (1982) 31 SASR 1 (FC)). See generally H Luntz, *Assessment of Damages for Personal Injury and Death* (3rd ed 1990) para 11.3.16. Note that interest on damages is not exempt from tax in Australia. Scottish courts apply the judicial, rather than a real, rate of interest. In Australia and Scotland interest is awarded only on pre-trial non-pecuniary loss and the relevant rate is halved to reflect the fact that not all the loss may have been sustained at the date of the accident, which is the time from which interest usually runs. Note the argument that it may be that, in truth, the low 2% rate is a compromise between awarding too much interest and awarding too little, a solution adopted by the English courts in preference to attempting to separate the plaintiff's non-pecuniary loss into that occurring before trial and that occurring after. Note further that interest on damages for bereavement in fatal accident claims is payable at the full special account rate from the date of death: *Prior v Hastie* [1987] CLY 1219; *Khan v Duncan*, 9 March 1989, *Kemp and Kemp*, vol 1, paras 16-031 and 16-032. In *McGregor on Damages* (15th ed 1988) para 612 the author argues that there is no good reason why the tax exemption on damages should lead to there being a low rate of interest on non-pecuniary loss but not on pecuniary loss.

[390] D Morgan, "Interest and Inflation in the House of Lords" (1983) 133 NLJ 821, 822, states that, immediately following *Birkett v Hayes*, judges typically responded to the new 2% guideline by stressing the importance of ensuring that damages for non-pecuniary loss *do* keep pace with inflation.

[391] See paras 4.30 and 4.34 above.

be entitled to recover interest at the full short term investment [that is, special] account rate, from the date of the accident.[392]

4.123   A further, and perhaps more powerful, argument in favour of applying a higher rate of interest than the net real rate, concerns the problem of delay and the role which the award of interest can have in encouraging the expeditious conduct of personal injury claims. Applying only a low, net real rate of interest acts as a disincentive to defendants (and their insurers) to settle, since far greater interest can be earned by delaying payment for as long as possible.[393] The availability of pre-judgment interest is one of the few incentives given to defendants to avoid delaying a settlement process in which defendants stand to gain more by delaying than do plaintiffs,[394] but at present it is extremely doubtful whether the 2 per cent rate has this effect. There is therefore a strong pragmatic argument in favour of applying a higher rate than the net real rate - either the commercial rate or, as is the case for special damages, the High Court special account rate. We recognise the force of this argument, particularly in the face of evidence suggesting that the settlement process in the context of personal injury is already weighted in favour of defendants and their insurers,[395] and that when compensation is received it is often inadequate for meeting an injured person's past and future losses.[396]

4.124   On the other hand, the reason for awarding pre-judgment interest is usually said to be to compensate the plaintiff for the loss which arises from being kept out of his or her money, rather than to encourage the expeditious conduct of proceedings.[397] Furthermore, we note that in the context of his review of civil procedure, Lord Woolf has already made interim recommendations for the award of interest at an enhanced rate above that which would otherwise be payable in cases where the defendant refuses an offer by the plaintiff to settle and the plaintiff then recovers a sum of damages which matches or exceeds the amount referred to in his or her

---

[392]   Preliminary Submission, p 17. Similarly, it was his view that non-pecuniary awards, other than those at the very top end of the range, are not adjusted regularly for inflation in Canada which in part led Mr Earl A Cherniak QC to dissent from the Ontario Law Reform Commission's recommendation that interest on such awards should accrue only at a real rate of 2.5%: Report on Compensation for Personal Injuries and Death (1987) pp 209-212.

[393]   I Goldrein & M de Haas, *Personal Injury Litigation Practice and Precedents* (1985) p 6; Dissent by Mr Earl A Cherniak QC, Ontario Law Reform Commission's Report on Compensation for Personal Injuries and Death (1987) p 210. See also the argument of counsel in *Wright v British Railways Board* [1983] 2 AC 773, 776C-D.

[394]   P Cane, *Atiyah's Accidents, Compensation and the Law* (5th ed 1993) pp 226 and 234.

[395]   Eg Harris *et al*, *Compensation and Support for Illness and Injury* (1984); H Genn, *Hard Bargaining: Out of Court Settlement in Personal Injury Actions* (1987).

[396]   See (1994) Law Com No 225.

[397]   Although the courts have certainly taken the effect of interest upon delay into account when formulating the guidelines for the award of interest upon damages for personal injury. See paras 2.42, 4.114 and 4.115 above.

offer.[398] Lord Woolf adopted the figures suggested to him by the Law Society of 10 per cent above the rate which would otherwise be payable up to £50,000, 5 per cent from £50,000 to £100,000 and then at an additional 2.5 per cent.[399] It is perhaps preferable that any proposals for applying a higher rate of interest than the current 2 per cent rate (or an alternative rate representing the net real rate) in order to encourage the early settlement of proceedings should take place within the context of a wider review of civil procedure in general, such as that being undertaken by Lord Woolf.

4.125 **We therefore ask consultees to indicate whether they consider satisfactory the 2 per cent interest rate which is presently applied to damages for non-pecuniary loss in personal injury actions. In particular, do they favour: (a) abandoning the "fixed" 2 per cent rate in favour of taking the net rate of return on ILGS over the relevant period; or (b) the application of a higher rate (for example, the commercial rate or the special account rate) than the net real rate of return on a low-risk investment, in order, for example, to discourage delay by defendants.**

10.   SHOULD DAMAGES FOR NON-PECUNIARY LOSS SURVIVE THE DEATH OF THE VICTIM?

4.126 The final matter for us to consider is the survival of damages for non-pecuniary loss for the benefit of the victim's estate. In Part II we saw that, where a victim of personal injury dies before his or her claim for damages is resolved, English law allows the deceased's estate to recover the full value of any pre-death pain, suffering and loss of amenity, whether or not death was caused by the injury itself and whether or not the deceased had commenced an action for damages while alive.[400] The survival of non-pecuniary loss, unlike accrued pecuniary losses, has been described as "controversial" and has on occasion been questioned.[401] When this Commission consulted on this issue in 1971, consultees were evenly divided as to whether non-pecuniary loss (other than for the then separate head of loss of expectation of life) should survive for the benefit of the deceased's estate.[402] Some

---

[398] *Access to Justice* (1995) ch 24, esp paras 7-13, and recommendation 118. The recommendations were not confined to personal injury actions.

[399] *Ibid*, p 196, para 10.

[400] See the Law Reform (Miscellaneous Provisions) Act 1934, s 1; and paras 2.48-2.52 above.

[401] See para 4.128 below. In its Report on The Effect of Death on Damages (1992) Scot Law Com No 134, para 3.31, the Scottish Law Commission recognised that "[t]he issues are controversial".

[402] See (1971) Law Com Working Paper No 41, para 67; (1973) Law Com No 56, paras 98, 101-107. This Commission recommended retaining the survival rule but we do not now find its reasons for so doing very convincing. These were: (i) to deny survival would cause injustice where the victim has spent in advance part of the damages for non-pecuniary loss which he or she expects to receive; (ii) to deny survival would require repayment by the estate of any interim damages for non-pecuniary loss where the injured person dies before final assessment and would thus prevent the courts from safely making interim awards

152

other jurisdictions either preclude the estate from recovering damages for non-pecuniary loss altogether[403] or only allow it to do so in certain circumstances.[404] In this section we consider whether English law ought to adopt one of these solutions.

4.127 The recent legislative history in Scotland on this issue is most illuminating. Between 1976 and 1992 damages for non-pecuniary loss were excluded from survival actions by virtue of section 2 of the Damages (Scotland) Act 1976.[405] Public concern at the effect of this exclusionary rule in cases of industrial disease (especially asbestos-related disease) led the Scottish Law Commission to reconsider the matter and as a result to reverse its policy against the survival of damages for non-pecuniary loss.[406] The policy against survival had been adopted in 1976 primarily on theoretical grounds, but also in the belief that it was unlikely to cause any injustice to or dissatisfaction among injured persons and their families, since it was envisaged that the expanded form of "loss of society" award introduced by the 1976 Act would lead to higher awards being made by the courts to the deceased's relatives in respect of their own non-pecuniary loss.[407] In fact the rule against survival gave rise to great public disquiet. The discrepancy between the damages which might otherwise have been obtained by the estate for the deceased's pre-death non-pecuniary loss on the one hand, and the comparatively low value of relatives' awards for loss of society on the other, both "heightened the sense of lost entitlement ... when death intervenes"[408] and gave rise to the perception that there was at least the

referable to non-pecuniary loss; (iii) relatives may have looked after the deceased and so not be undeserving of reward. See also the Pearson Report, vol 1, para 444.

[403] Damages for non-pecuniary loss do not survive the plaintiff's death in Ireland, nor do they in some of the Australian states, Canadian provinces and American jurisdictions: see paras 3.19, 3.25, 3.50 and 3.57 above.

[404] This is the law in some Australian jurisdictions and some Canadian provinces: see paras 3.25 and 3.50 above.

[405] As unamended. This implemented the recommendations made by the Scottish Law Commission in its Report on the Law Relating to Damages for Injuries Causing Death (1973) Scot Law Com No 31, paras 21-25.

[406] See Report on The Effect of Death on Damages (1992) Scot Law Com No 134. The industries involved in claims arising from asbestos-induced disease, notably shipbuilding and the construction industry, are well represented in Scotland. See para 1.9 of the Report. The Scottish Law Commission found that in Scotland in the period 1985-1989, 74% of damages claims in respect of supervening death were based on industrial disease (Appendix B, Table 1; and paras 1.8-1.10). Our own empirical research based on persons living in England and Wales found that work-related illness or disease figured much more prominently in claims following death (23%) than they did in claims by living plaintiffs (4%): (1994) Law Com No 225, para 13.4. However, as the Scottish Law Commission rightly notes in its Report, *op cit*, paras 1.1-1.11, the significance of the survival of damages for non-pecuniary loss in industrial disease cases is not merely quantitative but qualitative.

[407] See Report on the Law Relating to Damages for Injuries Causing Death (1973) Scot Law Com No 31, paras 23-24, and Report on The Effect of Death on Damages (1992) Scot Law Com No 134, para 2.33.

[408] *Ibid*, para 2.11.

potential for defendants to seek to delay the settlement of claims by persons whose death was impending, in order to minimise the amount of damages payable.[409] The Scottish Law Commission therefore recommended that damages for non-pecuniary loss should be allowed once again to survive for the benefit of the deceased's estate, although this time without restriction.[410] The Damages (Scotland) Act 1993, amending the 1976 Act of the same name, now gives effect to this recommendation and brings Scottish law back into line with the position which prevails in England and Wales.[411]

(1) Should the survival of damages for non-pecuniary loss be excluded altogether?

4.128 Those who argue that damages for non-pecuniary loss should not survive for the benefit of the deceased's estate do so primarily on theoretical grounds, by reference either to the nature of non-pecuniary loss or to the object of compensation for non-pecuniary loss. It is said that non-pecuniary loss is loss which is personal to the deceased and that, unlike pecuniary loss, it does not therefore involve a loss to the estate.[412] A variant of this argument is the contention that it is artificial and indeed impossible to award compensation for a person's suffering after his or her death, since he or she can no longer be comforted by the damages or otherwise benefit from the award.[413] On this view of the object of the award, damages for the deceased's past non-pecuniary loss merely constitute a windfall to the beneficiaries of the estate.

---

[409] *Ibid*, paras 1.2-1.3, 1.12-1.13, 1-18, 2.9-2.15, 2.33 and 3.1. The Scottish Law Commission found that *total* loss of society awards to one family (ie to the deceased's surviving spouse and children) typically lay in the range £5,000-£20,000. It contrasted this with awards of £40,000 and above for industrial disease likely to cause death. In England and Wales, the bereavement award (which is shared between those entitled to it) is fixed at £7,500; whereas serious cases of, eg, asbestosis attract damages for non-pecuniary loss of up to £47,500 (see the JSB *Guidelines*, p 17).

[410] Report on The Effect of Death on Damages (1992) Scot Law Com No 134, paras 4.7-4.10 and 4.22-4.28. Prior to 1976, damages for the deceased's pre-death non-pecuniary loss were permitted to survive only where the deceased had commenced an action for damages in his or her lifetime; see para 4.136 below.

[411] See s 2 of the 1976 Act, substituted by s 3 of the 1993 Act. The provision has retrospective effect for deaths occurring on or after 16 July 1992 (s 6 of the 1993 Act).

[412] Eg *McGregor on Damages* (15th ed 1989) para 719, who therefore regards the survival of non-pecuniary loss, and the desire to make the defendant pay for the full consequences of his or her actions, as punitive; K D Cooper-Stephenson & I B Saunders, *Personal Injury Damages in Canada* (1981) p 399.

[413] Eg *Andrews v Freeborough* [1967] 1 QB 1, 26G, *per* Winn LJ (dissenting)("Money can do little to ease the path of a departed soul"); W F Bowker, "The Uniform Survival of Actions Act" (1964) 3 Alta LR Rev 197, 199; Report on the Law Relating to Damages for Injuries Causing Death (1973) Scot Law Com No 31, leading to the exclusionary rule in the Damages (Scotland) Act 1976. Consultees to (1971) Law Com Working Paper No 41, who opposed the survival of damages for non-pecuniary loss did so mainly on this ground: see (1973) Law Com No 56, para 102.

4.129   The opposing theoretical view in favour of survival is that pain, suffering and loss of amenity are actual, past losses which have been experienced by the plaintiff and for which he or she is entitled to be compensated.[414] The fact of death is irrelevant to the actuality of the loss having occurred and merely makes certain the period over which it is to be measured. Just as with an accrued pecuniary loss, there is therefore nothing inherently objectionable in a rule which allows this loss to survive for the benefit of the estate; and it is irrelevant that the damages can no longer be enjoyed personally by the person upon whose suffering they are based. On the contrary, a rule which allowed death to extinguish the award would mean that actual suffering would go unrecognised and unacknowledged.[415]   One might also argue that the estate has suffered a real *pecuniary* loss in the sense that it has been deprived of the damages which the deceased would have been awarded had he or she lived.

4.130   Whichever answer is given to this theoretical dispute,[416] we would be concerned that a rule precluding the survival of damages for non-pecuniary loss could in certain circumstances have capricious effects and that it may for this reason be widely perceived as unfair by injured persons and their families. Whilst alive, the injured person undoubtedly has a right to recover damages for non-pecuniary loss and a rule which extinguishes that right in the event that he or she dies before resolving the claim may give rise to a sense of being deprived unfairly of an entitlement. This is likely to be heightened where the period between injury and death is long, and where either no other claims arise on death under the Fatal Accidents Act 1976 (for example because the victim dies some time after the injury from unconnected causes)[417] or where their value is small in comparison with the damages for pre-death suffering which could be recovered by the deceased's estate. Further, where it is known that the injured person may die (whether from the injury itself or because of extraneous circumstances), this may provide an incentive for defendants to seek to delay settlement in order to minimise their liability, "to the detriment of those pursuing claims in particularly distressing circumstances".[418] It also puts pressure on victims of personal injury, who are dying, to seek to settle their claims

---

[414]   (1971) Law Com Working Paper No 41, para 67 (as we hinted there, this argument becomes more compelling the longer the period between injury and death or the more severe the pain and suffering experienced); Report on The Effect of Death on Damages (1992) Scot Law Com No 134, paras 3.7 and 3.13; S M Waddams, *The Law of Damages* (2nd ed 1991) para 12.90.

[415]   Report on The Effect of Death on Damages (1992) Scot Law Com No 134, paras 3.7 and 3.13.

[416]   It finds a parallel in the question whether the living but permanently unconscious plaintiff should be permitted to recover damages for non-pecuniary loss. See paras 2.15-2.18 and 4.11-4.22 above.

[417]   See the telling example given by the Scottish Law Commission at para 1.19 of its Report on The Effect of Death on Damages (1992) Scot Law Com No 134.

[418]   The Scottish Law Commission found no evidence of deliberate delay by defendants, but reasoned, in our view correctly, that the very possibility of exploitation might be sufficient reason for reforming Scots law: *ibid*, paras 1.3 and 1.13.

as quickly as possible, so as to recover at least something for their non-pecuniary loss - which will often mean settling for less than the full value of their claim.[419] In addition, the knowledge or fear that a claim will be lost on death can exacerbate the pre-death suffering of the dying.[420] Some of the above considerations combine to make the victims of industrial disease a class of injured person which could be especially disadvantaged by a rule precluding the survival of damages for non-pecuniary loss.[421]

4.131 We find these arguments in favour of the current law compelling, especially in the absence of any pressing demand for reform. We think it instructive to remember that survival confers no new rights, but instead simply permits subsisting rights to survive for the benefit of the deceased's estate. Whilst it is open to plaintiffs to argue that a rule excluding the survival of damages for non-pecuniary loss unfairly *deprives* them of a valuable claim, we do not believe that it is open to defendants to complain that a rule which permits survival imposes an unreasonable burden upon them,[422] *except* in so far as it duplicates awards under the Fatal Accidents Act 1976. In our view, no such duplication exists. Where the injured person dies from extraneous causes, no action arises under the 1976 Act at all. Where death results from injury, the defendant may have to pay bereavement damages under the Act in addition to compensating the estate for the deceased's pre-death pain, suffering and loss of amenity: but these claims are juridically distinct since one relates to the injured person's pre-death suffering, whereas the other relates to a close relative's post-death suffering. If there were duplication the preferable way of dealing with it would be to offset the two awards against each other, not to preclude survival. In any event, it should be noted that the bereavement award is a relatively small, fixed sum of £7,500 and is available to a very small class of relatives.[423]

---

[419] *Ibid*, para 1.18. In its Report on Compensation for Personal Injuries and Death (1987) p 110, the Ontario Law Reform Commission thought that inducement to delay and pressure to settle early meant that "the abolition of survival actions would give rise to significant problems".

[420] Report on The Effect of Death on Damages (1992) Scot Law Com No 134, para 3.13.

[421] Asbestos-induced disease can develop many years after first exposure, with most deaths occurring in persons over 60. Diagnosis is difficult and death usually occurs shortly after - indeed diagnosis may only become define after death. The risk of death intervening before damages are obtained is therefore high in such cases, yet in the period before death the sufferer is typically in acute pain, severely incapacitated and (particularly if aware of impending death) much distressed, making the value of his or her non-pecuniary claim fairly substantial. See, eg, *Bryce v Swan Hunter Group plc* [1987] 2 Lloyd's Rep 426, 436; *Butler v Ministry Of Defence*, 10 October 1983, *Kemp and Kemp*, vol 2, para F2-102; and Report on The Effect of Death on Damages (1992) Scot Law Com No 134, para 1.2. The conventional sum for this type of injury can reach sums of over £40,000 (see the JSB *Guidelines*, p 17 and cases collected in *Kemp and Kemp*, vol 2, Part F2).

[422] It simply fails to relieve them of an existing liability.

[423] *Viz*, to a spouse or to the parents of an unmarried minor child. In the latter instance the parents share the award so that the defendant's total liability is always £7,500. Under Scottish law, in contrast, the class of persons entitled to claim a loss of society award is much wider, and awards are cumulative rather than shared. Nevertheless, in its Report on

4.132　The recent experience in Scotland and the arguments set out by the Scottish Law Commission in its 1992 Report[424] have particularly impressed us and ought to carry considerable weight when we ask whether the English rule should now be altered. Indeed as the Scottish Law Commission observed,[425] it is desirable that provision in the two jurisdictions should be comparable. Although there is an element of circularity in our seeking to justify our provisional conclusion by reference to this consideration, we believe that to reverse the present rule requires greater justification than is provided by the argument that the damages which survive to the estate can no longer be enjoyed personally by the person upon whose suffering they are based. **It is our provisional view that it is fairer to injured persons and their families, and not unfair to defendants, to allow an injured person's right to recover damages for non-pecuniary loss to continue to survive for the benefit of that person's estate. We invite consultees to indicate whether they agree with our provisional conclusion and, if not, to give their reasons.**

(2)　Should the survival of damages for non-pecuniary loss be subject to conditions?

4.133　Given our provisional view that damages for non-pecuniary loss should continue to survive for the benefit of the deceased's estate in cases of supervening death, the question then arises whether these should survive unconditionally or be subject to conditions. We canvass two possible restrictions which have been adopted at one time or another in other jurisdictions, namely: (a) allowing pre-death non-pecuniary loss to survive for the benefit of the estate in cases where death is due to extraneous causes, but not where it results from the injury itself, and (b) making it a condition of the survival of a right to pre-death non-pecuniary loss that the deceased should have commenced an action while alive.

(a)　Should damages for non-pecuniary loss be permitted to survive only where the supervening death is due to extraneous causes?

4.134　Some Australian jurisdictions draw a distinction between death which is caused by the injury in question and death which is due to extraneous causes, excluding the survival of damages for non-pecuniary loss in the former case but permitting it in the latter.[426] A rule of this kind was suggested to the Scottish Law Commission during its consultation exercises in 1973 and 1992. Although the Commission

---

The Effect of Death on Damages (1992) Scot Law Com No 134, para 3.28, the Scottish Law Commission still maintained that "Allowing the deceased's claim for [non-pecuniary loss] to survive as part of his or her estate cannot involve duplication of damages just because a relative who receives compensation in his or her own right may also take the estate" and therefore argued that "seeking to set off the deceased's claim against the relative's claim is misconceived".

[424] The Effect of Death on Damages (1992) Scot Law Com No 134.

[425] *Ibid*, para 3.36.

[426] See para 3.25 above. See also some Canadian provinces: see para 3.50 above.

accepted that the rule "has a certain logic," it rejected it on each occasion.[427] The rationale for this limitation to deaths which are due to extraneous causes appears to be that in this situation no new claims arise in favour of the deceased's relatives under the Fatal Accidents Acts, whereas they usually do when death is due to the wrong which caused the personal injury.[428] Where death is due to the injury itself, the deceased's own claim for damages for non-pecuniary loss is "transformed" instead into a claim for bereavement damages (or its equivalent) made by specified members of his or her family.[429]

4.135 We share the Scottish Law Commission's opinion that it would appear arbitrary and unjust to accord preference to certain claims on the basis of a distinction between one cause of death and another.[430] In particular the reasons which have led us to the provisional conclusion that the present rule in favour of survival should be retained, apply with equal force whatever the cause of the supervening death.[431] The problem that a rule which excludes the survival of non-pecuniary loss may provide an incentive for defendants to prolong negotiations or legal proceedings and at the same time put pressure on injured persons to settle early (and for less), is especially relevant in relation to injuries which result in death, since it is in these cases that it will usually be known that death is likely to occur. A rule of the kind proposed would also exclude the industrial disease cases which, as we observed above, pose special problems.[432] This, we anticipate, would be a source of public concern.[433] Finally, we find the rationale put forward for the distinction between death due to the injury and death due to extraneous causes somewhat unconvincing[434] and we note, as did the Scottish Law Commission, that where such a distinction is made

---

[427] Report on the Law Relating to Damages for Injuries Causing Death (1973) Scot Law Com No 31, para 24; Report on The Effect of Death on Damages (1992) Scot Law Com No 134, paras 3.6-3.9.

[428] J G Fleming, *The Law of Torts* (8th ed 1992) p 678, n 252; Report on the Law Relating to Damages for Injuries Causing Death (1973) Scot Law Com No 31, para 24; Report on The Effect of Death on Damages (1992) Scot Law Com No 134, para 3.7. Cf F Trindade & P Cane, *The Law of Torts in Australia* (2nd ed 1993) p 517.

[429] Report on the Law Relating to Damages for Injuries Causing Death (1973) Scot Law Com No 31, para 24.

[430] Report on The Effect of Death on Damages (1992) Scot Law Com No 134, paras 3.7-3.8.

[431] See paras 4.130-4.132 above.

[432] See para 4.130, n 421 above.

[433] See paras 4.127 and 4.130 above.

[434] One can argue that the claims are, and ought to be treated as, juridically distinct (see para 4.131 above). Further, a claim for bereavement damages does not arise in all cases of personal injury resulting in death and where it does it may still (at £7,500) compare unfavourably with the value of the injured person's own pain, suffering and loss of amenity. See para 4.127, n 409 above.

it tends to be criticised.[435] **We invite consultees to say whether they agree with our provisional view that there should be no rule limiting the survival of damages for non-pecuniary loss in personal injury actions to cases where the supervening death is due to extraneous causes.**

(b) Should damages for non-pecuniary loss be permitted to survive only in cases where the deceased has commenced an action while alive?

4.136 An alternative limitation would be a rule which would allow damages for non-pecuniary loss to survive only in cases where the deceased commenced an action while alive. This was the position in Scotland prior to 1976 and in Germany until 1990.[436] The rule is based on the idea that it is for the injured person to elect to sue for his or her non-pecuniary loss and that, by commencing an action, he or she provides clear evidence of an intention to claim damages. It is therefore a corollary of the view that non-pecuniary loss entailed by personal injury is inherently personal to the deceased.

4.137 We are equally opposed to the introduction of a rule to this effect. Like the Scottish Law Commission, we believe that it is likely to give rise to further difficulties (for example, what if the injured person is incapacitated and unable to act?) and that catering for these difficulties would entail creating a statutory scheme of some complexity.[437] In the case of persons suffering from industrial disease (such as asbestosis), diagnosis of the cause of the illness may only be made a very short time before death, or subsequent to death at post-mortem, and a rule which required the deceased to commence an action while alive would therefore disadvantage these and other injured persons whose injuries are difficult to diagnose. It also seems likely to encourage premature litigation and to discourage the negotiated settlement of claims.[438] In Germany, the rule in practice is said to have "caused much dispute and an unsavoury scramble to institute actions as soon as possible after the accident lest the victim die too soon."[439] It was repealed in 1990.[440] The Scottish Law

---

[435] Eg J G Fleming, *The Law of Torts* (8th ed 1992) p 678; F Trindade & P Cane, *The Law of Torts in Australia* (2nd ed 1993) p 517; H Luntz, *Assessment of Damages for Personal Injury and Death* (3rd ed 1990) para 9.1.4. See Report on The Effect of Death on Damages (1992) Scot Law Com No 134, para 3.8. However, the criticism is usually that the prohibition ought to extend to all cases of supervening death, rather than that it should apply to none.

[436] See Report on The Effect of Death on Damages (1992) Scot Law Com No 134, paras 2.17-2.18, 3.10-3.13 and 4.22-4.28; B S Markesinis, *The German Law of Torts* (3rd ed 1994) p 923; and W Pfennigstorf (ed), *Personal Injury Compensation* (1993) pp 67, 71, 200.

[437] Report on The Effect of Death on Damages (1992) Scot Law Com No 134, paras 4.24-4.27. See also B S Markesinis, *The German Law of Torts* (3rd ed 1994) p 923, discussing the situation which pertained in Germany prior to 1990 where the victim was unconscious in the period between injury and death.

[438] See Report on The Effect of Death on Damages (1992) Scot Law Com No 134, para 4.27.

[439] B S Markesinis, *The German Law of Torts* (3rd ed 1994) p 923.

Commission also reported a clear consensus among those it consulted in 1992 to the effect that, if the right to recover damages for non-pecuniary loss was allowed to survive, it should do so unconditionally. For all these reasons, **it is our provisional view that a rule which permits damages for non-pecuniary loss to survive for the benefit of the deceased's estate only in cases where the deceased has commenced an action while alive ought not to be introduced. We invite consultees to say whether they agree, and if not why not.**

[440] See para 3.77 above.

PART V
SUMMARY OF RECOMMENDATIONS AND CONSULTATION ISSUES

5.1 We set out below a summary of our questions and provisional recommendations on which we invite the views of consultees.

1. THE AVAILABILITY OF DAMAGES FOR NON-PECUNIARY LOSS

5.2 Do consultees agree with our strong provisional view that the courts should continue to award damages for non-pecuniary loss? (paragraphs 4.5-4.8)

2. THE CANADIAN 'FUNCTIONAL' APPROACH TO THE ASSESSMENT OF DAMAGES FOR NON-PECUNIARY LOSS

5.3 Do consultees agree with our provisional rejection of the 'functional' approach to damages for non-pecuniary loss? (paragraphs 4.9-4.10)

3. THE ENTITLEMENT TO DAMAGES FOR NON-PECUNIARY LOSS OF A PLAINTIFF WHO IS UNAWARE OF HIS OR HER INJURY

5.4 We ask consultees for their views as to the damages for non-pecuniary loss that should be awarded to plaintiffs who have been rendered permanently unconscious. In particular, should the amount of those damages be (a) nil; or (b) assessed, as at present, within a bracket that is at the top end of the judicial tariff of values; or (c) a low amount (say, for example, one tenth of that awarded to a conscious quadriplegic)? (paragraphs 4.11-4.21)

5.5 We invite consultees' views as to whether damages for non-pecuniary loss for a conscious, but severely brain-damaged, plaintiff who has little appreciation of his or her condition should continue to be assessed within, or near, the highest bracket of awards; or, on the contrary, whether a mid-range bracket or an even lower sum should instead be awarded to such a plaintiff for non-pecuniary loss. (paragraph 4.22)

4. A THRESHOLD FOR THE RECOVERY OF DAMAGES FOR NON-PECUNIARY LOSS

5.6 Do consultees agree with our provisional view (given that we are not recommending and, within our terms of reference, cannot recommend a trade-off with a new no-fault compensation scheme) that a threshold for the recovery of non-pecuniary loss should not be introduced? If consultees disagree, we invite them to specify the form of threshold they favour. (paragraphs 4.23-4.26)

5. THE LEVEL OF DAMAGES FOR NON-PECUNIARY LOSS
(1) The present level

5.7 Do consultees believe that the level of damages for non-pecuniary loss is too high or too low? If so, does that belief rest on anything other than intuition? If consultees

161

do think that the damages are too low we ask: (a) what would be the uplift required to render awards acceptable (for example, double or one and a half times the present levels)?; and (b) should the uplift be across the whole range of awards or confined, for example, to the most serious injuries? If, in contrast, consultees consider that the level of awards is too high, would they favour a legislative ceiling on awards for non-pecuniary loss in personal injury cases? (paragraphs 4.27-4.33)

(2)   The effect of inflation on the present level

5.8   We ask consultees whether they agree with our provisional conclusion that the exercise in paragraphs 4.35-4.50 provides some support for the view that, at least in respect of very serious injuries, damages for non-pecuniary loss have failed to keep pace with inflation when compared with awards 25 to 30 years ago. We also ask consultees whether they have any other evidence either to support or contradict the view that awards for non-pecuniary loss have failed to keep up with inflation. (paragraphs 4.34-4.51)

(3)   Raising the level of damages for non-pecuniary loss

5.9   At the risk of an overlap with answers to be given to questions posed in the next two sections, we ask consultees: if damages for non-pecuniary loss are too low, what should be done to rectify the position? (paragraph 4.52)

6.   A LEGISLATIVE TARIFF

5.10   We invite consultees to say whether or not they agree with our provisional view that, *if there is to be a legislative tariff*, its form should follow that of the present judicial tariff by fixing upper and lower limits and by laying down a non-exhaustive list of relevant discretionary factors for determining the precise award: and we invite the views of consultees as to whether there should be such a legislative tariff. (paragraphs 4.53-4.67)

7.   ASSISTING THE JUDICIARY IN FIXING THE AMOUNTS TO BE AWARDED FOR NON-PECUNIARY LOSS IN THE ABSENCE OF A LEGISLATIVE TARIFF

(1)   A Compensation Advisory Board

5.11   We invite consultees: (a) to consider the desirability, in the absence of a legislative tariff, of establishing a Compensation Advisory Board, for the purpose of setting new levels of compensation which better reflect the value which society places upon the non-pecuniary consequences of personal injury; and (b) to indicate whether they disagree with, or can foresee problems regarding, any elements of the model for a Board which we have outlined at paragraph 4.71 above. (paragraphs 4.68-4.72)

(2)   Guinea-pig jury trials

5.12   Do consultees agree with our provisional view that trial by jury should not be used as a means of providing sample awards for the judicial assessment of non-pecuniary loss? (paragraphs 4.73-4.76)

(3)   Greater reliance on medical "scores"

5.13   We ask consultees, particularly those with the appropriate medical expertise, for their views as to whether greater reliance should be placed on medical scoring systems in comparing awards for non-pecuniary loss. In particular, would it be possible and sensible to devise a special medical scoring system for use in assessing damages for non-pecuniary loss in personal injury cases? (paragraphs 4.77-4.79)

(4)   Computerised assistance

5.14   We ask consultees for their views as to whether greater use could be made of computers as an aid to the more consistent assessment by judges of damages for non-pecuniary loss and, if so, in what precise ways do they envisage computers being used? (paragraph 4.80)

(5)   Other ways of assisting the judiciary

5.15   In addition to the specific questions posed in this section, we ask consultees generally whether there are any other ways, that we have not mentioned, in which (on the assumption that a legislative tariff is not introduced) the judiciary might be assisted in fixing the amounts to be awarded for non-pecuniary loss. (paragraph 4.81)

8.   THE ASSESSMENT OF DAMAGES BY JURIES

(1)   The assessment by juries of compensatory damages for personal injury

5.16   Our provisional view is that the assessment of compensatory damages for personal injuries should always be a matter for the judge and should never be left to a jury. We ask consultees to say whether they agree with that provisional view. (paragraphs 4.82-4.85)

(2)   The assessment by juries of damages in defamation cases

5.17   In the light of the problems mentioned in paragraphs 4.96 to 4.99 - and subject to the views of consultees - we have reluctantly reached the provisional view that the Faulks Committee's recommendation to split the determination of liability and damages between jury and judge in defamation cases is unworkable. Nevertheless, we would welcome views, particularly from lawyers with relevant practical experience, as to whether there is any solution to the difficulties that we have referred to in splitting the determination of liability and damages between jury and judge in defamation cases. (paragraphs 4.86-4.100)

5.18   Do consultees agree with our provisional view that a judge, in directing the jury in relation to the assessment of damages in a defamation case, should inform the jury of the range of awards for non-pecuniary loss in personal injury cases as is conveniently set out in the Judicial Studies Board's *Guidelines for the Assessment of General Damages in Personal Injury Cases,* and that the same approach should be applied in any other (non-defamation) case where a jury is required to assess damages for non-pecuniary loss (for example, for malicious prosecution or false imprisonment)? (paragraphs 4.101-4.103)

5.19 We would welcome views on the further suggestion that has been made to us, that there should be a statutory ceiling on awards for non-pecuniary loss in defamation cases and, if so, what the appropriate maximum sum should be and how it should be kept up-to-date. (paragraph 4.104)

9. INTEREST ON DAMAGES FOR NON-PECUNIARY LOSS

(1) Awarding interest on damages for non-pecuniary loss

5.20 Do consultees agree with our provisional view that interest should continue to be awarded on damages for non-pecuniary loss in personal injury actions? (paragraphs 4.106-4.110)

(2) Awarding interest only on pre-trial non-pecuniary loss

5.21 We ask consultees for their views on whether the English practice should be changed so that a division is made between past and future non-pecuniary loss with interest being allowed only on the former. If it is considered that such a change should be made we ask consultees (after reading paragraphs 4.114-4.125) to say whether this change should be combined with the application of a higher rate of interest than the current 2 per cent rate and, if so, why; and/or whether the date of the accident should then be taken as the date from which interest runs and, if so, why. (paragraphs 4.111-4.113)

(3) The date from which interest is payable

5.22 We invite consultees' views as to whether interest on damages for non-pecuniary loss should be payable from the date of the accident rather than from the date of the service of the writ. (paragraphs 4.114-4.118)

(4) The current 2 per cent rate of interest

5.23 We ask consultees to indicate whether they consider satisfactory the 2 per cent interest rate which is presently applied to damages for non-pecuniary loss in personal injury actions. In particular, do they favour: (a) abandoning the "fixed" 2 per cent rate in favour of taking the net rate of return on index-linked government securities over the relevant period; or (b) the application of a higher rate (for example, the commercial rate or the special account rate) than the net real rate of return on a low-risk investment, in order, for example, to discourage delay by defendants. (paragraphs 4.119-4.125)

10. THE SURVIVAL OF DAMAGES FOR NON-PECUNIARY LOSS ON THE DEATH OF THE VICTIM

(1) The survival of damages for non-pecuniary loss

5.24 We invite consultees to indicate whether they agree with our provisional view that it is fairer to injured persons and their families, and not unfair to defendants, to allow an injured person's right to recover damages for non-pecuniary loss to continue to survive for the benefit of that person's estate; and, if not, to give their reasons. (paragraphs 4.128-4.132)

(2)   Conditions on the survival of damages for non-pecuniary loss

(a)   The survival of damages for non-pecuniary loss where the supervening death is due to extraneous causes

5.25   Do consultees agree with our provisional view that there should be no rule limiting the survival of damages for non-pecuniary loss in personal injury actions to cases where the supervening death is due to extraneous causes? (paragraphs 4.134-4.135)

(b)   The survival of damages for non-pecuniary loss where the deceased has commenced an action while alive

5.26   It is our provisional view that a rule which permits damages for non-pecuniary loss to survive for the benefit of the deceased's estate only in cases where the deceased has commenced an action while alive ought not to be introduced. We invite consultees to say whether they agree, and if not why not. (paragraphs 4.136-4.137)

11.   QUESTION FROM PART II

5.27   We would welcome the views of consultees, and particularly those with experience of personal injury litigation, as to whether the question of overlap (between damages for loss of earnings and damages for loss of amenity) raised in *Fletcher v Autocar and Transporters Ltd*[1] gives rise to difficulty and, if so, what the solution to that difficulty should be. (paragraph 2.38)

GENERAL

5.28   We invite consultees to comment on any other aspect of damages for non-pecuniary loss in cases of personal injury which they consider relevant to the general purpose of this paper, but on which we have not specifically sought the views of consultees.

---

[1]   [1968] 2 QB 322.